Languishing

Languishing

How to Feel Alive Again
in a World That
Wears Us Down

COREY KEYES

CROWN
NEW YORK

Published in the United States by Crown, an imprint of the Crown Publishing Group,
a division of Penguin Random House LLC, New York.

CROWN and the Crown colophon are registered trademarks of
Penguin Random House LLC.

Library of Congress Cataloging-in-Publication Data
Names: Keyes, Corey L. M., author.
Title: Languishing / Corey Keyes.
Description: First edition. | New York: Crown, [2024] |
Includes bibliographical references and index.
Identifiers: LCCN 2023048676 (print) | LCCN 2023048677 (ebook) |
ISBN 9780593444627 (hardcover) | ISBN 9780593735145 |
ISBN 9780593444634 (ebook)
Subjects: LCSH: Mental fatigue. | Executive functions (Neuropsychology) | Success.
Classification: LCC BF482 .K49 2024 (print) |
LCC BF482 (ebook) | DDC 152.1/886—dc23/eng/20231205
LC record available at https://lccn.loc.gov/2023048676
LC ebook record available at https://lccn.loc.gov/2023048677

Printed in the United States of America on acid-free paper

crownpublishing.com

2 4 6 8 9 7 5 3 1

FIRST EDITION

Editor: Leah Trouwborst
Editorial assistant: Cierra Hinckson
Production editor: Andy Lefkowitz
Text designer: Ralph Fowler
Production manager: Sandra Sjursen
Managing editors: Allison Fox and Sally Franklin
Copy editor: Lynn Anderson
Proofreaders: Kimberly Broderick, Megha Jain, Kristin Jones, Lori Newhouse,
Barbara Stussy, Bridget Sweet, and Caryl Weintraub
Indexer: Ina Gravitz
Publicist: Gwyneth Stansfield
Marketer: Mason Eng

This book is dedicated to my
"Nana" and "Papa"—Eva Marie (Pilon) Keyes
and Herbert Keyes Sr.—who, in their retirement,
adopted me and my sister and gave us
a home where the seed of flourishing was sown.

Contents

Running on Empty

As a quiet, curious teenager growing up in a one-stop-sign town in northern Wisconsin, I would tune my FM radio to listen to the *King Biscuit Flower Hour* on Sunday evenings. Staring at a water stain on the ceiling one night, I heard the song that would become my high school anthem: "Running on Empty" by Jackson Browne. He didn't use the words *lonely, sad,* or *anxious,* but he expressed the feeling, so familiar to me, of dully going through the motions of a life that seemed increasingly drained of color:

> *I don't know where I'm running now, I'm just running on*
> *Running on (running on empty)*
> *Running on (running on blind)*

Pinned to my bed, I felt profoundly seen for perhaps the first time in my life. There I was, sixteen years old, about to learn how to drive. Outwardly, things were going surprisingly well after a complicated childhood. My grades were strong. I had a loving relationship with my grandparents, with whom I now lived. Yet I couldn't shake the sense that something was off. Whether I'd had a good day or a bad day, after school my chest felt like a blown-up balloon—pressurized yet entirely empty of substance.

If this sounds like depression, I can assure you that it wasn't, though I would struggle with depression later in life. I wasn't hopelessly sad. I didn't have trouble getting out of bed in the morning. It was more like

I was on autopilot, compelled to keep *doing*, to throw myself at activity after activity, leaving little room for the thoughts that rose up when I was alone with myself. This feeling of restless emptiness eclipsed all aspects of my otherwise peaceful life. As a kid, it was disorienting, to say the least.

The specter of languishing continued to haunt me as I grew up, following me into adulthood—if not the feeling, then the fear of it returning. Ultimately, it led me to become a professor of sociology and embark on a long journey to understand just what this experience of "running on empty" was all about, and to find out whether it haunted other people, too.

The Power of a Name

About a year into the global covid pandemic, Adam Grant, an organizational psychologist and bestselling author, wrote a *New York Times* article describing the very term I'd been quietly studying for years. His piece was called "There's a Name for the Blah You're Feeling: It's Called Languishing." It began: "At first, I didn't recognize the symptoms that we all had in common. Friends mentioned that they were having trouble concentrating. Colleagues reported that even with vaccines on the horizon, they weren't excited about 2021. A family member was staying up late to watch *National Treasure* again even though she knows the movie by heart. And instead of bouncing out of bed at 6 A.M., I was lying there until 7, playing Words with Friends." For him and many others, languishing crept in after a period of extreme stress, grief, or loneliness—a sense of low-grade mental weariness that can be easy to dismiss, especially since indifference is one of its symptoms.

Languishing often sets in slowly and imperceptibly—and then suddenly, you're engulfed in it. The simple question "How are you?" can feel like an unwelcome pop quiz, leaving you casting about for a socially acceptable response, not quite knowing the answer yourself.

Grant's piece went viral, becoming the most widely read *New York*

Times article of the year. Clearly, there was a deep need for vocabulary to describe a struggle that millions of people—teenagers, frontline workers, parents, overworked professionals in all fields, and those grieving the loss of loved ones—were experiencing but found hard to put into words. Celebrities and royals alike tweeted about having bouts of languishing. Trevor Noah opened up about his own experience with languishing at a sold-out show in Madison Square Garden; the crowd of twenty thousand grew pin-drop silent.

Are You Languishing?

Do you find yourself nodding your head in recognition at the symptoms on this list?

- You feel emotionally flattened. It's hard to muster up excitement for events and milestones on the horizon.

- A sense of inevitability has washed over you. Your life circumstances seem increasingly dictated by external forces.

- You find yourself procrastinating on tasks at work and in your personal life as a why-try-anyway attitude sets in.

- More and more things strike you as irrelevant, superficial, or boring.

- You have the constant feeling of unease that you're missing something that will make your life feel complete again, but you can't figure out what it is.

- You feel disconnected from your own community and/or a greater purpose or cause.

- Your job once gave you a sense of meaning, or at least accomplishment, but it is starting to seem pointless in the grand scheme of things.

- You regularly experience brain fog (for example, standing in the shower and trying to remember whether you've washed your hair yet).

- Small setbacks that you might once have weathered fairly easily leave you feeling defeated. You feel restless, even rootless.

- You find yourself being convinced—or sometimes steamrolled—by people with strong opinions, because you're increasingly unsure of your own.

- It's hard to find the motivation to reach out to friends and family and to maintain relationships that were once important to you. You've been finding it more difficult to feel close to people.

- You don't have the ability to see and understand your strengths and weaknesses; you cannot figure out where you're doing well and what you should think about improving on. Your sense of self-worth is flickering or plummeting.

In a few pages, you'll have the chance to take a more formal assessment. But if more than a few of these experiences ring true for you or someone you love, this book will help you understand why—and what to do about it when you're stuck in a cycle you can't break.

What Languishing Isn't

Languishing might sound similar to depression, and both are characterized by a loss of interest in life, but there are crucial differences between the two. Depression is marked by a persistent sense of hopelessness or sadness every day or almost every day for at least two straight weeks, often accompanied by crying spells, sleeping too much or too little, and having suicidal thoughts. Yet millions of people are languishing who don't meet those criteria. You can be devoid of a sense of purpose in life and not have any symptoms of depression. Languishers are also more likely to feel out of control of their lives, uncertain about what they want from the future, and paralyzed in the face of decisions, large and small.

What about burnout, the word you might reach for after sending that last email at 12:01 A.M., watching your toddler erupt in yet another tantrum, or swiping on dating apps until it feels like you have robot fingers? Burnout might capture the prevailing mood of a generation—or a planet—although technically speaking, it's not a mental health condition, but an "occupational phenomenon" that describes a mismatch between your workload and the resources you have to do it, which allows chronic stress to build up. The two conditions can feel similar at times, but burnout is a much narrower term.

That said, burnout can leave you so demoralized that languishing takes hold. When you're constantly stretched too thin by work, it's hard to find joy or meaning in the activities that you once found greatly fulfilling. A parent's nighttime reading of *Where the Wild Things Are* to their four-year-old—perhaps even performing a full suite of character voices, to their kid's delight—can be disrupted by intrusive thoughts about a never-ending to-do list, making it all but impossible to feel present. The rush of anticipation a graphic designer once felt at seeing their advertising campaigns go live might feel like a distant memory when they're tied to their computer late into the night, churning out repetitive banner designs for a demanding client.

Our society is fond of admonishing us to "take personal responsibility" for our actions. If we're not happy, we should get up earlier, exercise more, get more sleep. But sociologists like me are more interested in understanding how systems can fail us than in placing all the blame on individuals. If we're feeling record levels of stress, anxiety, burnout, and, of course, languishing, how can it be only *your* fault? In fact, it is so often the system itself that robs us of our agency to create better lives for ourselves, and even to act in ways that line up with our values and identities.

One young doctor recognized that he was being demoralized—the demands being placed on him and his colleagues by our healthcare system were forcing them to sacrifice their professional values.

He wrote an opinion article for *The New York Times* about what could only be described as a moral collapse in his own profession, arguing that hospitals were "deliberately understaffing themselves and undercutting patient care while sitting on billions of dollars in cash reserves." An arcane medical billing system designed to maximize profit creates a skewed incentive structure—not to mention mountains of administrative work—for the providers in charge of making critical treatment choices for patients, making it extremely difficult to uphold the standards of care they'd sworn to. It's no wonder healthcare workers are reporting a sense of helplessness and lost purpose in mass numbers. "Our demoralization is not a reaction to a medical condition, but rather to the diseased systems for which we work," he wrote forcefully. Practicing medicine is wearing practitioners down from the inside out.

It's not hard to imagine a similar scenario playing out in other professions. A teacher at an understaffed, underfunded school might have always loved her job and her students, priding herself on her willingness to go the extra mile for her students. That kind of work ethic can carry a person for only so long, though, and over time, she might feel a sense of weary detachment set in. This isn't her; the system's failures have worn down her defenses.

Over time, under such conditions, our self-narrative—the story we construct to make meaning out of our lives and the world around us—begins to crumble. This weakened sense of self is sometimes described as "feeling dead inside." We have a deep psychological need not only to be accepted by our families and communities but also to accept *ourselves* and hold ourselves in high regard. What happens when we no longer like the person we see in the mirror? You can probably see how the vicious cycle plays out.

Have We Been Asking the Wrong Questions?

For a brief period in the late 1990s, I was involved with the launch of the positive psychology movement, even cohosting the very first summit on positive psychology in 1999. But as the movement has grown, I've seen it, like so many other self-improvement philosophies, focus inordinately on feeling states: *feeling* optimistic, *feeling* happy, *feeling* strong. What would happen, I asked myself, if we stopped measuring our well-being based on the presence of pleasant or unpleasant emotions? What if we directed our energy toward meeting a deeper set of needs?

My research on the conditions that lead to good mental health—which I call *flourishing*—has found that improving our psychological, relational, and social *functioning* builds well-being from the ground up. Learning to hold our emotions more loosely, change the stories we tell ourselves, become more accepting of ourselves and others, and form communities of care and belonging, creates a virtuous cycle, increasing our tolerance for stress, adversity, and the pressures of modern living. Over time, improving our functioning creates a deeper sense of life satisfaction and overall emotional well-being. In other words, you feel good because you are functioning well.

No simple task, you may think! Focusing on healthy functioning may require a shift in priorities, but in the second half of this book, we'll explore a set of simple but powerful practices to ground and recenter yourself—to go back to the building blocks of flourishing—every day.

A few years ago, I was contacted by a journal to review a paper submitted by Italian colleagues who were studying, among other things, the mental health of healthcare workers in Lombardy. Lombardy recorded nearly half of the almost thirty thousand deaths that happened in a three-month period during the early phase of the covid pandemic in Italy.

At the time, the healthcare system and medical staff in Lombardy were under siege. The researchers had found that languishing tripled the odds of frontline healthcare workers in Lombardy being diagnosed with post-traumatic stress disorder (PTSD); those who were languishing severely were the most at risk. But they also found that workers who were flourishing were almost four times *less* likely to come down with PTSD than those who were languishing moderately.

If languishing makes you more vulnerable to a wide variety of risks, such as developing PTSD, flourishing builds up a strong immunity to problems like this and so many others, giving you the resiliency needed to live in a world that too often grinds us down and takes too much from us.

Thirteen Reasons Why

Need more convincing? As you read the list below, frame each line in the following way:

Flourishing protects against . . . Languishing makes you vulnerable to . . .

- Delinquent behaviors (smoking, doing inhalants, drinking alcohol, skipping school, etc.) in middle and high schoolers

- Suicide attempts and suicidality (planning and having serious thoughts about suicide)

- Self-harming behaviors other than suicide (hitting or cutting oneself, pulling out hair, etc.)

- Wanting to quit school

- Depression

- Anxiety

- Post-traumatic stress disorder (PTSD)

- Relapse of mental illness (sliding back into mental illness after having reached clinical recovery following treatment)

- Mental distress from working in a high-conflict or very stressful work environment

- Reduced work productivity (missing days of work)

- Frequent healthcare visits (for physical and mental/emotional reasons)

- Activating a set of genes called conserved transcriptional response to adversity (CTRA) genes, which increase inflammation and decrease antibody production

- Premature death

These findings are based on my decades of research. Languishing not only impedes our daily functioning, trapping us in "loops" of inflexible behaviors, but is also a gateway to serious mental illness and early mortality. We cannot afford to leave that door open.

No one wants to add another problem to the menu of mental health issues we are worrying about. Before and after its viral moment during the pandemic, the media has been largely indifferent to languishing, letting it recede into the background. Yet we can't give in to the temptation to downplay languishing in the face of "real" mental health diagnoses and "bigger problems." Languishing poses a serious threat to public health.

Mental illness is a profound individual and societal burden. About half of the entire population will experience it in their lifetime. Yet for too long, well-meaning, well-trained psychiatrists have focused on diagnosing and treating the negative symptoms of mental illness. And after billions of dollars have been invested in the field, many leading medications are still less effective at treating symptoms of depression, anxiety, and psychological distress than physical exercise or meditation.

As someone who has been treated for depression and PTSD, who has contemplated suicide, who has been on psychiatric medications, I've dedicated my professional life to studying the *positive* components of mental health. My framework for flourishing recognizes that mental illness and mental health are two related but distinct dimensions. Health is not just the absence of disease; it is also the presence of well-being. And the medical field has too often overlooked the possibility that you can learn to function well in life—and even to flourish—without completely "curing" anxiety, PTSD, complex PTSD, ADHD, OCD, or other mental illnesses or disorders.

How is it possible, you might wonder, to be mentally ill and mentally healthy at the same time? It does sound odd, almost impossible. Indeed, languishing is more common among people being treated for a mental illness. Yet even among patients being treated for something as serious as schizophrenia, flourishing can and does happen. A recent study of patients in Hong Kong with schizophrenia found that 28 percent met the criteria for flourishing despite battling one of the most difficult mental illnesses out there. The sample size was small and perhaps not representative of all schizophrenics, but that's pretty good news for the rest of us who are battling our own demons, large or small.

I don't want to languish, and I definitely don't want to be mentally ill. I'm pretty sure you don't, either. But the questions we must ask are how to define our end goal: which metric we should use to assess mental health; and how we can get there—which methods are most effective.

As I've shared my work with the world over the years, flourishing also began to find me. One evening in Glasgow, Scotland, I gave a public presentation of my work. A group came up to me afterward to chat, thrumming with excitement. They proclaimed that they were part of the Mad Pride movement, a group with lived experience advocating for what they called "full" recovery from mental illness. They don't want to be merely free of their illness, nor do they want to be defined by it or stigmatized by it.

"This flourishing thing may be new to some people, but it is nothing new to us." For a few seconds, the academic in me felt a little put out. Then I realized how exciting—how profoundly significant—it was to be aligned on a vision of recovery: to belong, to contribute, to have purpose, to express our ideas and opinions, to be accepted and accept ourselves. A sense of pride washed over me—I, too, was living proof of Mad Pride.

For many of us, despite our best efforts to manage an extremely challenging condition and the possibility of its receding into the background for periods of time, mental illness will remain with us in some form—often a manageable one—throughout our lives. But we can expand our vocabulary, and with it, our potential. We can focus on levels of healthy functioning and on the positive steps anyone can take to create a virtuous cycle of flourishing.

A Holistic Measure of Mental Health

You may be curious to know where you fall on the scale of *positive* mental health. In the coming pages, you'll see a fourteen-point questionnaire I developed, which has been used by clinicians for decades as a holistic and reliable means of assessing well-being. (If you'd rather wait until the end of the book before holding that particular mirror up to your own face, feel free to skip this assessment for now.)

Each of the questions probes an important and fundamental facet of well-being. The first three evaluate *emotional* well-being; the next five test *social* well-being; and the final six measure *psychological* well-being. As you'll see, we don't have to have it all figured out, walking through life glowing with contentment, to meet the criteria for flourishing—and some components of well-being carry more weight than others.

Think about yourself and your life over the past month before answering the following questions:

CRITERIA FOR FLOURISHING

During the past month, how often did you feel	Never	Once or Twice	About Once a Week	Two or Three Times a Week	Almost Every Day	Every Day
Emotional Well-being						
1. happy	0	1	2	3	4	5
2. interested in life	0	1	2	3	4	5
3. satisfied with life	0	1	2	3	4	5
Criteria for flourishing: Can you circle 4 or 5 in response to at least one of these first three questions?						
Social Well-being						
4. that you had something important to contribute to society	0	1	2	3	4	5
5. that you belonged to a community (a social group, school, neighborhood, etc.)	0	1	2	3	4	5
6. that our society is a good place, or is becoming a better place, for all people	0	1	2	3	4	5
7. that people are basically good	0	1	2	3	4	5
8. that the way our society works made sense to you	0	1	2	3	4	5
Criteria for flourishing: Can you circle 4 or 5 in response to at least six of the questions above and below? (Since both social and psychological well-being are a measure of healthy *functioning*, high marks in either category can meet the criteria for flourishing.)						
Psychological Well-being						
9. that you liked most parts of your personality	0	1	2	3	4	5
10. that you were good at managing the responsibilities of your daily life	0	1	2	3	4	5
11. that you had warm and trusting relationships with others	0	1	2	3	4	5
12. that you had experiences that challenged you to grow and become a better person	0	1	2	3	4	5
13. that you are confident to think or express your own ideas and opinions	0	1	2	3	4	5
14. that your life has a sense of direction or meaning to it	0	1	2	3	4	5

Your goal should not be to check every box every single day. You only need six of the eleven functioning well—any combination of social or psychological well-being—along with one of the three facets of emotional well-being almost every day to flourish. The combinations are almost endless, so you can flourish in your own unique way.

If you are not flourishing, it means that you are—to some degree—languishing. Some people languish severely, while some languish only moderately. If you circled more 0's and 1's, you may be languishing severely; if you circled more 2's and 3's, your languishing is probably moderate.

But let me remind you: Wherever you are today, it doesn't mean you have to stay there.

A New Anthem for Our Time

Last summer, as I was sitting down to write this book, a new teenage anthem took over. "Numb Little Bug" by Em Beihold was a sensation, and as I listened to it for the first time, I couldn't help but imagine today's teenagers lying in their beds and feeling seen, as if a mirror were being held up to their faces. The most haunting reference to languishing and its accompanying sense of invisibility came in the line, "Like your body's in the room but you're not really there."

Throughout the song, Beihold asks if anyone else feels the same way as she does, "Like you're not really happy but you don't wanna die." Yes, Em, we do. So many of us do.

Naming something gives it power—and gives us power over it. We need to use language to describe a painful experience before we can fully recognize it in ourselves, much less feel validated in our suffering. But we need more than a word to move toward healing; we need to understand the psychology of languishing and its underlying causes. The first half of this book will help you understand why we're languishing and how it's impacting us, both individually and as a society.

We keep hearing that the pandemic fast-forwarded social and economic issues that had already been set into motion, and it's true. As the Harvard University historian Niall Ferguson wrote in a piece in *The Washington Post* in early 2023, "It would have been astonishing if the abrupt closure of real-world social networks had not been detrimental to the mental health of a gregarious species of naked apes." During those all-too-difficult pandemic years, billions of people retreated from one another, disappearing into the woodwork of their own lives. Being plunged into a state of mass loneliness, uncertainty, fear, grief, and sleep deprivation took a sharp psychological toll on our country and world.

Globally, emotional distress is on the rise, and socioeconomically disadvantaged communities and people between the ages of fifteen and thirty-five have been hardest hit. The number of high school girls reporting "persistent feelings of sadness or hopelessness" rose to 57 percent in 2021, a 36 percent increase since 2011. And it's not just teenage girls who are in trouble—in 2021, a record number of adults reported having experienced "a lot of stress" (41 percent) and "a lot of worry" (42 percent) the previous day.

The pandemic magnified our mental and emotional distress, but we've been traveling down this path for quite some time now. Had we actually planned to set up a modern world built to promote languishing, we could not possibly have done a better job. Many of us are hungry for richer, more meaningful lives.

Many of us are hungry to feel that our lives matter. We are hungry to belong. We are hungry for warmer, more trusting relationships. We are hungry to live in a society that accepts us for who we are. Everything we are hungry to receive must come from others who are also hungry for the same things. How can a society of hungry people feed one another what they need?

Part II takes up that question. I'll map out a path toward flourishing, drawing on stories of people across different ages, races, ethnicities, income levels, schedules, and personality types who broke out of long-established ruts. Across demographics and regardless of mental health diagnoses, the same five practices instill a renewed sense of meaning, connection, and personal growth—even if you can only carve out minutes of your day, or week, for them.

Flourishing acts as an alternative form of medicine. If you have ever been diagnosed with anemia, which means having a low iron level in the bloodstream, you know that it makes you feel weak, sluggish, tired—kind of like the physical equivalent of languishing. In the same way as you can treat anemia with iron supplements, you can treat languishing with what I call the Five Vitamins of Flourishing.

The best part? The research says that any movement on the spectrum of good mental health has value. If severe languishing is a 1 and flourishing is a 10, you don't have to figure out how to get from 1 to 10 before you turn the last page of this book. Every indicator of someone's life, health, and ability to function is markedly worse when they are languishing at the lowest level; moving toward flourishing, no matter how incremental the movement, can have a profound effect on your life.

Now let's go figure out how.

PART ONE

Mental Health Continuum: From Languishing to Flourishing

[1]

What Languishing Looks Like

Paul was in seventh grade when the trouble started—or at least when the phone calls to his parents from the principal really started to pick up. He and his classmates had all entered middle school the year before, but only for a few hours a day every other week, per the new covid restrictions in his district. They'd missed all sorts of milestones—graduation from their elementary school, a summer of fun in between, and an orientation in person at their new school—because of the pandemic raging around them. Most of Paul's classmates had never even set foot inside the main building before September rolled around.

Any chance of making new friends from the other local elementary schools had slipped away within the first few weeks of sixth grade. If students were learning in person, they were all masked up and leaving before lunchtime; if they were on Zoom, not a single kid kept their camera on the whole day. They'd never even seen their new teachers smile in real life—their faces had been hidden by masks. It felt hopeless and impossible to connect with new people and make a fresh start.

By the time seventh grade rolled around, Paul and his friends, most of whom were left over from his elementary school days, had started making trouble. Small trouble, at first: horsing around in the hallway, speaking out of turn in class, sort of normal seventh-grade stuff, or so his parents thought. But then things started ticking upward. Various destructive TikTok trends were taking off in schools all around the country—paper towel dispensers were getting ripped off walls, horsing around in the hallways turned into full-body tackles, and bathrooms were getting trashed on a regular basis. Paul kept getting caught—for petty vandalism, low-level violence couched as fun. His grades were slipping. Nothing dramatic, such as regularly ditching school, was happening, but his grades had been A's and B's, and now there were a whole lot of C's sprinkled throughout his report card.

At home, things weren't much more hopeful. Paul was spending hours alone in his room, or if he did come out, he slunk around with his hoodie up, refusing to talk to his parents beyond a cursory hello or goodbye. The silence unsettled them; he could barely meet their eyes at dinner. When he came home from school, he'd climb right into bed with his laptop, saying he had homework to do, but he also seemed to be missing school assignments left and right. He was just so still all the time, his mom told me, as if he didn't have the energy to move his limbs. It was unnerving. His high-achieving parents were distraught—this wasn't the kid they knew.

Something about the isolation many kids feel at that time in their lives—things in middle school are, at best, hormonal, confusing, painful, stressful, and anxiety producing—was causing Paul to act out in ways he never had before. One day, to the horror of his parents, they found out that he'd bought a real-looking fake gun and posted about bringing it to school on social media. His classmates had immediately told their teachers, and the school had gone into lockdown mode before 9:00 A.M. It was a joke—of course it was a joke, the gun was just a toy, for God's sake, and he didn't even bring it in!—he told his frantic mother. But that joke would get him expelled from school before noon that day.

Why would he do such a shocking thing? Paul's parents wondered. It was clear that, despite his hiding under his hoodie, he was screaming out to be seen. Underneath his defiant façade, he was feeling powerless and purposeless, more alienated than integrated, his parents began to realize. How, in this nonstop, disorienting, status-obsessed online world, could he feel that he liked most parts of his personality, believe he had something important to contribute to society—beyond an edgy Snapchat post or a dumb hallway prank—or form warm and trusting relationships with others? These are the building blocks of flourishing, and they too often feel hopelessly out of reach for adolescents growing up today.

It makes sense, then, that a languishing teen would rather experience the wrath of their principal, the disapproval of their parents, and the humiliation of getting kicked out of school—than the deadening sentiment of feeling nothing at all.

Who Else Is Languishing?

Languishing is particularly likely to occur during three phases of life, affecting as many as 50 to 60 percent of us. The first is adolescence (ages twelve to nineteen)—a difficult time of transition. The second period is young adulthood, between twenty-five and thirty-four, when people are starting their careers and families. Finally, after the age of seventy-five, languishing creeps back up again. Many older adults are not only mourning the loss of loved ones, but also the loss of their former mobility and independence, beset by a variety of ailments and indignities.

In this chapter, we'll take a close look at how languishing affects us at different ages. As our social and physical environments evolve, what risk factors rise and fall?

Can Young Children Languish?

It's hard to imagine a two-year-old feeling an inner void. At such an early developmental stage, how could a toddler be emotionally or cognitively mature enough to show signs of a more serious mental health shortfall? If we understand languishing as the absence of emotional, psychological, or social well-being, however, the sad truth is that yes, young children can demonstrate what researchers call a "failure to flourish." In fact, in rare cases, toddlers can show signs of major depression, though the symptoms are easy to miss. They might not even seem sad to their parents: Symptoms can range from a "flat affect" to increased clinginess.

In recent years, as the mental health of young adults has deteriorated at alarming rates, clinicians and researchers have begun studying early tells of distress in young children more closely. A growing body of the healthcare community has also shifted toward using holistic measures of health, such as flourishing, that encompass not only physical and cognitive health, but also the social and environmental factors that impact well-being.

A 2022 study of more than eighteen thousand children conducted by the U.S. Census Bureau examined the prevalence of flourishing—and its predictors—in one- to five-year-olds. Parents were asked four questions about their child's emotional health and functioning. First, does your child bounce back quickly when things don't go his or her way? Second, would you describe your child as affectionate and tender toward you? Third, does your child show interest and curiosity about learning new things? Fourth, does your child smile and laugh? A child was considered to be flourishing if the answers to all four questions were "always" or "usually."

The good news was that 63 percent of children met those criteria. But nearly four in ten children were demonstrating a failure to flourish: They lacked resilience, felt disconnected from their parents and others, were uninterested and disengaged, or rarely laughed or smiled.

Children in the study who'd been diagnosed with a physical illness, a developmental disability, or an emotional or behavioral problem were at higher risk. Researchers also found that the failure to flourish was more common among children from socially and economically marginalized families—particularly those experiencing food insufficiency or sleep insufficiency, and whose parents felt a lack of social support.

Young children, more than any other age group, have the natural capacity to flourish. But families need a society that supports them if we, as a society, expect them to nurture that natural capacity. When parents are forced to work multiple minimum wage jobs with unpredictable hours; when they don't have access to parental leave, limiting bonding time in the early months of a child's life (and later, opportunities to interact with childcare providers and teachers); when extended family, friends, and others in the local community are overtaxed and underresourced, limiting their availability to help parents in desperate need of support; and when neighborhoods don't have playgrounds, libraries, and other shared spaces for families to spend time together and form strong support networks, we're not only failing entire communities, but also our tiniest children.

Teenage Wasteland

We are at the dawn of a new millennium. A crowning achievement of the preceding century was increasing life expectancy by thirty years on average. We have added more years to our life expectancy in the last hundred years than in all prior centuries combined. Congratulations are truly in order.

But we've also inherited a world plagued by uncertainty, and the pressure of making sense of it all—and living with integrity within it—weighs heavily on our adolescents, eroding the sense of self so crucial to their healthy functioning. In the United States, I found that the failure to flourish steadily increases from 37 percent among one- to five-year-olds to 51 percent among kids aged twelve to fourteen, then up to 60 percent among high school–aged teenagers.

Weighty questions surround them that feel outside their scope to answer:

"What sources of information should I trust to stay informed about current events?"

"How can I express my opinions without offending or alienating others?"

"Why do I feel like I'm on a different level than my peers?"

"What if being authentic means losing friends or social status?"

"Am I being a good friend?"

"What is my sexual orientation? Am I straight, gay, bisexual, or something else?"

"Why do I feel responsible for my parents' depression?"

"Do I need to go to college to have a successful career?"

"How can I help stop the planet from burning when it seems like one individual can hardly make an impact?"

Our youngest teens—the twelve- to fourteen-year-olds—are sending out subtle signals of warning to all around them who might care that something is wrong. One of these signals is intentional self-harm. A recent study of Hungarian youths ages twelve to twenty found that as the severity of languishing increased, so did the prevalence of hair pulling, cutting, pinching, biting, burning oneself, and suicidality.

Another warning sign is the early onset of problem behaviors such as substance use and delinquency. Typically, delinquency emerges and increases in the late teens, during high school. But languishing middle school kids between ages twelve and fourteen are *already* engaging in more delinquency, especially the kind that adults aren't always aware of. They weren't always doing things that would get them arrested, but they were starting to skip school, drink, smoke cigarettes and marijuana, and experiment with inhalants.

Lack of social support from peers leaves children especially vulnerable to languishing. The number of adolescents reporting increased loneliness has nearly doubled over the last decade. Fewer middle and high school students report having friends who invite them to their homes, miss them when they aren't at school, tell them explicitly that they are a friend, share their secrets, and would choose them to be on their team at school. As teens navigate their own identities, deal with self-esteem issues, and experience heightened self-consciousness, they're often drained of the emotional energy necessary for nurturing and maintaining close friendships.

PBS aired a documentary about just such an unsettling trend in the lives of teenagers in a suburb of Atlanta, Georgia, in 1999—a year that might feel eons away, but the forces at work back then have only intensified in the intervening decades. Between 1996, as Atlanta prepared to host the Olympics, and the spring of 1999, a series of disturbing events occurred in Rockdale County. A sixteen-year-old boy was killed in a fight at a strip mall parking lot. An adolescent boy, wielding a shotgun, went on a shooting rampage at Heritage High School in Conyers, Georgia, wounding six fellow students. Another seventeen teens in Rockdale County between the ages of fourteen and seventeen tested positive for syphilis, and two hundred teens in total were exposed to the sexually transmitted virus.

Rockdale County is small and affluent and consists of mostly white, suburban, middle- to upper-class families. The children of Rockdale lived comfortable, privileged lives. Heritage High School, where the shooting and several of the syphilis cases occurred, was ranked among the best schools in Georgia. But a public health investigation of the syphilis outbreak revealed the hidden reality of these privileged teens' lives: group sex, alcohol abuse, and drug use abounded.

Alarmed experts searched for explanations. PBS's *Frontline* producer said that she and her colleagues came to see the syphilis outbreak in Rockdale County as a sign of a much deeper problem affecting adolescents. Wherever they went, they kept meeting kids who were lonely, drifting, empty, searching for something to fill that void inside.

Doesn't that sound achingly familiar? The teens felt a void, an emptiness, and nobody saw it until they acted out, badly. The absence of meaningful relationships in the lives of Rockdale's youths was—ironically—a reflection of their parents' economic success. Those kids, by and large, had parents who were successful, busy, and hardworking.

But although the parents could provide for their children's material needs, they were left with little time, energy, or (sometimes) inclination to provide for their emotional or existential needs.

A recent study of more than thirty-seven thousand eleven- to thirteen-year-olds found that languishing was strongly related to the quality of parental-child relationships. The teenagers were asked five questions: Are there people in your family who care about you? Will someone in your family help you if you have a problem? Do the adults in your life listen to you and take your views into account? Do your parents consult with you when making decisions about your life or that affect you? Do you feel safe at home?

Languishing went up as teens said "no" to more of those five questions. I remember how bad it feels to have nothing to go home to. When I was their age, and before I was adopted by my grandparents, I, too, would have had to say "no" to all five questions.

On the flip side, positive relationships with parents act as a protectant against mental health woes, predicting higher empathy, emotional regulation, problem-solving skills, and clearer goals and higher aspirations for the future.

Many parents struggle to breach the invisible impasse between their world and their child's—which is no easy thing, I'll admit—or are too deeply mired in their own suffering to fully connect with their children.

The Canaries Go to College

When Taral was around nineteen years old, an undergrad in college, he went through something I call his "YouTube phase." He didn't have a name for it necessarily, he just knew he didn't want to get out of bed. But he admitted that those days of "chill" had never really made him feel any better. More often than not, they mostly made him feel guilty for wasting his time, for "really not doing anything productive."

Taral noted that he wasn't depressed at the time—he remembered some periods of depression and anxiety in high school, when he was officially diagnosed with the condition, but this time around was different. Back then, his parents had been putting a lot of pressure on him, getting after him to figure out "his future." When he finally got to college, he thought he was doing okay. But the sense of pressure to figure things out still lingered, and he just couldn't seem to force himself to make a choice. He still didn't know what he wanted to do with his future—astrophysics had too much math, and the computer science department was filled with kids who had been coding since they were in grade school. Mostly, he was confused as to where he should be putting his energy, his focus. Sometimes he wondered whether there even was a path for him. So he postponed making any decisions at all and got stuck in some sort of middle place, unable to retreat but with nothing and no one to push him forward, either.

Taral felt paralyzed with indecision and avoidance. His junior year, he started living alone, though he had enjoyed having a roommate the previous year. But the solo life didn't help—he found he could go a day or two, sometimes more, without leaving his dorm room. Some friends would think to check on him if they hadn't heard from him in a few days, but if he didn't reach out to anyone, he could go without human contact for days. He would order in food and do his classes online, and he spent a hell of a lot of time watching YouTube.

* * *

Whether their kids leave high school flourishing or languishing, parents rank getting a good education and finding happiness as their greatest wishes for their college-aged child. In fact, research shows that the closer parents saw themselves to achieving those goals, the higher their *own* psychological well-being.

But our fixation on happiness is a concern of mine. Feeling good, when you aren't functioning well, will not solve your languishing. Parents who are unduly focused on eliciting positive emotions from their children, rather than with their overall well-being, might be missing something important.

What happens when a parent's aspirations put their kid's mental wellness at risk? The figurative family report card can put too much pressure on already fragile teens. Over the past thirty years, college students have reported a 40 percent rise in perceived parental expectations, along with increased levels of parental criticism. Rates of perfectionism have gone up in tandem. Students who hold themselves to unreasonably high standards can come to see life as a series of pass-fail propositions, eroding their sense of self and narrowing their personal goals and interests. Perfectionism is linked to eating disorders, anxiety, self-harm, and depression—and once ingrained, it can become a lifelong trait.

Today's students are faltering under ferocious internal and external pressure. Between 2013 and 2021, rates of depression on college campuses increased by 135 percent and anxiety rates went up by 110 percent. Indeed, the overall number of students who met the criteria for one or more mental health issues *doubled.* Only 38 percent met the criteria for positive mental health. You don't have to be a math major to figure out what that means: that 62 percent of college students are *not* flourishing.

When asked how often they felt they lacked companionship, 64 percent of students answered "Some of the time" or "Often," with 68 percent feeling left out either some of the time or often. You can have all kinds of social connections, even friendships, and still feel intensely isolated; later in the book, I'll look at the qualities that make a connection intimate and meaningful.

I wanted to dig into the implications of this data more deeply to try to understand how college students think about mental health. In my own research, in a representative study of students in the United States, I found that they considered all five aspects of *social* well-being—making a contribution to society, being integrated, making sense of the world, accepting other people, and growing socially—to be the *least* important. What they considered most important was *emotional* well-being: feeling happy, satisfied, and interested in life. That was what they yearned for above all else.

Psychological well-being—having a purpose in life; building warm, trusting relationships; self-acceptance—was considered more important than social well-being but still less important than feeling good. In other words, if this had been an Olympic medal ceremony, feeling good would have won the gold medal by a long shot; functioning well psychologically (the "I") would have had to make do with the silver medal, and functioning well socially (the "we") would have had to settle for bronze.

I'm not surprised that my students felt that emotional well-being was more important than anything else. For the past several decades, this has been the primary if not sole focus of most of the popular work in the field of positive psychology. But that obsession lays the groundwork for languishing—and kids have so many other things to worry about these days.

On top of the emotional, social, and psychological concerns of college students, there are extensive societal and economic stressors weighing them down: the demands of getting into a "good school," followed shortly by relentless competition and achievement anxiety throughout those four years of college, which take a heavy toll. Anxiety begins to tick upward when teens have to focus on getting into college; depression and substance abuse increase around age twenty-one, when they've been in school long enough for chronic worry about grades and post-college opportunities to set in. Many students I have known throughout my twenty-five years of teaching leave college with as many unanswered questions and as much uncertainty about their future as when they began.

Of course, most parents push their children to succeed out of genuine concern. They're understandably anxious over today's hypercompetitive job market and determined to ensure their kid doesn't fall down the social or economic ladder. Getting a college degree today is seen as the equivalent of the lifetime economic security once granted by simply finishing public school with a high school diploma. More children are sacrificing their childhoods to create résumés that will get them into "the best" schools. Higher education is also diminishing the savings of many families, as well as creating stress and anxiety among all members of the household.

We can all agree that being a child and spending carefree afternoons swimming, fishing, biking, and just playing would probably bring more happiness to more youths than taking yet another extra AP math class or an SAT preparation class. But is that an option anymore when outdoor playtime doesn't count for much in the admission departments at four-year universities?

Attending a top-ranked college matters less for long-term financial stability than many worried parents believe, with many employers speaking openly about shifting their hiring focus away from high-status degrees and toward soft qualities such as good writing, communication, and problem solving, and with major companies such as Google sometimes waiving degree requirements. It would be a far worthier ambition for high school students to spend their time and energy choosing a school with an environment conducive to flourishing, a place that cares as much about the mental capacity and growth of its students as it does their SAT scores and GPAs.

This much seems clear to me: When a university starts to measure student success in terms of flourishing as well as GPAs, we may finally have a university system worthy of the moniker "higher" education.

So what should a flourishing university actually be tracking? When students walk across that stage, take their diploma, and graduate, they should feel happy and engaged in their lives, with a sense of direction and personal growth, accepting of themselves and others, and eager to contribute to not just their community but society at large. Universities can and should create flourishing students. Now wouldn't *that* be a worthy outcome of an expensive college education?

Why do various published annual rankings include student–professor ratios, tuition costs, alumni giving rates, and first-year incomes but not, for example, the ratio of mental health counselors to students? The statistics on mental illness diagnoses and attempted suicides? What about a column on the mental health–related student dropout rate? Shouldn't that information be available? And if not, shouldn't concerned parents have the right to demand it?

The rising wealth of many universities and colleges has done little to improve the mental health and happiness of their students. Top colleges throw their weight into recruiting—buying up—the most talented research faculty in the world. But those prestigious faculty are less and less likely to spend much time with their students either inside or outside the classroom.

If the assumption persists that a four-year college degree is going to be a requirement in order to get a good job, universities will have no trouble filling their seats. Can we at least agree that more students should be flourishing as a result of attending a college than when they arrived? Those are the kinds of college graduates who will help contribute to the society we all should be dreaming of.

Tallying Up the Cost of Languishing

Languishing impairs students' ability to function in countless ways. One study of medical students found that languishing increased their odds of having suicidal thoughts, dropping out of school, and engaging in unethical behaviors once they were doing medical rounds in their fourth or fifth years of schooling, including:

- Allowing another student to steal answers from their exam during a closed-book examination

- Taking credit for another student's work

- Reporting a lab test or X-ray as pending when it had not been ordered

- Reporting lab results as normal when they had forgotten to inquire about the need for the test during the patient examination

- Not apologizing or taking responsibility for mistakes

Languishing and unethical behaviors may go together in medical settings because both are symptoms of a larger cause of overwork, competitiveness, and prioritizing profit. It is plausible that languishing may cause medical students to make mistakes and then not want to admit to them or apologize for them. When we lack a sense of purpose, belonging, and social contribution, the thought of admitting to a mistake can be overwhelming. To confess wrongdoing could create an even greater gulf in one's sense of belonging or contribution to the hospital and one's medical team. A "win," such as correctly requesting a lab test that finds a result that helps solve a patient's medical problem, is probably what a languishing medical student is hoping for.

Those medical students had worked very hard to reach their clinical training years. Despite all they'd accomplished, languishing prompted them to think of quitting before they ever had a chance to start a career. And if those medical students were willing to engage in such professionally risky behaviors, can you imagine what languishing might be doing to countless others as they settle into their careers?

The Canaries Have Flown the Coop

So you made your way through compulsory schooling and completed your launch into the "real world." In their mid-twenties, thirties, and forties, young adults face uncharted territory time and time again, including budding careers, new marriages, and, perhaps most uncharted— learning how to parent. This is one of the three stretches of life when languishing is at its highest.

To echo Tolstoy's famous line that "each unhappy family is unhappy in its own way," our unique stressors, traumas, communities, and personalities twist us and bend us in different ways. In the next chapter, we'll unpack the impact of racism and discrimination on languishing. But there are, of course, commonalities to our experiences. Daily stressors seem to keep accumulating and never abating.

During the pandemic, mothers in particular experienced a huge uptick in the amount of mothering they were being asked to do, with little to no support during the months of isolation, leading to—no surprise—an increase in languishing.

Postpartum depression (PPD) is now recognized as a serious problem and monitored in many women after they give birth. Worldwide, the estimate of PPD is 17 percent. But should we also be paying attention to the quieter but pernicious effects of postpartum languishing (PPL)? A study of mothers in Spain not only found that 40 percent of participants were languishing, but that these mothers were more likely to feel low "maternal confidence" than those with PPD, meaning they doubted they were capable of caring for their child in the ways the child needed. Low maternal confidence not only places enormous stress on mothers, but can also impede their ability to form healthy attachments with their newborn, feel a strong sense of maternal identity, and find satisfaction in their role as caregivers. The study found several important protective factors against PPL: higher levels of self-compassion, psychological flexibility, resilience, and social support from partners and families.

As children grow older, parenting doesn't get any easier. For example, school stress takes a heavy toll on parents as well as students. Choosing the best school for their child, with scarce data available, can involve countless hours of research, cost-benefit analysis, and general agonizing. Other so-called "invisible work" takes a toll on us as well. As adults, we are also tasked with navigating an increasingly labyrinthine tax system, attempting to curate a newsfeed that we can trust (without exposing ourselves to an overwhelming firehose of information), installing software update after software update, rushing to change passwords after data leaks, and so much more. Somehow, we keep being asked to do more with less, until sometimes we feel we have nothing left at all.

Besieged by so many stressors, it's no wonder adults today report difficulty savoring experiences and finding fulfillment in the blur of day-to-day life. Many of us find ourselves questioning the choices we have made as we come to terms with the reality of what our lives will look like. Did we choose the right place to live? The right person to partner with? The right career? The right friends? The right balance between work and life and friends and family? Have we neglected important emotional connections in service of our work, our wallets, our retirement plans? *It's too late to start over*, the voice in our heads tells us. Some of us must face the fact that we made all the "right" choices—we have everything we thought we wanted—yet we still feel unfulfilled. The markers of success we worked so hard to achieve turned out to be besides the point.

When we lose a sense of meaning in our lives, it's sometimes difficult to mentally rewind to a time when things *did* matter—when we felt the rush of learning new things, experiencing something for the first time, or expanding our worldview earlier in life—digging us deeper into the hole.

When Work Doesn't Work

Sociologists have observed a curious development in work in recent years: Everyone, regardless of pay or number of hours logged, reports more job-related stress today than ever before. What is strange on the face of all of this is that the average number of hours worked weekly hasn't changed all that much. Today, compared to the 1970s, people still work, on average, around thirty-five to forty hours per week.

Averages can be deceiving. The numbers hide the fact that some people are putting in many more hours a week while others are putting in many fewer. The percentage of people working fifty-plus hours a week has gone up, as has the percentage of people working thirty hours or less a week.

People in high-level service jobs—doctors, lawyers, financial advisers, and other professionals—have more work and higher pay than ever before, while people in low-level service jobs—janitors, waiters, bartenders, daycare providers, and others—are working slightly less, often because they cannot find enough work, or high-paying enough work, to make ends meet. The difference is quite small, though—in the United States, the top 10 percent of earners work an average of 46.6 hours per week, while the bottom 10 percent work just over four hours fewer, 42.2 hours per week. Internationally, it's a slightly different story—in one study across twenty-seven countries, the data showed that the top 10 percent of full-time workers actually work an hour less per week than the bottom 10 percent of earners.

Regardless of the exact number of hours worked, both groups of workers are stressed, one because they work too much and bring their work home at night and on weekends, the other because they cannot count on stable, continuous work, they cannot find enough work, period, or they are working more than one job and often doing it as the lone provider in a single-headed household caring for at least one dependent child.

My research has found that, in the United States, adults who are languishing miss six more days of work per year—called "absenteeism"—than the general population, adding up to *twenty-three years* of lost economic productivity every year. But when it comes to presenteeism, where someone left early or was less than productive due to mental or emotional reasons, languishing accounts for more than *fifty-two years* of lost work each year in the United States.

Protection Against Work Stress

Earlier, I touched on how flourishing builds up a strong immunity to high-stress environments. The strongest evidence for that finding comes from a longitudinal study of Australian employees, which found that positive mental health is either a vulnerability or a source of resilience, depending on its level. The study tracked the impact of high-stress or high-conflict workplaces on employees' psychological distress—feeling nervous, hopeless, restless, fidgety, worthless, depressed, or that "everything feels like an effort."

You won't be surprised to hear that languishing employees exhibited higher levels of distress. But I was more interested in another finding, one I found truly amazing: The researchers found that employees who had high levels of positive mental health—those who were flourishing— had the lowest levels of distress over time *regardless of their job stress.*

What *did* impact their mental health on the job was the level of support they got from their colleagues. We need coworkers we get along with, who are there for us, who understand that we all have bad days, and who create an atmosphere of collegiality—warmth, trust, and openness.

In other words, working in a high-demand, high-stress environment that is *not* supportive will undermine your well-being and make it more likely that you will languish.

Is Stress a Prerequisite for Languishing?

Years ago, I remember tuning in to the beginning of *The Oprah Winfrey Show* just as Oprah asked a question that stopped me in my tracks: "How many days have you felt grateful for your nice home and your healthy children and your caring husband, but you still feel like a piece of the puzzle is missing? You feel there is a hole somewhere, and you think to yourself, 'Is this all there is?' It's because your heart feels a longing for something more. If you can relate to that, you're not alone, because we couldn't believe how many women share this silent struggle."

The women who spoke on that episode clarified the challenges of languishing in life, of the feeling of emptiness that pervaded their days. Even those with strong marriages, healthy children, good jobs, and nice homes in good neighborhoods felt adrift. One woman said, "Oprah, I'm a happily married woman and a mother of two children. I've been blessed with my health and my financial stability. I'm looking for ways to satisfy an unsettling feeling. It's like *a void in the center of my soul.*"

Another woman said she asked herself, "Why am I here? My spirit keeps telling me *there's more to this life.*"

Still another said she was "looking for direction in my life, a sense of purpose, something that defines who I am. *I want something more; I just don't know how to get there.*"

Then a woman spoke to how languishing created a craving for something more, a feeling I recognized all too well; she said she had "tried to find and fill the void with food, money, love, sex, possessions, self-help groups. I still have this feeling there should be *something more.*"

That episode that I happened to catch so many years ago feels remarkably fresh and relevant today. I recently connected with an acquaintance, Andrea, who told me that she felt she was languishing. When I asked her to elaborate, she—a busy mom of two young boys—took the time to write me an eloquent response, outlining an experience that Oprah might have featured on that very same show:

> Languishing feels like being on an airplane, circling above the runway but unable to land. It doesn't feel like I'm in imminent danger—I'm strapped into my seat and generally fine, but there's a sense that I'm waiting for a resolution that is taking forever to come. Strangely, I'm not even sure what it is. Anxieties that were never there pop up. (Did another plane crash on the runway? Are we going to run out of gas?) Languishing puts you squarely in the present and makes you aware of all that is going on around you, but it's not mindfulness; it's hypervigilance.
>
> In moments of pause, it starts to feel like you aren't really living like you once did, and too many things feel out of your control. (When will this plane ever land so I can get on with my life?) Yet all the tedious tasks of daily living stay piled high in front of you (I'm still so damn busy! And tired!). It feels like every day you're putting out a hundred little fires and never getting to do the things that really matter, the fulfilling things you remember doing pre-pandemic. The world has largely returned to normal, but somehow I'm still stuck in a pandemic state of mind.

Both my friend Andrea and these women on Oprah understood that many of their lives were objectively enviable but lacking the elements of flourishing. Were they expecting too much of themselves and their lives? Are we all? Is it naive to think true flourishing is attainable in this messy, chaotic world? The word *flourishing* might paint a picture of blissful calm and round-the-clock happiness, but you need only seven of the fourteen signs of well-being to flourish. Moreover, many elements of flourishing—for example, purpose in life, acceptance of self and others, belonging—are basic human needs for living a decent life. No, I don't think high expectations are the main problem. And a robust body of research supports the argument that flourishing is attainable for people from all walks of life and a diverse array of circumstances.

Languishing Late in Life

Flourishing peaks between the ages of sixty and sixty-five, as many stressors diminish. But at the same time, one's sense of purpose and contribution begins to decline. Parenting and work both provide bulwarks against the sense that life is meaningless. If you live long enough past the age of seventy-five, which more and more people are doing, languishing creeps back in.

My research on languishing in this age group has found that the increase in life-threatening diseases such as diabetes, hypertension, stroke, cancer, and heart disease was *not* a significant cause of increased languishing. Instead, another set of physical ailments that pose fewer health risks but can cause pain and embarrassment and limit one's independence is to blame: constipation, hemorrhoids, back pain, sleep difficulties, and foot injuries, for instance.

I have a dear family member who is now eighty-eight years old who no longer flies and therefore no longer comes down south to visit me and my wife in Atlanta. Why? Because he has had bouts of incontinence and is understandably worried that it will happen during the two-hour flight, which would embarrass him deeply. As a result, we do not visit with one another as much as we used to, and we all miss that form of connection during these years.

The decline is such that by some estimates, after the age of seventy-five, we may spend an average of only 10 percent of most days in direct contact with other people, let alone with someone we love and care about.

This is a real cause of concern. But there's a silver lining. Something very interesting happens as we get older: Relationships tend to be perceived as more intimate and satisfying. In fact, in some cases, the reduction in the quantity of social contact is a deliberate attempt to improve the *quality* of social contact.

Endings matter. When we have a sense that time is abundant, we tend to take it for granted, not thinking too carefully about whether our life and behavior reflect our priorities. But when we approach the end of our story, we start to focus on what truly matters to us. A by-product of growing older is a shift from an almost limitless subjective time frame to a compressed one.

As we grow older and recognize we have less life left to live, we are more likely to assess others based on whether they can provide emotionally close and satisfying contact. We no longer suffer fools gladly, and we choose to spend less and less time with people whom we do not admire, care about, or have feelings for. There is also evidence that we are better able to prevent unpleasant interpersonal exchanges as we age. Couples learn to discuss sensitive topics in ways that prevent the instigation and display of negative feelings.

Chapter six will explore how anyone can nurture the kinds of relationships that contribute to flourishing, which are characterized by a mutual sense of equality and emotional closeness, and by connections across age and class lines.

As the mortality data shows us in stark terms, older adults who continue to flourish, who feel that they still have a purpose in life and have a strong sense of contributing to society, live not only longer but also more meaningful lives; they add quality to the quantity of longer life they've been granted.

Languishing: A Once Deadly Sin Returns

As a Catholic boy, I spent the better part of my youth in confessionals on Saturdays admitting to and atoning for my week of sins. Happiness, I was taught, would follow only after purging all the bad stuff inside me and reciting my rosary prayers.

I never once confessed to being empty, to languishing, to feeling *blah*—but perhaps that would have been appropriate. During particularly "naughty" weeks, I started to feel empty inside because I hadn't honored myself or God with good works and good behavior. In better weeks, I felt contented and filled with pride, and I would glow on Sunday as I worked alongside Father Henry as his altar boy.

Languishing was once, believe it or not, considered the eighth deadly sin, although of course there is nothing remotely sin-like about this very real sense of suffering. We all are familiar with vanity, envy, gluttony, lust, wrath, greed, and sloth. But many centuries ago, *acedia*—the historical equivalent of feeling blah or languishing—was also on the list.

Acedia is derived from the Greek term *akēdia*, meaning an absence of care, whether for life or one's self. The influential early Christian monk Evagrius Ponticus (345–399 A.D.) described it as a restless boredom that tempted monks to disengage with religious life. Early Syrian writers equated acedia with a despondent spirit, and John Cassian (360–435 A.D.), a Christian mystic of the fourth century, described acedia as a weariness of the heart. Whatever you call it—acedia or languishing—it stops you from feeling or performing at your best, and, to make it doubly difficult, powerless to change your circumstances.

Acedia vanished from the list of deadly sins in the sixth century at the hands of Pope Gregory the Great, lost in the mists of time from

Western thought. (It appears that it was folded into the category of sloth.) Nevertheless, acedia continued to plague people from all walks of life throughout history.

Languishing is just as bad for you today as it was in the past, though it is (mercifully) no longer framed as sinful. Correctly understood, languishing isn't a sin at all; it is a personal and global public health problem—as we'll see in the next chapter.

[2]

How Did We Get Here?

When Scott hit his ten-year work anniversary, he turned on his computer one morning to find an email from his boss: "You are required to attend a well-being and resilience program. Please sign up here."

"Screw that" was the only response Scott could muster. And he deleted the email. At that point in time, he was just barely getting by. He was in the middle of finalizing a contentious divorce from his former wife. They had been very financially comfortable as a couple, but since the breakup, he had gone from financially secure to basically destitute. There he was, trying to build a new home and life for his four young children, and he could barely afford salt shakers. He tried to blame it on his ex-wife, who he felt was "taking him for everything," because blaming someone else felt good, at least temporarily.

Scott would have been the first to tell you that he was the poster child for the anti-well-being movement. He had spent a decade working as a prison guard in a large women's prison in southern Australia, and although at one point he had loved his work, these days he didn't want to be at work at all. When he was there, he was simultaneously combative and withdrawn. If someone challenged a decision he made or the way he handled a situation, he wasn't interested in listening or discussing the matter. He just went on the offensive, trying to win an argument, not by proving his point but by being more aggressive than his opponent.

Although he loved his kids immensely, his home life wasn't all that different. He had been raising his boys much the same way as his father had raised him. There was no room for discussion or dissension—it was his way or the highway, and he was fine with that. There was, he'll admit, a lot of yelling. And there was little room for joy or fun, sharing or caring. He focused on work and home, and he went to bed every night ready to do it all over again—to make it through without a major problem.

Unlike in a lot of rock-bottom stories, during that period, Scott actually quit drinking. It was as if even his old vices couldn't make him feel anything anymore. He knew he was in a bad place mentally, but he didn't have the energy or ambition to get himself out of it.

It took a nudge from a good friend who had already completed the program and knew he would benefit as much as she had, to get Scott to finally sign up. Faye, who had worked with Scott for years, had nearly lost touch with him during Scott's period of languishing. He had stopped spending time in the break room, he had bailed on after-work drinks, and he had kept his head down in the hallways, barely looking up to greet his colleagues.

He had always been one of the friendlier guys at work, and Faye hated to see him that way, disconnected and silent, almost distrustful. One day, she showed up in his office and told him she thought he should stop fighting the higher-ups on the well-being program and just sign up. He needed it, she told him. Scott had always liked Faye, even if they hadn't seen much of each other lately, so he begrudgingly agreed.

It was just the nudge he needed. Scott's experience in that room a few weeks later would open his eyes to a new way of being. The people in the room with him—both during the program and in the hallways later—weren't his enemies. They didn't think he was an idiot—at least he didn't think they did. Why did he insist on fighting with them? In fact, why was he always spoiling for a fight? Wouldn't working together be far more productive? He hadn't trusted them—hell, he hadn't trusted anyone during those brutal months following his wife's decision to leave—but did they deserve so much of his vitriol? Hadn't he once been one of the best-connected, most well-liked guys at work? Hadn't he believed they were all there for the same reason—to make a difference in whatever way they could?

Scott couldn't say when he stopped caring about outcomes at work. He had once truly cared about the women in his prison, hoping they would find some meaning during their time there and use the experience to build a better life for themselves once they got out. But he'd just been punching a clock lately. So he'd just assumed everyone else was, too.

When had he lost sight of the needs of the humans around him? Why did both work and home feel like an endless list of chores to be slogged through, not places to contribute something to? Why was he refusing all connections with those he loved and liked and admired? Why had he shut down his caring gene? Where on earth was all his anger and isolation and giving-no-fucks getting him? Nowhere, he realized. He sat in that room and looked around him at all the people he had once felt so connected to, and he resolved to soften his heart, to open his eyes, to believe in something once more.

The Well-being and Resilience Program trainer reminded them that this was a program designed for them to participate in and actively learn about themselves. They were told to make themselves comfortable throughout, to get up if they needed to stretch, and to walk around if necessary. No rules, no restrictions. To Scott, this was a classroom game-changer. They were in that room for the students to learn, not just for the teacher to hold court, the way he remembered school—this was a completely different experience, one much more suited to his learning style.

He also appreciated the training's intense focus on the growth mind-set. They worked hard on starting to name and understand their own strengths, which really opened his eyes to how he was perceived, as well as how he viewed himself. After just a few hours, he was reminded that one of his strengths was that he was *good* with people—he used to be anyway. It dawned on him that he could grow that skill again—that he could grow in many ways, in fact.

He felt utterly changed. Just a few hours in that program—it was as though someone had dumped a bucket of ice water on his head. He was awake now. And he had no desire to keep the experience to himself. He went to see Faye to thank her; then he took a deep breath and asked another question: Would she be willing to take yet another well-being course with him, this time with the goal of becoming trainers themselves?

Scott didn't know it then, but he had already taken his first steps toward flourishing: He started to connect with his colleagues again, Faye above all, and he thought he might have found his purpose: connecting with people and working with them to find their own strengths. The program also focused on mindfulness training and meditation practices. He began to look inside himself with compassion and objectivity, to calm himself in any given moment, to focus on what he could control, rather than lament over what he couldn't. He started to see and understand himself, others, and the conditions that shaped them more clearly in these quiet, introspective moments. He couldn't help but think that others could benefit from everything he was learning, too. He began to think of his job as caring for the inmates and their well-being, not just guarding them.

The women in his prison had been through hell and back, and he knew all too well how the traumas they had experienced had affected their well-being. He had already reconnected with Faye. He thought it might be worth a try to connect with the women again and perhaps help them find the things they had lost in their own lives—the kinds of connections, meaning, and purpose none of us should live without.

Loneliness Is Part of Languishing

Scott's transformation is a story of moving from feeling defeated, bitter, and retreating from life to regaining a sense of purpose and something to live and fight for. There is a sweetness to life when we find something bigger and better to live for.

The last chapter gave a close-up view of the causes and costs of languishing in specific communities and age groups. In this chapter—"How Did We Get Here?"—we'll look at broader forces at work, focusing on the decline of warm, trusting relationships and the brain and body's response to loneliness, as well as racism, discrimination, and other forms of adversity.

You've probably heard that loneliness is now considered a public health epidemic, associated with shorter lives and a host of mental and physical health problems. Put simply, the "war on loneliness" is really about the need to address the absence of warm, trusting relationships in our lives, of a sense of belonging, and of acceptance within a community. Loneliness is only a part—an important one—of a bigger problem that is the epidemic of languishing.

In a 2021 study, when respondents were asked if they had felt very lonely frequently or most of the time in the month prior, 36 percent responded in the affirmative. For those between ages eighteen and twenty-five, the number rose to an alarming 61 percent, with 43 percent reporting an increase since the pandemic had begun.

In August 2020, the Bureau of Labor Statistics reported that people over the age of fifteen were spending one more hour alone, measured as time not spent in face-to-face contact, increasing from 6.1 hours in 2019 to 7 hours in 2020. Adults with a spouse or partner but no children saw an increase of just under an hour—forty-eight minutes—while adults with a child age eighteen or younger at home saw the smallest increase, just over a half hour—thirty-six minutes—of time spent alone in 2020 compared with 2019. (That said, the 2020 studies on loneliness also pointed out an alarming statistic: that 51 percent of mothers with young kids reported serious loneliness.)

The statistics also showed that people spent less time socializing with people outside their household, indicating that social isolation—having less contact with fewer people—increased during the pandemic. People tend to meet the people who will become their best friends, on average, at the age of twenty-one, and these days, people are finding it harder and harder to make new friends as they get older, move around, and hit different life phases.

We can see that in the data, too; studies show that loneliness increases as we age. Close relationships disappear as we get older due to death or moving from home into a nursing home. Social disconnection can also be tied to our living arrangements. Prior to the twentieth century, living alone was uncommon, and it remained so until about the last half of the century. Our ancestors slept together, worked together, and fought together. Researchers have documented a dramatic uptick in living alone, which began in the United States and other industrialized economies and has continued unabated ever since. In some countries and cities, as much as 60 percent of all living arrangements are solitary. People already living alone have been steadily getting less face-to-face contact since 2003, and the pandemic magnified this trend for this cohort, jumping from 9.7 hours spent alone in 2019 to 11.3 hours in 2020.

We consider people to be socially isolated when they have few friends and relatives or have little or infrequent contact with them. People can be isolated socially because they don't have many (or any) people to spend time with, or they may have relationships but cannot spend much time with those people. As time spent alone increases, social isolation is assumed to increase.

The truth is that they only correlate modestly. Spending a lot of time with people does not mean that it is time spent with people with whom there are the love, warmth, trust, and other qualities that make for meaningful relationships. You can feel lonely when you spend a lot or most of your time with people with whom you are not close. Or you may spend more time alone, but what little time you spend with others is with people you are close to; you do not feel lonely because you experience loving, warm, trusting relationships with other people.

That said, loneliness, social isolation, and living alone all lead to premature death. One review of seventy studies of over three million subjects concluded that living alone increased the chances of premature death by 32 percent (compared to living with others), social isolation increased the chance of death by 29 percent (compared to people with larger social networks and more frequent contact), and loneliness increased the chances of death by 26 percent in all age groups.

Loneliness rarely happens in a bubble. Take my friend Jonas, who was in his eighties. After his first glorious decade of retirement, he began to lose his sense of purpose in life, which happened because he came to believe he had nothing left to contribute to society. I told him again and again that that was a false message from the world. "You do not have to believe you have nothing left to give to your community." He confessed to me that he had begun spending less time in his social clubs and participating in his leisure activities; he had also begun to withdraw from his community after his long-term partner had died not long after his best friend had passed away.

His pulling back from society had ripple effects. He had started to be less accepting of himself; he had begun to dislike more parts of his personality, even ones he had formerly liked. He had become less confident, and he had stopped feeling that he was growing as a person. He told me that he had begun to think that his life was over and that living longer was not a gift but a curse.

Jonas was languishing not just because he was lonely but in part because he was disconnected—from himself, from others, from his sense that his life mattered. Loneliness rarely happens alone because it goes hand-in-hand with—sometimes as a result of, sometimes as a cause of—loss of purpose, personal growth, social contribution, mastery, autonomy, and so on.

The Pain of Being Alone

We know from quite a bit of research that being alone in a room is pretty uncomfortable for many people, especially these days. According to a much cited 2014 study, when participants were asked to store any belongings that might be entertaining (cell phones, computers, writing implements, etc.) and to spend some time being "alone with their thoughts" for several minutes, the results were almost comically surprising. More than 57 percent found it difficult to concentrate, and 89 percent felt their mind wandering, even though there was nothing to concentrate on but themselves. Even more troubling: Nearly 50 percent of the participants rated their enjoyment of the task at or *below* the midpoint of the scale.

But it gets worse. When the experiment started, the participants were offered the chance to self-administer electric shocks—entirely at their own discretion—during their time alone. The experimenters were astonished to find out that more than a few participants would rather undergo electric shocks than be alone with their thoughts; a full 67 percent of men and 25 percent of women gave themselves at least one electric shock during the thinking period.

This study might be familiar to you, but I want you to try to look at it anew, as I do, through the lens of languishing. Basically, the study nudged people into a state of languishing by removing any possibility of an outside connection, leaving them alone with themselves. The result? The enforced isolation—the situational induction of temporary languishing—caused a bout of nonsuicidal self-harm. The subjects chose to hurt themselves in order to feel something rather than nothing.

Silence and stillness can be forced upon you by circumstances or by others. I remember a truism spoken often and widely when I was growing up that "Children are to be seen, not heard." I was a high-energy child, and the traditional classroom was a daily prison sentence for me. I recall being reprimanded too many times to count for not being quiet or sitting still. My exuberance—what the teacher called disruption—was a punishable offense. I would have to wear the "dunce hat"—yes, a conical hat fashioned of paper—and sit still and quiet in the corner of the classroom.

Too much quiet and stillness for too long feels aversive; it inevitably begins to feel like punishment. We have all been in a meeting, exposed to an awkward pause that lingers for so long that it motivates someone to break the silence, speak up. Our natural aversion to quiet happens because being still and quiet for too long can morph into emptiness and stagnation and become a source of deep pain.

The pain psychologist Rachel Zoffness speaks eloquently about this state of emotional distress and how it feels much like physical pain. Her expertise is in how cognitive, emotional, social, and environmental factors, including adverse childhood experiences, discrimination, loneliness, the stories we tell ourselves about pain, the ways we ruminate on it, and our conscious and unconscious coping strategies, from physical clenching to opioids, can affect the way the brain and spinal cord process pain signals.

Zoffness tells us that the more often you label mental or physical distress as a "bad" thing, more and deeper pain pathways are created that heighten the sensitivity of your central nervous system to pain. When those so-called pain pathways become too well trodden, even the smallest stressors—emotional, psychological, social, or physical— are interpreted by the brain as a huge burden.

Evolution did not favor creating separate and multiple systems in the brain for processing different kinds of pain. The neuroscientist John Cacioppo made similar findings in his research on "social pain," which is the pain of loneliness and disconnection. The more intensely our thoughts and feelings reflect disconnection or problems with connection, the more likely those thoughts are to cause pain. It doesn't matter to your brain whether it is a nurse's needle puncturing your skin to inject a necessary medicine or you are feeling ashamed, thinking you are unlovable, or imagining your future as hopeless; the same pain center in your brain is being activated and sending an aversive signal to order the body to engage in some "repair" activities.

Who can honestly say that a broken bone hurts more than a broken heart? It hurts to live in fear without safety and security. It hurts to be ostracized, to feel shame, to feel unlovable. It hurts to experience discrimination that's demeaning. Such hurt can be accompanied by a feeling of being overwhelmed, as if you are being threatened or attacked. That is why stress hormones can course through our veins when we feel distress and pain no matter what is causing the pain and distress.

That hurt, that pain, that stress reaction try to encourage us to do something constructive—say, therapy—to alleviate the memories and thinking patterns that are causing the pain. Too many people are stuck, cannot afford therapy, cannot respond, and they are likely to turn to drugs or alcohol to mask the pain. Gabor Maté, in his book *In the Realm of Hungry Ghosts,* describes many addictions as functioning like "emotional anesthetics" for those craving relief from the pain of social ostracization. He writes of one patient who said that the first time she experienced the drug of her choice it felt like a "warm, soft hug."

Connection from injection (heroin), connection from ingestion (alcohol or food)—whatever our drug of choice, we try to find the feeling of connection from addictive substances and behaviors when we cannot get it from the real thing, especially when the real thing has been a source of great pain.

Connection can cut both ways. The absence of it can cause pain, and, for some of us, the presence of it can be a source of trauma and pain that we try to mask.

Feeling Disconnected

Disconnection was profoundly distressing for Scott. He wanted to blame the pain of the divorce on his wife. Like Scott, we want to find something obvious to blame. Social media is an obvious target. As smartphones came into wider use, the amount of time people spent in in-person interactions plummeted. But social media is both a medium and a tool, and we can choose to use it or not. All craftspeople, from carpenters to electricians, know they need the right tools in their hands to get the best results. I know I have used a smartphone when it was the wrong tool and didn't get the best results. I have used email and texting to "get things off my plate." I wanted things done quickly when instead I could have made direct contact, during which I could have given and received more warmth, built more trust, and created more belonging.

And some key indicators of connection were already declining well before smartphones and platforms such as Facebook appeared on the scene. David Brooks, the writer and journalist, has written extensively about the collapse of social trust and how nations that are higher functioning on a number of fronts have higher-trust societies. In his view, civic engagement is the key to a functioning society, one in which we all feel connected and share a sense of the common good. The declines that Brooks talks about have been happening steadily over the past several decades. Some of those declines appear to be a receding from an abnormally high level of reconnection that happened in response to the rebuilding of society and life after World War II.

For example, membership in religious groups and communities has been dropping precipitously for years; according to a recent Gallup Poll, as of 2020, only 47 percent of Americans belonged to a house of worship, whether a mosque, a synagogue, or a church. Just before the pandemic, in 2018, that number was 50 percent, which was a steep drop from 70 percent in 1999, well before anyone in the country knew what a coronavirus was.

Another recent study argued that the steep drop in religious participation in this country happened in parallel with an increase in deaths of despair—suicide, alcohol abuse, and drug overdoses—which the researchers linked to this loss of community and the attendant increase of loneliness and isolation. As the political scientist Robert Putnam has been telling us for decades, as bowling leagues—literal and metaphorical—were falling out of favor, trust in our schools, our government, even our fellow Americans was ebbing. Back then, Putnam wasn't able to foresee what the advent of personal technology and social media would do to and for us, both good and bad.

Building Connections Requires Skills

Like so many of us searching for warmth and goodness during the pandemic lockdown, I started watching *Ted Lasso*. (Skip the following paragraph if you don't want spoilers.)

At the end of the second season, Ted's former assistant coach, Nate, took a turn to the dark side. His shift into villainy—to win at all costs—caught many of the show's fans by surprise. But I'm sad to say that although I found it disheartening, I wasn't all that shocked. Nate had been bullied for so long; wasn't his desire for power and status a pretty natural response to the deep-seated insecurity created by years of being tormented by others?

We are a lot like Nate these days. Our response to a polarized world—the way we go on the offensive—is more of a defense mechanism. We ache from a deeply ingrained insecurity we feel but don't want to admit to—so we sometimes look to hurt others rather than be hurt.

Sometimes when I peer out into the world these days, it appears that we are sharpening our cruelty rather than working on our empathy. We all know that negative or divisive comments, headlines, and social media posts garner more likes and muster up more interest. The worry is that we are practicing the wrong skills. We are building a world—especially online, but it is leaking into our everyday lives as well—in which cruelty is becoming normative, even reflexive. The win-at-all-costs theory of modern life leads to us shedding our kinder, gentler selves in favor of a tougher competitor who can help us get ahead—or if not, at least hold others down to suffer alongside us.

We tend to think that having more social connections will reduce our loneliness because social connections make our lives meaningful. But a lot rides on what both sides can bring to the relationship. Recently, I was spending time with a friend of mine, a Zen Buddhist monk, who was talking about how Buddhists believe that most of life is an acquired skill. You have to practice things to get good at them. We both concluded that forming satisfying social connections characterized by warmth, trust, patience, mutual understanding, and empathy requires skill. Being alone more and "doing" more of our lives alone means that we may be losing our skills for getting what we really need from our social connections.

Countless books have been written about emotional intelligence skills for a reason; experts know that these are skills we must build—being more attuned to others and learning how to connect with others through empathy and perspective taking. Therapists and clinicians have been worrying about learning losses in these areas, not just among kids and youths but among adults as well. But as most of us know, it is really hard to find other people with whom we share interests; the ability to be vulnerable and supportive and communicate in a healthy way, especially around conflict, is far from a given. Making new friends in adulthood requires time and effort; exposing yourself to unplanned interactions, which can be especially challenging after having kids or moving to a new city, isn't all that easy for anyone, no matter how social you wish to be or how hard you're willing to try.

But connection is also about shared interests and shared values, or at least acceptance, tolerance, and curiosity, when some of those things aren't shared. We are sharing more than values and interests when we connect, because we are sharing some of ourselves and our life with another person. The question is whether we have something meaningful to share. I happen to think we do.

Social Connections and a Meaningful Life Are Mutually Reinforcing

It is tempting to think that social connections cause meaning in life, not the other way around. Sometimes, the causal arrows can go both ways. Flourishing is the combination of connection—warm and trusting relationships and feelings of belongingness to a community—with purpose in life and a variety of other markers of a meaningful life. A meaningful life with meaningful connections is what we are aiming for; it may be the answer to the modern problem of living and working alone, feeling lonely, and languishing.

It would make sense that isolating people and making them spend too much time alone erode the meaningfulness of life. Experimental evidence suggests that temporarily causing people to feel isolated by making them feel rejected or ostracized—excluded—causes a loss of their meaning in life. Restoring their feeling of belonging and being accepted by others increases their sense of having a meaning in life.

In other words, feelings of loneliness are tied to our sense of purpose as much as the quantity of our social connections is. What is it about having a meaningful life that motivates you to connect with others? One cross-sectional study—meaning it was done at a single point in time—has shown that measuring meaning in life explained 25 percent of the loneliness scores, while measuring social connections explained only 14 percent of the scores. The researchers also found that, altogether, having more connections and having a more meaningful life predicted loneliness, or the lack thereof, with even more precision.

We seem to be making our own beds, so to speak. Even though we know we crave and require meaningful human connection to thrive, we keep making decisions that lead to our being and feeling more alone. Connection makes our lives meaningful; a meaningful life makes us want to connect and share it with others.

Discrimination and Flourishing

For some, the world is not only an alienating place, but an actively hostile one. Discrimination—whether on the basis of race, ethnicity, sexual orientation, gender identity, gender expression, or socioeconomic status—highly suppresses seven of the fourteen components of flourishing, making it more difficult to:

1. feel that society is becoming a better place (social growth);

2. make sense of what is going on in the world around you (social coherence);

3. feel that you belong to the larger community (social integration);

4. hold yourself in high regard (self-acceptance);

5. feel confident to think and express your ideas and opinions (autonomy);

6. feel you can manage your own life (environmental mastery); and

7. have a trusting and positive attitude toward others (social acceptance).

Black Americans report particularly low levels of social acceptance—55 percent less than white Americans—a perfectly rational response to a society that's given them every reason to mistrust it.

How can we begin to calculate the full toll of facing stereotyping, prejudice, injustice, and brutality (or the threat of brutality) throughout your life? The stark disparities in rates of physical disease and mental illness speak loudly and urgently. But research also points to more insidious effects.

Even outward success can come at a cost to people who overcome the odds stacked against them. John Henryism, a term coined by social epidemiologist Sherman James, describes the prolonged stress of learning to cope "well" with social and economic adversity, unemployment, underemployment, low incomes, less education, poor housing, segregated and violent neighborhoods, and so on. The scale to measure JH coping consists of twelve statements. Respondents indicate the degree to which each item is "true" or "false" of their disposition toward life. The statements include:

- I've always felt that I could make of my life pretty much what I wanted to make of it.

- Once I make up my mind to do something, I stay with it until the job is completely done.

- I like doing things that other people thought could not be done.

- When things don't go the way I want them to, that makes me work even harder.

- I don't let my personal feelings get in the way of doing a job.

- Hard work has really helped me to get ahead in life.

Being asked to prove your worth again and again, to show the world how "resilient," "strong," and "inspiring" you are, and to simply shield yourself from the toll of discrimination, builds up chronic stress over time. Sherman James correctly hypothesized that JH coping would not only be more common among the Black community, but would also explain the community's higher rates of hypertension and heart disease.

Researchers, including myself, have long been puzzled by a phenomenon called "The Black-White Paradox of Health and Illness." Despite facing greater social inequality, discrimination, stress exposure, and physical morbidity, Black Americans report lower rates of mental health disorders and higher levels of flourishing than the white population. How could that be? And what story do those numbers really tell?

Some studies have pointed to the role of two protective factors against languishing: Black Americans report higher levels of both self-esteem and social support than white Americans. Social support works in two important ways—it is both a belief *and* a reality. It is the belief that *when I tell others I have a problem or they learn about my tragedy, those people will come to me to provide help and comfort.* Believing that you have others you can count on promotes well-being even when you do not need that social support, much like the calm of knowing you have money in the bank or a retirement account that is growing steadily over your working years.

And social support is of course also a reality—having a ready, able, and motivated group of people to lean on when you need it. Black parents are more likely than white parents to believe that they, as parents, are role models to their own and other children; to say being a parent is the most important aspect of their identity (42 percent of Black and 38 percent of Latinx/Hispanic parents report this, compared to 25 percent of white parents); and Black and Latinx/Hispanic parents are more than twice as likely to say that parenting is always rewarding and enjoyable than both white and Asian American parents.

Every year, the Healthy Minds Network surveys tens of thousands of undergraduate and graduate students on their mental health—including the prevalence of languishing—as well as their likelihood of seeking help, quality of treatment, and beliefs and attitudes regarding mental health conditions. Their 2021–2022 findings were consistent with the so-called "Black-white" paradox; Black students were 1.36 times as likely to be flourishing than white students. Other studies, however, indicate that this "advantage" disappears with age, suggesting that life in the U.S. adult world wears people down. (A similar phenomenon has been observed in the Latinx/Hispanic immigrant population. Early arrivals to the United States see improved health outcomes, but the longer they remain here, the worse their health—and that initial advantage has shrunk substantially since the onset of the covid pandemic.)

When looking at rates of languishing—or any health outcome—within historically marginalized groups, it's important to contextualize those numbers by considering their lived experiences of being dismissed, underdiagnosed, and undertreated by the healthcare industry. Doctors routinely judge Black patients' pain as lower than white patients', prescribing them less pain medication, and at lower doses. Among those with a mental health problem, Black students in the Healthy Minds study were 73 percent less likely to get a diagnosis after seeking help than their counterparts, and were more likely to seek support from family, friends, and other informal sources than to seek clinical care.

Researchers analyzing the study also stressed the role of personal and perceived public stigma in receiving mental health treatment. Sixty-three percent of Black students agreed with the statement that "Most people would think less of someone who has received mental health treatment"—the highest out of any racial or ethnic group—while Black students reported the lowest levels of *personal* stigma (6 percent), and Asian American and Asian international students reported the highest (23 percent and 35 percent, respectively). Across the board—unsurprisingly—stigma was higher among men than women.

The spike of anti-Asian hate crimes and verbal harassment in the wake of the pandemic will forever stain our nation's history. Psychological distress has skyrocketed among Asian Americans, many of whom report the grueling mental and emotional toll of years of hypervigilance—and the strain of hypervisibility. "At one point [in 2021], I bought a panic button and started wearing it on a lanyard around my neck, a tiny weight that I would rub absentmindedly to self-soothe," the writer Esther Wang recounted in a piece in *New York* magazine.

The fingerprints of this acute stress were clearly visible in the Healthy Minds survey: 68 percent of Asian American students were languishing, more than any other racial or ethnic group. They were also the least likely to seek clinical care, with roughly 80 percent of mental health cases going untreated—and those who did seek treatment exhibited the highest rates of distress at intake, followed by Latinx, Black, and then white students—though therapists and psychiatrists have reported more Asian American patients coming through their doors (or virtual doors) in recent years.

Another finding of the Healthy Minds survey was that a staggering 87 percent of transgender/nonbinary/other gender individuals were languishing, and were 52 percent less likely to be flourishing than cisgender men. Meanwhile, heterosexual students were 61 percent more likely to be flourishing than lesbian, gay, and bisexual students, a chilling indictment of the pain wrought by school bullying, lack of family support, bigotry, and overt violence they may face from an early age. The rate of mental illness is double for LGBTQ+ students: 20 percent of LGBTQ+ males compared with 9 percent of heterosexual males and 29 percent of LGBTQ+ females compared with 15 percent of heterosexual females.

This grim picture of the costs of discrimination across these various groups should, more than anything, galvanize cries for political and social change. As Sherry C. Wang, an associate professor of counseling psychology at Santa Clara University, told *The New York Times,* "While a new generation of Asian Americans can forge a different conversation about mental health, measures like therapy cannot solve a problem they did not start." The most restorative self-care routine in the world isn't a solution to the cultural blight of intolerance, ignorance, racism, xenophobia, and homophobia—nor is it a reparation for the inconceivable harm done to vulnerable communities.

Yet as we fight for a more safe, equitable, and antiracist world, we still have bodies and emotions, desires, and fears. Health equity is a social justice issue, and it calls for both systemic change and immediate care.

In recent years, reseachers have begun to recognize the profound role of social and environmental factors in determining health outcomes. We are not mere biological entities untethered from our surroundings, in other words. This understanding has guided my work on flourishing. To get a full picture of mental health, we need to look at the quality of our relationships—are they warm and trusting?—and the strength of our community ties—do we feel seen and supported? Mounting research has shown that these social "resources" are *especially* protective against adverse health outcomes in socioeconomically disadvantaged communities that may have fewer alternative resources to call on. That is, higher levels of flourishing have a more dramatic impact on quality of life for some than others.

One 2021 study found that the racial mortality gap between Black and white Americans disappeared among adults who meet the criteria for flourishing. (Black Americans live, on average, to 71, while non-Latinx/Hispanic white Americans live, on average, to 76—a galling figure.) The authors hypothesized that, "because Black Americans are disproportionately exposed to social conditions that deplete psychosocial resources, including poverty, residential segregation, neighborhood insecurity, and racism," and flourishing replenishes social resources that are powerful protectants against early mortality, the Black community benefits more from flourishing than the wider population.

This is not to suggest that flourishing can "erase" the wrongs of overpolicing, disproportionate incarceration, income inequality, and the prolonged stressors of discrimination, but rather, in the interest of immediate care, creating the conditions for flourishing advances health equity—and individual efforts and public health policy interventions can go hand in hand.

Responding to Adversity

The genetic response to adversity—whether it is the accrued trauma of a lifetime of discrimination, losing a job without having a financial cushion, or experiencing the pain of prolonged loneliness and isolation—is known as the conserved transcriptional response to adversity, or CTRA. When our mind senses a threat, it activates the genes that create inflammation and decreases the expression of antiviral and antibody genes that help keep us healthy. The CTRA functions much like our stress system's fight-or-flight response, directing all of the body's resources and energy to the most immediate task at hand, which is to survive for another day.

Inflammation is a useful bodily response to injury and infection that helps with the process of recovering and healing, but it is not a helpful response to emotional, social, or financial stressors—and in fact, it compounds the toll of prolonged adversity.

All kinds of stressors that do not represent threats to our life can activate our stress system and CTRA. Violence and financial insecurity pose very real dangers, of course. But other forms of adversity that the modern human experiences, such as ending a relationship with a partner, are not real flight-or-fight situations—yet the body acts as though they are. In most cases, the CTRA is a maladaptive response, increasing the risk of developing cancer, diabetes, heart disease, and mental health issues. For instance, studies have found that lonely people have more inflammation and less effective immune responses than people with close connections. To which you might ask, "So it's not enough to be miserable—I have to worry about chronic disease and early mortality, too?" It's a cruel twisting of the knife if you are languishing.

How can we better moderate our CTRA in times of stress and anxiety? Researchers have been looking for characteristics and qualities of people who do this well, because CTRA expression is almost invariably harmful. You might not be surprised when I tell you that flourishing has emerged as one of the leading predictors of a more muted CTRA.

To be clear, it is not the "feeling good" or "happiness" component of flourishing that helps modulate the CTRA, it is the *functioning well* part. In several studies across various cultures, researchers have found that it was not *just* the quick hits of joy and contentment—say, the elation of getting a good grade on a test, the rush of positivity that accompanies a nice compliment, the enjoyment of sitting in the sunshine with friends, having a beautiful meal—that made the difference. It was psychological well-being—the sense that one is living a life that has meaning and importance—that counted. Indeed, the research showed that when people with higher psychological well-being are highly stressed, their inflammation genes aren't ramped up and their antiviral genes aren't tamped down as much as those of people with low levels of psychological well-being.

In addition to affecting gene expression of the CTRA, higher levels of functioning well have been linked to related levels of biomarkers from blood samples. Researchers used data from the English Longitudinal Study of Ageing to determine whether levels of certain biomarkers that are linked to aspects of inflammation varied by level of emotional well-being. Once again, happiness and satisfaction (feeling good) were unrelated to participants' levels of C-reactive protein (CRP) and white blood cells (WBC), both of which are unhealthy biomarkers. But the participants who had higher levels of the indicators of psychological well-being (functioning well) had lower levels of CRP and WBC.

The data gathered in these and other studies pointed to the same conclusion: People who score high on psychological well-being have a much healthier response when they are experiencing adversity and stress. Basically, when you like most parts of your personality, when you have warm and trusting relationships, when you are being challenged to grow and become a better person, when your life has purpose, when you are confident about thinking and expressing your ideas and opinions, and when you can manage your life, you have higher psychological well-being. Psychological well-being is powerful "medicine," isn't it?

[3]

The Feelings Trap

Don't be fooled by happiness;
on its own, happiness is not the
North Star to flourishing.

We humans often get fooled by feelings. I think often of a lovely line from Henry David Thoreau: "Happiness is like a butterfly. If you chase it directly, it will elude you. But, if you turn your attention to other things, it will come sit softly on your shoulder."

In other words, we tend to focus too much on being happy. In typical American fashion, we try to achieve it as quickly and directly as possible, usually by chasing feeling "good." But that butterfly of happiness keeps flittering away. Perhaps a better approach, and one I am advocating for in this book, is to focus on achieving happiness by working on the functioning well aspects of flourishing. If you focus on improving how you are functioning in life (increasing your purpose in life, along with self-acceptance, social integration, and other ingredients of flourishing), happiness will come to you as a result of functioning better in life.

This is a lesson I try to teach my students every year. On the first day of a new semester, I often give the kids in my Sociology 352 class, The

Sociology of Happiness, a challenge. I ask them what they seek most. Inevitably, most of my students admit that what they seek most is happiness. Of course it is! The ancient Greek philosophers knew this; Epicurus (341–270 B.C.) was the first philosopher who championed pleasure. Guess what—twenty-first-century college students know it, too. Who doesn't want to feel good?

"Great!" I tell them. "Here is your first assignment. This afternoon, go out and do something that makes you happy. Then I want you to see if you can make your happiness last an hour; better yet, the whole afternoon." My students love this assignment. No reading? No papers? Just go and chase some metaphorical sunshine? Done. They walk out of the classroom with smiles on their faces.

When they come back to my classroom, I ask them how their assignment went. Lo and behold, they all failed. None of them were able to make happiness last an entire afternoon. The students might have remained in a good mood, enjoyed their day—but none of them could tell me, in all honesty, that they had felt happy for more than an hour or so. They just couldn't keep it going. And if they tried to, it felt unnatural. Why? Are my students all failures? Are they sad, hopeless creatures, destined for lives of misery?

Of course not. "Happiness is an emotion," I remind them. They look at me blankly. Of course happiness is an emotion, Professor— I can almost see them rolling their eyes at me. "So is sadness. Fear. Anger. Disgust." I name all six of the basic human emotions to underline my point. Then I challenge them to dig deeper into what an emotion really is.

In one study, pictures of hundreds of people expressing different emotions were placed in front of people from nearly every culture around the world. Six basic emotions were identified accurately by almost everyone in the study.

Every basic emotion—anger, fear, disgust, surprise, happiness, and sadness—has evolved to serve an important purpose. All emotions, not just the good ones, are vital. Sadness is an emotion we feel when we lose something of significance or importance; perhaps we have to relocate and leave a loved one behind, or someone we love dies. My students feel sad after graduating from college, when they have to leave it and their friends behind. Sadness motivates us to reflect, often quietly and alone, upon our lives, the nature of life, and how or why we feel as we do. Fear is another useful emotion because it marshals our attention and physical resources to respond wisely to an active threat to our life or well-being—although our fear response can be highly oversensitive, as I've discussed.

Does Happiness Serve Us?

What purpose or function might the emotion of happiness serve in our lives? The answer to this question eluded me and many others for decades until researchers began to understand the nature of addiction, alcoholism, and the role of dopamine in our brain. When we get something we want or need, we experience a rush of dopamine, which signals pleasure and reward in our brain. The outward sign of such pleasure is often happiness, though sometimes it can be expressed as joy, satisfaction, or contentment.

Regardless of how it might be expressed and felt, pleasure and the dopamine rush that accompanies it help our brain remember the details of the experience that brought that reward. For our ancestors, the source of pleasure was pretty rudimentary: food to eat, belonging to a tribe that helps keep us safe, warm, and fed. It is as simple as that: Our brain makes sure we feel happy when we get what we want, because it knows we will need more of it in the future to sustain ourselves and enjoy our lives.

"Emotions are, by definition, fleeting," I remind my students. "They aren't built to last." They're like wind socks at an airport—they blow in all different directions, and they are only telling you which direction the wind is blowing at any given time, so you can direct your activity accordingly. Ideally, we allow them in to do what they're supposed to do for us and then release them. We move on.

Feeling Nothing at All

The neuroscientist Antonio Damasio has written extensively about a patient of his who lost the ability to feel any emotion. Marvin, a onetime cheerful, loving husband and father, had a stroke when he was fifty-six-years old that paralyzed one side of his body.

Far more upsetting to his wife, though, was when his doctors told her that the stroke had damaged a vital part of his brain. That area—where the signals of the emotion the body is producing reaches the prefrontal cortex, the process by which our brain becomes aware of the emotion, then causes us to feel that emotion—had died. The bridge was out; the signal had stopped reaching the prefrontal cortex because of the damage. As a result, he was forever cut off from his feelings.

Usually, the rational decision-making brain works to reduce the enormous realm of options from which the rational brain must decide. Emotions, as gut feelings, allow us to reduce the possibilities from which to choose by ruling out all the patently bad ones, allowing our rational brain to make better decisions. Without the ability to feel emotions before we make decisions, the rational brain can

The problems begin when our emotions start to become pathological. If an emotion lingers too long and becomes too strong, we start to get into some trouble. If fear persists, it can turn into anxiety. If sadness lingers, it can turn into depression. Even happiness can last too long and get too strong; we call it mania.

My students in the afternoon-of-happiness challenge, alas, were stuck in an impossible situation. They were trying to sustain something that is not sustainable. As a society, we've placed pleasure, which is fueled by dopamine, and happiness, which is linked to serotonin, on a pedestal. If we aren't chasing positive feelings, advertisements for fitness classes, new tech gadgets, and luxury vacations seem to ask us, then what is the point of life?

make rather bad ones. Marvin could no longer be trusted with the family finances, nor could he hold down a job. Marvin's wife was now reckoning with a future in which her husband was alive and reasonably healthy but completely unrecognizable to her. This was no longer the man she had spent her life with and it never would be again. His stroke had cast him into a permanent state of languishing.

When Marvin and his wife looked at wedding pictures, he could not figure out how he should feel. He knew logically that he should feel something, but he could not. He remembered getting married, but he could not feel the way he had when he had gotten married.

When you are languishing, you might feel a bit like Marvin. Your loved ones might wonder whether you're even in the room with them or if you even care about being there, as his wife felt. You might look at your own wedding photos on your anniversary and forget the love you once shared with your significant other. You might not be able to take into account the disappointment a co-worker might feel when you fail to contribute to an important project. You might not be able to cheer your child on in their basketball game or even remember afterward how they played. Even in a crowded room, you might always have the sense that you are alone.

Happiness and pleasure seeking can literally morph into an addiction. The psychiatrist Dr. Anna Lembke wrote about this in her fascinating book *Dopamine Nation: Finding Balance in the Age of Indulgence*, explaining the many and surprising ways we can get hooked on dopamine. Whether it's reading erotic novels, playing video games, or buying so many things that it culminates in a shopping addiction, quick dopamine hits that leave us wanting more tempt us from all sides. As she put it, "We've transformed the world from a place of scarcity to a place of overwhelming abundance . . . the increased numbers, variety, and potency of highly rewarding stimuli today is staggering." If we're not happy, well, we can just chase the next hit, right? We're like greyhounds pursuing a mechanical rabbit around a never-ending track—never completing our quest and never in control of the outcome.

Rewriting the Cultural Scripts

We Westerners love the idea that we can control our emotional lives, curating what we feel and for how long. Headlines boast eleven strategies you can try to control your emotions, books promise a happier life if you just follow certain steps to attain "wellness," and apps give you a space to think through your feelings, but only if you pay a fee first. Thus, we may see emotions as expressions of ourselves and our identity—even our effort level—rather than justifiable reactions to the world and what is happening around us.

But we can't control the world around us, and when we demonize difficult or uncomfortable emotions—which are natural responses to difficult and uncomfortable events—we end up demonizing our own minds, feeling ashamed about our anger, afraid of our grief, or anxious about our anxiety. Busy trying to curate our feelings, we might have only a clouded awareness of our internal and external experience in the present moment, and without confidence in our ability to cope with uncomfortable feelings, minor stressors can feel more high stakes than they really are.

Unlike those in most of the Western world, many Eastern cultures have reservations about the single-minded pursuit of bliss, encouraging us instead to prepare the mind for the inevitable pain life brings. Some interpretations of the Quran conclude that an outsized sense of desire is the root cause of human suffering. Contrast the Islamic approach with, for example, the American Prosperity Gospel. In this belief system, being aligned with God and the spiritual path shows up in this life as abundance—of wealth, success, and happiness.

The psychologist Steven Hayes, who helped develop what is known as acceptance and commitment therapy, takes a quite Buddhist approach to meeting the full spectrum of human emotions. He encourages people to stop mentally suppressing uncomfortable feelings, which leads to psychological inflexibility—a factor that, alongside loneliness, leaves us more vulnerable to stress. In the face of overwhelming global social, political, and economic upheavals and nagging worries about health, safety, financial security, childcare, and so much more, it's both harder and more important than ever to be mentally flexible.

When we welcome the tough stuff in, we can learn to get comfortable with it. This doesn't mean *liking* the experience of grief, shame, or anxiety but simply letting it be without denying, judging, or immediately trying to change it. A Buddhist would counsel us not to fuse ourselves with our emotions but simply allow them to come and go. We can then stop *reacting* when negative thoughts pass through and learn to *respond* to negativity according to our deepest commitments and values—a core component of psychological well-being and thus flourishing.

Research has shown that Americans are the least dialectical in their emotional lives. Dialectical means, in this case, the ability to hold two opposing ideas or emotions in one's head at the same time. People in other cultures are far better at accepting the idea that there will be good times, there will be bad times, and often such experiences of good and bad can happen in the same day or even within the same hour. Good and bad events and feelings can happen in the same moment—bittersweet ones. As Susan Cain put it beautifully in her book *Bittersweet: How Sorrow and Longing Make Us Whole,* "The place you suffer . . . is the same place you care profoundly—care enough to act." Does the ability to feel different things simultaneously spur bigger, better things in all of us?

I recently sat shiva with a friend who was mourning the loss of her beloved mother. She and her husband greeted all the visitors with a hug, a smile, and, more often than not, a laugh. The Jewish culture, they explained to me, treats mourning as an opportunity for drawing a community close, for sending messages of support and love by physically showing up for someone, for sitting with them through this time of pain.

This happens in my own religious faith and traditions, and I suspect it happens to varying degrees in yours as well. Visitors arrive, cookies and food in hand, smiling and laughing as well as crying and hugging, recounting memories and times together. When mourning, people who might otherwise be nondialectical in their emotional life embody a dialectical approach, holding sadness and happiness, and memories of bad times and good times, in their heart all at once. It is a beautiful thing to watch, and even better to experience, because it helps us make sense of the complexities of a life as we say goodbye to it.

The benefits of moments like these, when positive and negative emotions are muddled up together, can be beautiful but difficult to experience.

I have friends who are parenting teenagers in this strange modern moment, and they are struggling to teach this lesson to their children. Their daughter has a friend who is leaving her out in the cold, or their son didn't get invited to a cool party over the weekend—for a teenager, it feels like the end of the world. How can parents teach their children to accept that they will be sad sometimes, they will be lonely sometimes, but that it doesn't mean they will be sad or lonely for all time? There is great wisdom to be wrung from these moments of struggle, for both parents and teenagers, to know that we can feel difficult things, but that there is a real opportunity for growth that comes from such suffering.

If we were all capable of this sort of approach—believing that our most difficult moments are opportunities for understanding ourselves and our world better—mixed emotional profiles might not be any less healthy than purely positive ones. If we could mitigate and control our emotions, thereby escaping the gravitational pull of our innate negativity bias, we would cease to prioritize merely feeling good (the absence of negative emotions) and focus our energies on functioning well. As we know, functioning well is the key to finding our way to the "North Star" that is flourishing.

Eudaimonia, or Functioning Well, as Good Mental Health

The word *epicurean,* which hearkens back to the ancient philosopher Epicurus, describes someone with a fondness for the self-indulgences and sensual pleasures of life. Epicurus's teachings ruffled some feathers—particularly as Christianity, with its emphasis on self-discipline, took root in Europe, condemning many hedonistic pleasures as shameful.

The philosopher Emily Austin refers to Epicurus as a "psychological hedonist" because he believed that humans are fundamentally wired to avoid pain and pursue pleasure above all else. In her book *Living for Pleasure: An Epicurean Guide to Life,* she wrote:

> Picture a human infant cast screaming from the womb into the great hurly-burly of this world, red with rage. It is hungry, over-stimulated, and suddenly very cold and uncomfortable . . . What it wants, and what we want to give it, is whatever will chill that baby out. It needs sustenance, a warm embrace, snuggles, music, the sound of the tap running, to be bounced around, a soft hat. Epicurus thinks that this brute desire for secure comfort never leaves us. An infant who lacks foundational security struggles to experience easy joys, and Epicurus thinks the same is true for humans at all stages.

Pursuing pleasure has gotten a bad rap, for sure. So please throw away your preconceived notions about the word *hedonism,* because this perspective on happiness is not about bacchanalian self-indulgence or epic feasts that turn into wild orgies. The word derives from the ancient Greek word for "emotions," *hedone.* Tranquility, in Epicurus's view, was the pinnacle of the good life.

His contemporary Aristotle (384–322 B.C.) didn't deny that happiness was appealing, or that people desired pleasure and wanted to avoid pain. But he didn't prioritize happiness as the be-all, end-all destination. Rather, he saw feeling good as a by-product of more important pursuits: growing as a person; having the self-awareness, freedom, and discipline to live out your values; being connected to a community; and functioning well. The word that Aristotle used to refer to a good life was *eudaimonia* (pronounced "you-die-MOH-nee-ah"). The word consists of two parts: the "eu" refers to something good, and in the ancient world, the "daimon" referred to something like an internal spirit or potential.

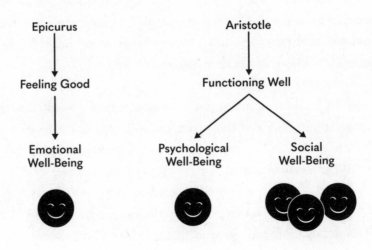

Flourishing, you may recall, encompasses all three kinds of well-being I mentioned earlier: emotional, psychological, and social. I call this the tripartite model of well-being, and it draws on both Epicurus and Aristotle's writings. It is a lifelong challenge to try to live a life in which we feel happy, satisfied, or interested in it while *also* being able to function well, with purpose, belonging, contribution, acceptance, and so on. Our job is to pursue excellence.

Aristotle argued that every object or thing in this world has a particular function. A handsaw cuts wood straight and clean; a car helps us get from one place to the next safely and quickly. Humans also have a particular function that sets us apart from all other sentient creatures, Aristotle argued—our minds—and in particular the unique structure we today call the prefrontal cortex (PFC). The PFC is the seat of our ability to make plans, to understand, to reason or exercise rationality, to learn from the past and apply those lessons to our future, to have a conception of ourselves and our personalities, to think about and try to live according to our sense of purpose in life, to judge right from wrong and then behave according to such judgments. The PFC does a lot; it makes us uniquely human.

A vital part of human nature comes from something we have in common with all living creatures: the primitive, or limbic, emotional brain, where pleasure, pain, stress, and survival are paramount. But we are no ordinary animal that is preprogrammed to live and act in specific ways that aim only to help us survive, procreate, and feel good. Well, we are that, of course, but we are also, as a species, singularly capable of quite a bit more. Unlike many other creatures, we humans can forgo the desire for immediate gratification, a fact so delightfully exhibited by some children in the well-known and important Marshmallow Experiment.

The PFC, or neocortex, the part of the brain that evolved most recently, is layered around and over the limbic cortex of the brain. There is a complex "highway system" of two-way streets that connect the limbic cortex and neocortex that allows each to exert control over the other. The children in the Marshmallow Experiment were asked to hold off on eating the one marshmallow sitting in front of them until the experimenter returned many minutes later. If they left the marshmallow untouched until the experimenter came back, they could experience even greater pleasure; those who waited would receive a second marshmallow to eat.

The children who managed to wait were using their PFC, and at a very young age, to overcome temptation; they were exhibiting the better part of their potential, or eudaimonia. The experimenters discovered that, later on in life, the kids who had demonstrated that ability would eventually get better grades and better college entrance exam scores, and they accomplished a host of other things that eclipsed what the children who couldn't resist the one-marshmallow temptation would.

To get anywhere in life, having potential isn't enough. To grow and become a better person, or a better anything—athlete, student, friend, sibling, employee, spiritual person, and so on—requires work, practice, time, dedication, and then more of all the above. Indeed, it takes a lifetime to become the best version of the person you were meant to be.

Developing into a more excellent version of yourself is an achievement. For the sake of prompting discussion in my classroom, I often play the "I can grant you a wish" game with my students. I tell them I can give them all the positive qualities they wish for in themselves, right away. You might be surprised to know that the majority of my students refuse to let me grant them the wish. Why? Because they would rather develop those good qualities on their own. They want to achieve their eudaimonia, not simply be given it.

You and Aristotle agree on this one, I tell my students. Then I ask them another question: "Dear students, do you now understand why Aristotle cautions us about putting the cart before the horse? That is, why we should not put hedonic happiness first, before we try to prioritize eudaimonia and work to develop ourselves into better people?"

"It would be like we all live as if there is just one marshmallow in life and we always choose to eat it right away," my students told me. Indeed, there will be a lot more marshmallows in life if we realize that they will come as a result of working on ourselves to become a better person. Aristotle—and perhaps my students—would argue that as I work to become the better version of myself, it will be as if the experimenter is coming back throughout my life and giving me a second, a third, maybe infinitely more marshmallows throughout life. The pleasure, the happiness, the joy, and the contentment I will feel from constantly trying to become a better person means so much more than the pleasure I would feel from having someone simply give me all the qualities of a good person in one wish-granting morning seminar or an all-you-can-eat marshmallow buffet.

I can't help it. Every time a new class comes to this conclusion, I grin from ear to ear. My students are proclaiming that they want to be challenged; they are willing to accept that they will sometimes fail, that they will not always be perfect.

The Six Domains of Human Excellence

Functioning well does not mean you have to be perfect, exceptional, or constantly exhibiting qualities of good mental health at the highest levels. For us mere mortals, the real challenge is to exhibit positive qualities in the right amount and in as consistent—over time and context—a manner as possible.

There are six domains of human excellence that are the foundation of how I measure the functioning well side of flourishing. These six key domains determine whether we get high marks on psychological and social well-being: acceptance and autonomy, connection and competence, and mastery and mattering.

1. **Acceptance:** Are you accepting of yourself as you are—your personality, your strengths and weaknesses, your behavior, and your full range of thoughts and emotions? Are you accepting of other people? This doesn't necessarily mean that you like them, agree with them, or approve of their choices, simply that you accept the reality of who they are without trying to change it.

2. **Autonomy:** When a situation calls for self-direction, are you comfortable thinking for yourself, expressing yourself, and doing your own thing? Because it is a form of independence from society and social influence, autonomy is measured as a form of psychological well-being. (If I were creating my questionnaire today, I might add a question about your ability to en-

gage in cooperative thinking and action that could reflect the social well-being side of confidence. Cooperative thinking seems to be in even shorter supply now than it was then.)

3. **Connection:** Are you able to cultivate warm, trusting relationships? Are you part of a larger community? As a social species—because 80 percent of our evolutionary history has been spent in small hunting and gathering tribes—human beings thrive best when they feel connected to others.

4. **Competence:** Are you able to manage the tasks of daily life? This is the psychological component of competence. Socially, competence is the ability to be able to make sense of complicated events and a complex social world.

5. **Mastery:** Are you motivated to learn and grow? Getting better at something is innately rewarding to humans. Functioning well as an individual requires both wanting to grow and being part of an environment in which that growth can occur.

6. **Mattering:** Do you believe that you and your life are significant and that you're making a contribution to this world? For many of us, this contribution often comes from raising a family or through our passion for or success in our careers.

The second half of this book will show you how to work toward mastering these different domains of human functioning. As you work on them, remember: Directing our energy toward functioning well, even when we are not feeling good—when stress nips at our heels or grief surges up at unpredictable and inopportune times—will have the most immediate and profound impact on our well-being. Doing so requires a great deal of faith in the process and courage in the moment. But time and time again, research I've done, along with other colleagues, has supported this approach. This eye-opening chart makes the case visually far better than I can in words.

FUNCTIONING WELL VS. FEELING GOOD

Percentage of college students diagnosed with a mental illness

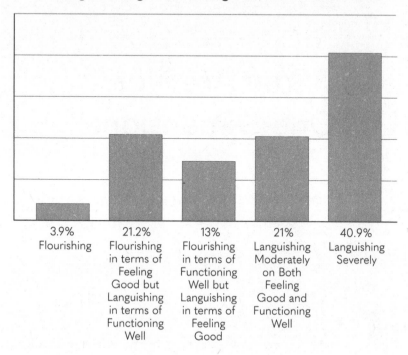

| 3.9%
Flourishing | 21.2%
Flourishing in terms of Feeling Good but Languishing in terms of Functioning Well | 13%
Flourishing in terms of Functioning Well but Languishing in terms of Feeling Good | 21%
Languishing Moderately on Both Feeling Good and Functioning Well | 40.9%
Languishing Severely |

Together, feeling good and functioning well are necessary—to the surprising extent that the prevalence of mental illness in the college students in the study was under 4 percent when they were flourishing. But as you can see, when they were languishing, even moderately, their mental illness was several times higher. Students who only felt good also had much higher rates of mental illness.

This is why flourishing is your North Star. Do not be fooled by the promise of happiness alone. Many studies measure happiness based on a certain set of social criteria and, as a result, praise various cultures for their success in achieving "happiness." But they—and we—should be more cautious. Cultures are just like people: They might feel happy in a moment—even a lot of moments—but if they are not also functioning well, they are not fully reaping all the benefits of flourishing.

[4]

You Are Not
One-Dimensional

Health is not just the absence of disease;
it is the presence of well-being.

The ancient Greeks told the story of the origin of medicine through the myth of Asclepius and his daughters Panacea and Hygeia. Each daughter represented a distinct branch of medicine: Panacea represented the branch of medicine that sought ways to remedy or remediate illness and disease; Hygeia was the daughter who represented the branch that sought ways to increase or maintain the presence of health and well-being.

The staff of Asclepius, which symbolizes medicine and public health, has what is, to many people, an unexpected symbol: a snake. Why? Then and now, snakes periodically shed their old skin as they grow to unveil new, healthy skin. The snake, therefore, represents the importance of promoting and maintaining good health.

From its inception, medicine was supposed to be practiced by two complementary branches, each with its own foci and techniques, that aimed for human flourishing. One branch was pathogenic, focused on combating the presence of illness, and the other was salutogenic, focused on promoting the presence of health.

The pathogenic approach is derived from the ancient Greek word *pathos,* meaning "suffering." The salutogenic approach comes from the Latin word *salus,* meaning "health," considered to be a positive state. Vaccinations are a great example of a salutogenic approach to health. Vaccines are designed to increase the strength of our immune system by exploiting a quirk in it.

A vaccine does not cure an infection once it has occurred; it helps prevent a serious infection in the first place. As such, it uses "tricks" learned from Hygeia; by introducing a small dose of an infectious agent into the body, it enables the immune system to use its innate health-building, health-strengthening abilities. As our immune system grows stronger, our immune system is "mostly positive"; anything negative, like a virus, that may now enter the body is far outweighed by the positive—our immune strength. A flourishing immune system can be created by vaccination, as well as through a healthy lifestyle including mitigating stress and maintaining a healthy diet.

Our mental health works the same way as our physical health. The pathogenic model views mental health as the absence of mental illness and therefore devotes its resources to understanding the etiology (or causes) of illness and disease in order to remedy such sources of human suffering. The salutogenic model views good mental health as the presence of positive feelings toward, and good functioning in, life and devotes its resources to understanding and creating flourishing.

A third and complementary conception of health derives from the word *hale,* which means "whole," which strikes me as the right way to look at our lives. Are we whole?

As a scientist, of course, I know we need reliable, valid measures of the presence and absence of good health. When I began my career, there were countless measures of illness, both physical and mental, but I could not find a single measure of good mental health. I created my mental health continuum questionnaire—the one you filled out in the introduction—to help measure both simultaneously.

Before I published my research on the mental health continuum, many scholars assumed that depression and well-being were highly correlated—so highly correlated that they belonged to one dimension. This one-dimensional view means that if a counselor or psychiatrist had a way to lower symptoms of depression and did so, then the expectation was that the patient would immediately regain their well-being— their flourishing. In other words, if there is a such a strong correlation between depression and well-being, then lowering depressive symptoms would mean that a patient would immediately default to increased levels of well-being.

But to many people's surprise, that was not what the research found. The correlation between depression and well-being is surprisingly modest, so modest that we can say without a doubt that lowering depression symptoms usually *will not increase levels of well-being.* What does this mean?

It means that our mental wellness actually exists on two dimensions, mental illness and mental health. We have found that it is possible to have low mental illness *and* low mental health, just as it is possible to have high mental illness *and* high mental health. We are working with two scales here; people's mental wellness can lie all over this map.

Here's one of the many implications of the dual-continua model: Even if we had a cure for mental illness—which we do not—people might then be free of mental illness but not necessarily anywhere close to flourishing. Remember Em Beihold's story as it is told in her song "Numb Little Bug"? The song talks about someone who is in therapy, waiting on more medication to arrive. The song appears to be arguing that the numbness, the languishing, may be caused by the psychiatric medication. Indeed, studies are now showing that an unintended side effect of medications for some people is emotional blunting. What this means is that psychiatric medications can numb all emotions, even the positive ones. The medication may turn the volume down on your sadness, a good thing if you are depressed, but it also turns the volume down on feeling

High Mental Health
Flourishing

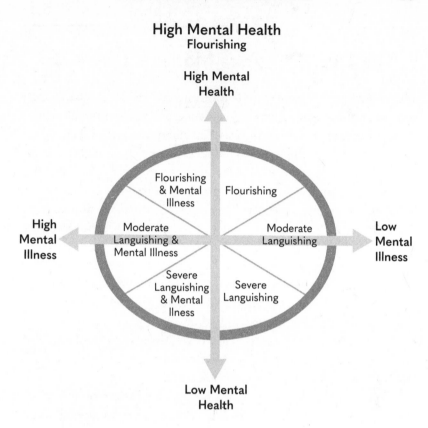

good, leaving you languishing. If you want to cut down on the depths of your misery, you won't be able to experience the highs of joy, either.

It turns out that our brain and its emotional life are built upon the dual-continuum model, which is rooted in the way the brain operates. Neuroscience has shown that the brain structures that light up when we feel sad are not the same brain structures that go dark—meaning they shut down and are not activated—when we feel happy or feel good. There is some overlap in the brain activation of sadness and happiness, but overall, the conclusion is that happiness is not the opposite of sadness when it comes to how the brain is wired.

Hence, the absence of the negative (sadness) does not mean the presence of the positive (happiness), nor does the presence of the negative preclude the presence of the positive. In other words, mental health is not a black or white issue. Mental health is a goddamn rainbow.

The Dual-Continua Model Is Inside Us

We have a lot of "nasty" or infectious agents inside us, all of which represent the negative axis of the dual-continua model. However, those nasty agents do not hurt us if our immune system is flourishing. When our strength is far greater than our vulnerability, we remain healthy and may even grow and become stronger from the fight. Muscle mass and strength are built through a similar quirk. When we exercise, which is a salutogenic process, we engage in small doses of muscle destruction that activate a process of rebuilding.

Our cholesterol system works on the dual-continua model as well. There is "bad" and "good" cholesterol. We now know that people will have the best heart health outcomes when their levels of bad cholesterol are lower and their levels of good cholesterol are higher. The best cholesterol profile is what someone like me might call "flourishing cholesterol," where there are low levels of bad cholesterol and high levels of good cholesterol.

Yet another example of the positive dimension of the dual-continua model has to do with our telomeres. The fragile ends of our chromosomes are capped with telomeres, and each time our cells divide, which continues the process of life, it takes a toll on

Can We Be Destined to Languish?

There is yet more evidence that the dual-continua model goes very deep into our biology. Since 1995, I, along with my colleague Dr. Kenneth Kendler, the renowned biological psychiatrist who has studied the behavioral genetics of mental illness, have been studying a representative sample of U.S. adult same-sex twins in order to figure out whether my mental health scale measured something that was heritable—genetic—and whether the dual-continua model was encoded in our DNA.

Recall that my mental health continuum questionnaire assesses them. Telomeres help us understand some of the mysteries of stress and aging. Experiencing a lot of psychosocial stress accelerates the damage to your telomeres, thereby encouraging pathogenesis, the creation of disease and illness that can shorten your life.

Telomerase is a substance that coats the telomeres to protect them from the damage of cellular division and stress. As telomerase levels increase, so does the level of protection; low telomerase levels mean less protection and more damage.

The importance of telomerase was showcased in a study reported by Elissa Epel in the National Geographic documentary *Stress: Portrait of a Killer*. The study focused on the long-term impact of stress on mothers who were long-term caregivers to a child with severe developmental disabilities. Caregiving for a loved one with health issues is a chronic stressor, and chronic high stress is the worst kind of stress for your health and longevity. Yet in the face of such a strong pathogenic factor—high chronic stress—the study found that telomerase levels were higher in the mothers who participated regularly in social support groups than mothers who remained caregivers in isolation without social support. The telomerase and social support did not get rid of the chronic stress, but it reduced the chronic stressors' ability to create damage.

three kinds of well-being: emotional, psychological, and social. It turns out that flourishing and languishing are just as heritable as depression or anxiety. Studies of mental illnesses such as depression have found estimates that around 60 percent of depression is genetic. My research on flourishing (and its absence, languishing) found that it was also in the 60 percent range of heritability, and the three kinds of well-being share the same genetic source.

Keep in mind, though, that to say that any condition is highly heritable does not mean that it is determined by genes and genes alone. Indeed, there is very little evidence for genetic determinism when it comes to depression. Many people who have a high genetic risk profile for depression never come down with it, and many people with a lower genetic risk profile for it become clinically depressed. It takes exposure to highly or chronically stressful experiences to activate the high genetic risk to create depression; that set of circumstances could also overcome the low genetic risk and create depression in an unlucky soul.

I wanted to know whether there was a strong correlation of the heritability of mental disorders and of good mental health. Just under half of the genes that predict mental illness (specifically depression, anxiety, and panic attacks) overlap with the genes that predict levels of mental health (as measured more holistically by my questionnaire). This is good news!

It means that having a high genetic liability to mental illness does not preordain an individual to low levels of subjective well-being. That said, inheriting a low level of genetic risk for mental illness by no means guarantees that an individual will flourish in life. In other words, just because you're not destined to be depressed, it doesn't mean that you inherited a high genetic potential to flourish. The two-continua model is in our DNA.

The Human Capacity for Growth

The positive dimension of the dual-continua model also represents our capacity for growth in terms of neurogenesis and neuroplasticity. This is called the regenerative capacity of the body; there is an entire branch of medicine now emerging called regenerative medicine. We have learned that stress can damage and destroy neurons in the brain, but we have also recently figured out that our body is capable of generating new neurons and new connections between them. We can literally help build new neurons and shape where they grow in our brain—and we can do this in all sorts of ways, further proof that someone who is suffering from a mental illness can move up the scale from languishing to flourishing and increase their mental wellness.

David Snowdon's Nun Study of aging and Alzheimer's disease, a 1986 longitudinal study of 678 Catholic nuns, all over seventy-five years old, found that postmortem, some of the nuns had levels of brain damage that should have caused dementia while they were alive. The researchers discovered that the difference was explained by the nuns' level of engagement with life. The nuns who had been active and engaged in more domains of life—physically, mentally, socially, spiritually—and who remained that way through late life were unwittingly stimulating neurogenesis and neuroplasticity that helped their brains remain a healthy platform for life, despite damage to some parts of their brains. When I think about how those healthier nuns engaged actively with one another and the world around them, creating more and more opportunities for mental growth, I cannot imagine a better example to explain how people can move from languishing to flourishing.

Another fascinating study that demonstrates our potential for neuronal repair and growth is constraint-induced movement therapy (CIMT). For years, stroke patients who lost the use of limbs were thought to be unable to recover the ability to use those limbs. Then, in what appeared at first to be a cruel approach, CIMT emerged. In patients who retained the use of a limb on one side of the body after a stroke, the therapy would constrain (prevent) its use and force the stroke patient to use the damaged limb. If the stroke had not completely wiped out the nerve connections between the brain and the damaged limb and the patient was then forced to use—in minuscule, precise, gradual steps—the damaged limb, neurogenesis and neuroplasticity occurred. As new neurons and connections were created by constraining the use of the good limb and forcing the use of the damaged limb, the patient recovered some use of the damaged limb.

The positive dimension of health—the underappreciated Hygeia—represents our capacity to regenerate, restore, and strengthen ourselves. This strength can be used to protect ourselves, our health, and one another. Whether in our immune system, our cardiovascular system, our brain and neurogenesis, or our cells and telomerase, we humans can build strength and resilience by experiencing manageable challenges.

When the body's ability to repair and grow outpaces the damage done

by adversities—whether infection, organ system damage, or psychosocial stress—we remain healthy or become healthier. When adversities are
extreme and the resulting damage exceeds our capacity to repair and
grow, the process of pathogenesis, the creation of illness, begins. Nobody
goes to sleep healthy and wakes up with a full-blown disease or illness;
we become ill over time. The creation of an illness, especially a chronic
disease, is a gradual process during which the sum of our adversities,
unhealthy habits, and damage (all pathogenic processes) exceeds our capacity to rebuild, restore, or grow (all salutogenic processes).

But strength is not just physical. Strength is not created only by and
for our internal organ systems. Our mental health works the same way
as all the other biological processes. This hearkens back to the discussion about Dr. Rachel Zoffness, the pain psychologist, who reminds us
that pain isn't biomedical but in fact is biopsychosocial—partly in our
body and partly in our brain: "Neuroscience research reveals that negative emotions, catastrophic thoughts, and unhealthy coping behaviors
actually amplify pain, exacerbate symptoms, and keep you stuck in a
cycle of fear, inactivity, misery, and pain. Said another way: stress, anxiety, depression, catastrophic thinking, negative predictions, focusing
on pain, social withdrawal, lack of exercise, and activity avoidance *all
make pain worse.*"

A placebo operates in the completely opposite way from negative
thoughts; a placebo carries the expectation that it will make you better,
so it encourages biological healing. Think of a placebo as the mind
becoming hopeful of getting better, and then that hope helps to make
it so. We can work to strengthen our mental health, our wellness, our
positivity, in order to gird ourselves against the difficulties we might
face. The stronger we are, the more ready we'll be to fight whatever
comes our way—body and mind.

The dual-continua model is, to me, an incredible discovery and a
reason for optimism. If we start to see our life on the languishing-to-
flourishing continuum, focusing not just on mental illness but also on
our mental health, we can imagine a different path forward. We can
shift our focus from what's happening *inside* us to what's happening

around us; we can start to figure out how to function well, rather than merely obsessing over how to feel good.

We need to cultivate the strength that comes from hope. When we begin to have hope, a seed is planted; we start to believe that something better is possible.

The Medicalization of Our Minds

As the twentieth century was coming to a close, the World Health Organization (WHO) published the results of a historic study called the Global Burden of Disease (GBD) study. The study focused on more than one hundred acute and chronic medical conditions and illnesses to determine how much each illness contributed to a new outcome it called the disability-adjusted life year (DALY).

The DALY reflects the total number of years lived and how much of that time was spent living with disability. For example, perhaps you were alive, but you were unable to hold down a job or perform normal activities of daily living, such as bathing yourself, cleaning your home, buying and putting away your groceries. Before 1996, the WHO had focused only on the number of years a life was curtailed due to an illness—in other words, it counted only the number of years that lives were cut short or people died prematurely from a specific health condition or illness. Mortality, put simply, had been the gold standard by which to judge the seriousness of an illness; illnesses that caused more premature mortality were ranked higher in the top ten list of public health priorities.

When mortality was the only standard, mental illness never showed up on the top ten public health lists. Finally, the WHO and others realized that although by the end of the twentieth century we were living longer, living longer did not necessarily mean living well. Miracles of modern medicine could keep more people alive who had diseases that in previous decades had ended people's lives. Heart disease is one such example; many heart conditions could now be managed—they were survivable—but they had become chronic conditions.

As the twentieth century was coming to a close, our mindset started to shift. We began to focus more on adding quality to life, not just quantity. When the WHO added a measure of disability along with mortality to create its new top ten list of priorities, depression showed up for the first time. In 1996, depression was the fourth leading cause of DALYs. By 2004, when the WHO performed the study again, depression had moved even further up the list. Depression was right up there with heart disease and cancer as causing the most DALYs. Today, in a majority of countries around the world, depression is the leading cause of DALYs, a bigger problem when it comes to disability than either heart disease or cancer.

A recent CDC study looking at the years 2015 to 2018 found that 13.2 percent of adults eighteen years and older had taken antidepressants in the past month, with the rates among women (17.7 percent) higher than among men (8.4 percent), with women over sixty accounting for the largest percentage (24.3 percent of that age group had used antidepressants in the past thirty days).

What's more, the average age at which people experience their first bouts of mental illness has gotten lower. Anxiety disorder typically strikes first, now usually around the age of fourteen. Substance abuse, which includes alcoholism, first strikes around the age of twenty. Mood disorders, which include depression, first strike around the age of twenty-six. It doesn't matter if you are growing up in Mexico, Brazil, or Turkey, so-called developing countries, or in the Netherlands, Germany, or the United States, so-called developed countries, these numbers are consistent around the world.

Those are numbers that should raise eyebrows and force us to focus on the issue of mental illness from a societal perspective. For so long, government figures and political leaders insisted on clinging to the delusion that mental illness was none of their concern. There was disbelief, possibly tinged with some anger, at any attempts to call our attention to the prevalence of this devastating disease: "How can depression be almost as serious as heart disease?" "Why should we spend money on depression when cancer is what is killing people?"

Over time, the governments of some countries came to the stage of acceptance and began to put more money toward easing the epidemic of depression. Where did the money go? They pushed for more treatment, of course. Pharmaceutical and talk therapies have existed for quite some time, but barely half of the people in some survey studies who met the criteria for depression said they were getting any treatment for their mental and emotional problems.

But therein lies the problem. Most of us have assumed—and this is a big assumption—that treatments for mental illness were effective, beneficial, and basically the best—and only—option for dealing with the problem. In the United Kingdom, "The Depression Report: A New Deal for Depression and Anxiety Disorders," published in 2006, therefore celebrated the fact that "The good news is that we now have evidence-based psychological therapies that can lift at least half of those affected out of their depression or their chronic fear." According to that report, as many as 75 percent of individuals in the United Kingdom with depression or anxiety do not receive any treatment and therefore "continue to suffer, even though at least half of them could be cured at a cost no more than £750."

Cure depression? Nothing could be further from the scientific truth—we cannot in good faith call *any* mental disorder treatment a "cure." In 1996, the U.S. Congress passed the Mental Health Parity Act, which provided insurance coverage for mental illness treatments, in the hope that treatment would help. But in 2006, the director of the National Institute of Mental Health, Thomas Insel, would publicly state that the current effect of all known treatments for mental illness was palliative at best.

Insel went on to review evidence that there had been no progress in reducing the prevalence and burden of mental disorders. It seemed that researchers in the mental illness field were content with achieving incremental change by trying to improve existing medications; often, making small improvements to existing drugs meant that they could boast fewer side effects. According to Insel and his colleague, "While there can be little doubt that we have not fully utilized the available treatments, it is important to recognize that the available treatments are insufficient. . . . All current medical treatments for mental illnesses are palliative, none are even proposed as cures. . . . We suggest that in mental illnesses, as in other medical illnesses, we need to aim for a goal of recovery defined by a complete and permanent remission." Permanent remission means a cure; Dr. Insel was proposing that we seek what he called "cure therapeutics" for mental illness.

The first time I read the U.K. depression report and Dr. Insel's article, both in 2006, I was confused as a scientist and livid as a patient. I had been told that the medication I'd been taking was the best available treatment for my own mental disorders. I'd been told I had a brain dysfunction—a chemical imbalance—that would be balanced first by taking Prozac, and then "a cocktail" of two medications that focused first on serotonin and then on dopamine. When that cocktail had stopped working, I had been put onto another, newer version of a medication called Pristiq. I was experiencing firsthand what Dr. Insel meant by incremental improvements in the science of mental illness treatment.

Why are these medications not helping to reduce the burden of depression and other mental disorders? Simple: No medication for mental disorder has ever been designed in the correct sequence of understanding the problem.

Normally, to create a true cure, one must discover the underlying pathology causing an illness. Once that is understood, the etiology, or internal cause, of the illness leads to the investigation of the best treatment. The etiology determines the creation of an effective treatment.

Scientists have been doing this backward with mental illness from the start. And this hasn't changed from 2006 to today. All current medications for mental disorders, from schizophrenia to anxiety and depression, originated from the observation of potentially beneficial side effects of a treatment or medication created to treat something else entirely.

During World War II, the Germans ran low on rocket fuel and created an alternative called hydrazine. After the war, chemists at the pharmaceutical manufacturer Hoffmann-La Roche created two drugs from hydrazine. Those drugs, called isoniazid and iproniazid, were found to be effective against the bacillus that caused tuberculosis (TB). But doctors also noticed a consistent set of side effects of iproniazid: TB patients became more energized, and their mood improved. They came to be seen as potentially beneficial side effects to treat depression, and the psychiatrist Nathan Kline was the first to use iproniazid on depressed patients. He found that it lifted his patients' moods and also energized them. Hence, a beneficial treatment was born before any understanding of the etiology of depression.

Next, scientists turned to pharmacology, the study of how drugs work in the body and brain. Pharmacology showed that iproniazid increased body levels of the neurotransmitter called serotonin. Serotonin deficiency—or "chemical imbalance"—was turned into an etiological explanation from observing that the medications increased (which is what antidepressants do) or decreased (which is what antipsychotic medications do) levels of specific neurotransmitters.

There is no disputing that taking antidepressants changes the body's levels of a neurotransmitter, but this does not mean that a patient had low levels or an imbalance before taking the medication. It just means that the neurotransmitter is now at a level that is higher than it was before the patient took the medication.

I can't put this any more plainly: There is *still* no scientific evidence whatsoever to support the chemical imbalance theory of any mental illness. What the public learns about this hypothesis is from direct-to-consumer advertising on television that gives the *appearance* that science supports the chemical imbalance theory. Television ads, not science, have convinced the public of the chemical imbalance theory and, thereby, the brain disease hypothesis of mental illness.

If you are wondering, as I did when I started taking Prozac, why I felt my mood and energy improve, because the same thing happened to you, we are not alone. I have scoured the research literature, and the best available science suggests that you and I may be among the 25 percent for whom medications may be necessary and even beneficial for long-term recovery. Or perhaps we benefited from taking our medication because we believed it would help us; our minds, through the placebo effect, expected us to feel and function better, and so we did.

Hundreds of later studies on placebos showed that 50 percent of improvement in patients with depression is due to their expectation that the medication they are taking will indeed make them feel better. Another 25 percent of improvement in patients taking antidepressants is due to what is called "natural recovery," meaning that some patients feel better with time and being put on medication has nothing to do with the improvement. At most, the studies suggest, 25 percent of improvement in depression can be attributed to the effects of the medication.

It should be unsurprising that, as Dr. Insel's review of the literature concluded, all current mental illness medications are palliative at best, and none comes close to a cure. Nothing in terms of etiological research has changed since the publication of Dr. Insel's 2006 paper.

We are no closer today to understanding the underlying pathologies inside the brain or body that cause depression or, for that matter, any of the other myriad mental disorders. Medications claiming to correct chemical brain imbalances are still widely prescribed. Research on new psychiatric medications continues to attempt only to improve upon existing medications—the same drugs that were intended to alleviate other, usually physical, conditions, that then produced side effects that seemed to help mental illness patients.

The truth is that depression and many other mental disorders are like chronic diseases: Despite efforts to manage them and the possibility of their receding into the background for periods of time, they are recurrent throughout life.

After coming down with depression for the first time in your life, the chances go to about a 50 percent chance that you will have a second bout in your lifetime. If you do have that second bout, the chances go up to 70 percent that you will have a third episode of it in your lifetime. If you have a third episode of depression, you now have a 90 percent chance of having a fourth bout of depression in your lifetime. The relapse data is especially concerning; it suggests that for individuals with a previous episode of a mental disorder, the chances of a relapse happening in their lifetime is very high.

The problem is no longer whether we can agree that mental illness is a serious public health issue. There have been so many studies on the burden of depression that one would risk professional credibility to claim that it is not a serious public health issue. Rather, a more sobering choice now awaits all of us about how to reduce the level of suffering of those who are diagnosed with depression.

This is where the dual-continua model can help us. We are now starting to understand that languishing might be an even bigger problem in the world than depression—more widespread yet profoundly undercounted.

We know that depression is a very difficult disease to solve; but we also know that if we can move patients up the scale from languishing to flourishing, their level of mental health can increase, even if they suffer from a mental illness. We are also aware that flourishing helps prevent depression. The question isn't: Why haven't we fixed depression yet? The question is: Why aren't we paying attention to languishing?

By promising medical miracles, our healthcare system encourages Americans to deprioritize maintaining our health in the hope that a brilliant doctor or expensive procedure will be able to fix it for us later. But deprioritizing our health is too costly for too many families, and it costs our economy millions in lost productivity and ingenuity. Now that we have made some progress with the Affordable Care Act, it is time to take the next step. We need a system that will encourage and support our right and responsibility to maintain our own good health and use it to live a better life. Americans should invest in a system that focuses more on flourishing and health than only illness.

Are other countries doing it right? Have other nations come around to the idea that medicating away our mental illness isn't going to work? Not in any robust way, unfortunately. At least now we know that smart people all around the world are starting to think about these issues in intelligent ways. But even if we have the best of intentions, there are still roadblocks standing in our path.

There are positive signs that we are headed in the right direction. The WHO and United Nations have joined a growing coalition that is calling for more attention to be paid to social determinants of mental health. Psychosocial treatments, including peer support groups and other kinds of more nuanced therapy options, are gaining ground. There has been an increase in schools, universities, and workplaces paying much more attention to funding mental wellness support programs for their communities. They're all good steps. But we need more.

It Is Time for a New Map

Even as we throw around terms such as *mental health* and *depression* and *psychiatric counseling*—as if to show that we are paying attention, we are handling the problem—we aren't looking at the issue the right way. Neither changing our mindset to think more optimistically nor treating the mind as a cocktail of brain chemicals and synapses will unlock sustained mental health—not for most of us. We need different tools if we want more people to flourish.

So much of our life is lived out of our consciousness, our understanding of ourselves, not just our physical bodies. Over the last several years, countless studies have demonstrated that changing our thoughts can profoundly affect our physical and neurological states, even healing seemingly intractable problems. Studies of students who are told shortly before they take a math test that they are, in fact, good at math, have shown improvements in their final score. Housecleaners who are told that their job should be considered a good workout lost more weight and showed improvement on a variety of health measures than others who are not told the same thing. This aligns with the much older Buddhist perspective that the mind, through concentrated effort, can heal the brain and body—the downward causation argument.

The medicalization of mental illness strips hope from so many people: I have depression, I am depressed, I am a depressed person. But I would remind you: That is not all you are. People who suffer from mental disorders are indeed capable of achieving some level of good mental health; some people with a mental disorder can even flourish.

We are not one-dimensional creatures who are either mentally ill or not mentally ill. The discovery of the second dimension—what I call the *mental health continuum*—gives us a better, richer language for our lives and a new approach to creating a mentally healthier world.

A Day in the Life of a Flourisher

What should people be prioritizing in their daily lives in order to be flourishers? I have been asked this question countless times over the years; for a long time I had no answer, and it frustrated me to no end.

Then one day an acquaintance of mine sent me an email, requesting that I review an article for a journal based in part on research related to my work. I get a dozen such requests a month to review articles, and I have to pick and choose among them. For the first time in a long time, I was immediately drawn in by the title of the paper: "A Tuesday in the Life of a Flourisher."

Most academic, scientific articles have the most boring, long-winded, pretentious titles. (Academics can suck the fun out of anything.) But this title intrigued me, and I read on.

Every Tuesday, the participants reconstructed the day before, identifying and articulating the details of important episodes and moments that had made up their Monday. They were asked whether, during those moments or episodes, they had learned something new, helped someone, or socialized or connected with another person and to what degree—from not at all to very much. For spirituality, they were asked if they had prayed, worshipped, or meditated during that important moment or episode. For playing, they were asked whether they had played a game, participated in a sport, or practiced a hobby.

The participants then indicated how they had felt while doing various activities, five of which mattered: playing, spirituality, connecting with others, learning or growing, and helping others. Participants who had done more of those activities reported having had a better day; they had felt more joy, excitement, hope, and interest in life when they had done little or none of the five activities. It didn't matter if the participant was depressed, languishing, or flourishing. If they continued the activities each week, people moved closer to flourishing.

If a participant did very few or none of the activities, they had a poor day; again, it didn't matter if they were flourishing, languishing, or depressed. If participants were flourishing and they cut back or stopped the activities, they began slipping into languishing.

Why Moving Toward Flourishing Creates Your Base Camp

Of course, bad days and bad things will happen. Flourishing can't protect us from experiencing daily stressors, but having a high level of well-being—getting closer and closer to flourishing—has been shown to stop bad experiences from mushrooming into a truly foul mood. One study followed participants as they experienced sources of stress ranging from interpersonal problems to conflict at work or home, health or financial issues, or being evaluated negatively at work. The study then measured the participants' negative mood by asking them how depressed, anxious, or angry they had felt that day.

Not surprisingly, they found that on the days the participants experienced more sources of stress, they reported more negative moods. But even on the days when nothing went wrong or very little "shit hit the fan," the participants who were flourishing or closer to it reported a better mood than languishers. On days with more sources of stress, participants had much more negative moods if they were languishing or closer to languishing. Flourishing doesn't protect you from having bad things happen, but it prevents those bad things from creating a really bad mood that ends in a bad day.

When you're flourishing, bad things have trouble getting inside you and sticking around. Flourishing, or getting closer to it, is like having a base camp for a summit attempt on a particularly difficult mountain. When bad weather strikes, you are protected from disaster; you can simply return to base camp, partway up that mountain. And then, from there, you can regroup and try again.

The Logic of the Internal Path

My decades of work in this field have shown me that people pursue happiness along two distinct paths. The first path is external; it's where we become "good at" something—a trade, a profession, a career—that enables us to make a living. We create a résumé of our skills and accomplishments that signals our value in the economic, business, and work worlds.

The external path is where we keep count of our worth. We count scores and wins, we count our salaries, we count our belongings. We tend to focus a lot on this external path, as we often believe that we can earn or acquire happiness through the social status that money and toys represent, along with the sense of power that tends to accompany this path.

This is not the logic of the internal path. What matters here is the kind of person you are or the one you are trying to become. Whereas the external path is about economics, the internal path is about ethics. The external path values success and winning; the internal path values substance and sharing. On the internal path, we earn our happiness not by being admired for the quantity of things we've acquired but for the quality of the virtues we've attained. Becoming a better person, a good person—not to yourself or only for yourself—but *to and for others* is the basis of true and genuine flourishing.

People who meet the criteria for functioning and feeling well incorporate five simple but meaningful activities into their lives. They see themselves as lifelong learners and carve out time to pursue intrinsic interests (say, googling "how to land a plane" and seeing where it leads, or experimenting with an adventurous cocktail recipe); they prioritize psychologically satisfying friendships that are marked by attunement, reciprocity, collaboration, and compromise; they practice unconditional acceptance and direct "kind attention" toward themselves and others; they find purpose in fulfilling an unmet need in their family, community, or world; and they find small moments for free play, whether they're learning to make latte art, going a little crazy with a charcuterie board, or driving to the next town to discover a new antiques shop—all of which can effectively quiet the mind and ease our preoccupation with outcomes, deadlines, and goals. I call these the five vitamins of flourishing. Instead of holding yourself to a rigid routine, aim to incorporate them into your week, even if it means stealing mere minutes from a busy schedule.

Even better, these daily vitamins can help us work toward balancing the internal path with the external one.

For example, you can learn something new (Vitamin no. 1) in order to showcase your knowledge, advanced degrees, and a sense of superiority, or you can become humble, honest, and vulnerable and embrace your imperfections.

You can connect or socialize with others (Vitamin no. 2) to look cool, and then post your coolness on Snapchat or Instagram, or you can connect deeply and meaningfully, and provide care, nurturance, and patience to others.

You can engage in spiritual practices (Vitamin no. 3) in order to get to Heaven or avoid Hell, to make business contacts, or to pad your résumé, or you can immerse yourself in spiritual and religious practices to become a better person.

You can follow your purpose by, for example, helping others (Vitamin no. 4) because it makes you look selfless or your résumé look better. Or you can help others because it represents a purpose in life, a cause you are selflessly dedicated to, one in which you are motivated to bring happiness to others.

Lastly, you can play (Vitamin no. 5) to win and keep score, or you

THE FIVE VITAMINS FOR FLOURISHING

1. Follow Your Curiosity to Learn Something New
For bolstering your sense of competence and rewriting your self-narrative through personal growth

2. Build Warm and Trusting Relationships
For a deeper sense of belonging, intimacy, and being "truly known"—and remember, quality matters more than quantity

3. Move Closer to the Sacred, the Divine, and the Infinite (through Contemplation, Meditation, or other Spiritual Practices)
For awareness of your union with all living things, unconditional acceptance and generosity towards yourself and others, and appreciation of the mysteries of life

4. Have and Live Your Purpose
For finding personal significance in the mundane, calm in the face of setbacks, and a profound sense of "mattering" to your community and world

5. Play (Make Time for Activities Where You Enjoy the Process, Not the Outcome)
For rediscovering joy, reconnecting with your imagination, practicing active leisure, and breaking away from achievement obsession

can play more because it is enjoyable for its own sake—we call that intrinsically satisfying—and because it expresses and develops good qualities: sharing and caring (kindness). You can engage in play because the act itself brings you joy and delight.

The bottom line is that the clarity of your intentions affects the purity of your actions. It's simple, really. A thoughtful life comes down to just that: intentions and actions. Think about living more of your life truly in the moment. Instead of adding things to your life, you might need to subtract them. Then perhaps the path in front of you will become more clear.

Flourishing is your North Star. It's your guide out of languishing. The flourishing vitamins are the five activities you can practice each day. Set your intention each time you take your vitamins; you may find something more beautiful than you ever imagined if you take that internal path.

PART TWO

The Five Vitamins of Flourishing

[5]

Learn: Creating Stories of Self-Growth

Ethan moved from downtown Brooklyn to rural upstate New York to quarantine with his parents during the pandemic, part of the larger exodus from New York City. He'd been alone in his apartment for too long, for too many hours, and he felt as if he hadn't seen sunshine in months. Walking around during the day felt too risky, so he'd kept his wanderings to the evening hours, when the streets were quieter. The long sunset walks helped, but not enough. He was feeling alone in a way he'd never felt before. His job, working in media for a benevolent British communications company, had lost its meaning; all of the other employees seemed to be checked out, and the work, which he'd always found important and exciting, felt trivial in the face of the global catastrophe. Almost all of his friends had already fled the city, but he'd held out as long as he could. He had always prized—nay, coveted—his independence, but at that point, it didn't feel worth the price. So he packed a few months' worth of clothes into a bag and headed north.

Ethan was a city boy through and through. He didn't have a driver's license, certainly didn't own a car. Houseplants had always felt like far too much of a commitment for his single, bachelor-esque existence, and other than a few months of surprisingly fertile mushroom growth in a very damp, leak-prone downtown Manhattan apartment bathroom, he was about as far from the gardening type as you could imagine. But shortly after his arrival, his mom started getting the garden ready for summer. And to his great surprise, her love of roses, cosmos, columbines, and daylilies started to rub off on him.

A few years later, both he and his mother remain somewhat obsessed with their garden. Now Ethan is the family's unofficial weekend gardener/unpaid groundskeeper—at last count, he has thirty-five different cultivars of daylilies planted around the yard, not including a recently planted test bed of hybrids he's been experimenting with.

Learning something new, of your own choosing, on your own time, for your own reasons is a surprisingly potent antidote to languishing. We naturally associate education with formal schooling and often think that chapter is closed when we embark into the working world—but there is great joy to be found in learning new things into our old age. We can even find meaning in *required* learning at any point in our lives if we can find a connection between the knowledge we are gaining and our lives or interests, even more if we can look back on any personal growth we have achieved with a real sense of pride.

You don't have to get sucked into an expensive sailing habit or spend countless hours (and money) learning to play golf. You can just google "daylilies" and see where your curiosity takes you. Knitting gets expensive only when you start to get a taste for Scottish yarn, and you can knit during a boring Zoom meeting any time of day or night. You can decide how much time, money, and collaboration your new habit will require. But trying something new is within all of our grasps, right now, today. My one caveat: Make sure you are learning and growing for the right reasons.

External path: Learning new things to acquire a skill, to show off, to best someone else.

Internal path: Learning something new to become a different person, to change your definition of yourself, to alter what you thought you were capable of doing.

The Self System

The ability to improve ourselves, let alone the knowledge that we are capable of it, is something I would call self-enhancement, which is a core component of a positive self-image—one of the gateways to flourishing. Ethan figured it out as soon as he moved back to Brooklyn, when instead of staying up late to binge Netflix shows, he spent the wee hours educating himself on how to get a delicate rosebush to survive a harsh upstate New York winter. He was a gardener now—by mistake or on purpose, he wasn't sure. But by learning and growing of his own volition, he had altered his sense of self—for the better.

I think of the self as a system, kind of like the heating, ventilation, and air conditioning (HVAC) system in your house. Your HVAC system keeps track of the ambient temperature in your house. After you program in temperature settings, one part of your HVAC system collects information, another part compares that data against your chosen settings, and a third part reacts by heating or cooling the house.

Much like an HVAC system, the self is a system designed to collect information about our strengths and weaknesses, who we are in various situations and with different people, how we're perceived, and who we're becoming, and then compare it to the self-narrative—or "temperature settings"—we've internalized.

As the psychologist and Northwestern University professor Dan McAdams put it, we start to become "historians of the self" in adolescence, reconstructing our past experiences into coherent stories that give us a sense of meaning. These stories can evolve, of course, but they "often take a decisive form, and people will often make decisions in their lives based on narrative assumptions." One strand of your narrative identity might be that you are *not* going to be like your mother; that "everything goes your way," a conviction that becomes a life mantra; that you are always late to appointments and can never get your life in order; or that you have a particular competency: *I know some-*

thing about flower-growing conditions in the climate of the northeast or *I am a burgeoning amateur expert on daylilies.* McAdams wrote:

> Life stories are psychological resources. We use them to help us
> make decisions and move forward in life. It's great when those
> stories affirm positive messages: when they affirm hope for the
> future, when they tell us that we are good people, when they
> celebrate our achievements and our triumphs, and when they
> help us overcome suffering—that's all good. Yet, the story also
> has to be true to your lived experience. And so, if you're going
> through really horrible things in your life right now, coming up
> with some sunny reconstruction of it that exudes a kind of
> strong optimism will not work immediately. It's not true to who
> you are. You're fooling yourself in those kinds of situations.

Though difficult life events can shape our self-narratives in unhealthy ways, we're wired to want two things from them. The first is self-consistency. Research shows that when we are presented with feedback that is inconsistent with our self-concept, we rush to provide evidence to restore it. If we think of ourselves as honest and we're suspected of lying, we will be highly motivated to find or create opportunities to display our honesty, to prove—to both ourselves and others—that our sense of self is intact.

We also have a deep psychological need for a favorable or positive view of ourselves (self-enhancement), leading us to seek out desirable, positive, or flattering information about ourselves. Studies have found innumerable ways in which people try to create and maintain a positive self-image, from taking credit for successes (either our own or others') and attributing them to skill rather than luck to making excuses for our failures, attributing them to bad luck rather than skill. Ultimately, most people want to perceive themselves as above average—and they do, a phenomenon known as *illusory superiority,* though it's much more prevalent in North America than in other parts of the world. Indeed, studies have found that the majority of Americans rate themselves as above average in numerous ways, whether in creativity, intelligence, dependability, athleticism, honesty, friendliness, or driving skills.

What kind of information are we collecting with these stories, and what do we do with it? There's social comparison, which is just what it sounds like: judging how we measure up to other people. We often try out different self-narratives in the context of our interactions with friends, parents, teachers, and coworkers. We also compare versions of ourselves over time (temporal self-comparisons), using a "back-to-the-future" system to go back months or years into the past to think about facets of ourselves and how they've improved or declined over time. Once we have traveled back in time through reconstructive memory, we then compare that version of the self with our self in the present.

Like your HVAC system, which has reactors that turn on heating or cooling, the self-system also has its heating and cooling reactors. In this case, researchers often refer to the emotional system as the heating component and the cognition, or thinking, system as the cooling one. Unlike the HVAC system, however, the self can activate both at the same time and go ahead at full speed.

When information or an experience can be judged as uniformly good or uniformly bad, an individual's feelings and thoughts about that experience are consistent. When feedback and information about oneself are a mixture of good and bad—which we all might admit happens quite a lot—feelings and thoughts can be incongruent. You can feel one way but think another.

Imagine having been studying for months for an important exam, one that you are sure will make or break your chance at the career you have long dreamed of. One day, right before the exam, a very old friend surprises you when they come to town to see the band you both loved wildly play a stadium show nearby. They have one spare ticket, and they convince you to drop everything for the opportunity to see your favorite band play; it's the final show of a sold-out tour. You go. It's an experience you'll cherish forever. Of course, it feels good in the moment—amazing, even—but when you wake up the next morning, you are exhausted, a little hungover, and consumed by negative thoughts.

You might feel that you deserve an occasional reward, but you also feel guilty about taking so much time off studying, and you're disappointed in yourself for having had a few beers and not being in tip-top studying shape. What if you fail the exam just because you thought you deserved one big night off? Even if it was for a once-in-a-lifetime opportunity to share a cherished, unforgettable moment with a dear friend?

You know that it's possible to feel bad and have positive thoughts at the same time; likewise, you can think negative thoughts but have positive feelings at the same time. Maybe you should have studied more. But maybe—just maybe—that other moment of learning was worth more in the long run?

The Learning Paradox

Every day, students around the world go to school to (hopefully) soak up new knowledge. If learning something new were good in and of itself, our youths should be the happiest, most flourishing population in the world. But that is not the case; languishing is highest in the life span when youths are finishing high school, going through college, and beginning young adulthood, a period of a lot of learning as they begin their careers.

To contribute to psychological well-being, learning has to be an autonomous decision to understand something that is personally meaningful or relevant. Adults are constantly exposed to new challenges, such as raising a family, staying healthy, managing their finances, and even moving up in their careers, which can require developing expertise in a domain and learning new skills.

The wisdom we accumulate as we age never stops accruing; it just ebbs and flows and changes across our life span. Just because you never went to law school doesn't mean you quit learning after your high school or college graduation. Give yourself the credit you are due! Learning is a choice, and you can keep choosing it. It's important, however, to assign value to the knowledge you have accrued for it to contribute to a positive self-image. That growth in knowledge and the accompanying boost in your self-image can be found in all sorts of surprising places, and when you least expect it.

What Bravery Looks Like

A lovely acquaintance of mine just started playing the violin last year. Sheila, who recently turned fifty-five, was growing increasingly aware that her youngest child was just about to head off to college, leaving her and her husband as empty nesters. Her husband still works a busy job, and with his closest family members living abroad, he has to travel quite a bit for both work and family obligations. In recent years, Sheila had a lengthy struggle with a very difficult autoimmune disease, the lack of control over which left her feeling frustrated and depleted. She is healthy now and lives a full and busy life, and she has always enjoyed the feeling of being heavily wrapped up in her community and her children.

But she felt a lingering sense of emptiness. Was it the memory of her illness still casting a shadow? Was it that she could sense a change coming when her last child soon leaves home? Whatever it was, she didn't like it. She decided she wanted to do something for herself for the first time in a long time. Her children had abandoned so many of their childhood pursuits years earlier, so there was a closetful of beautiful musical instruments gathering dust in her spare room. Was it possible—could she—? She decided that yes, she could. She would learn to play the violin.

It's been over a year since she started now, and all the struggles of "teaching an old dog new tricks" are—she laughs when she says this—entirely true. Learning a new thing as an adult is hard! She told me that she had her first big recital coming up. The majority of the other performers are in their teens. Not infrequently, one of the parents of the children in her group tells her they admire how "brave" she is—they keep marveling at her willingness to keep at it, to embarrass herself ever so slightly, to show up week after week to try something new.

"Do you get angry when they call you brave?" I ask her.

She chuckles. "No, I am brave!"

Sheila tells me that she has long fought against feeling marginalized, as a woman of color in a small, insular town. She has wanted to feel that she has a presence that matters, an opinion that counts, an identity outside that of a wife, a mother, or a PTA parent. When she gave up her career years ago in order to raise three children, she didn't intend to give up any voice of her own.

The violin has given her a voice again, she says. It has made her feel younger, more vibrant, more independent, somehow less at the mercy of the world and more in control of her own life, all at once. She's learning and growing, and the idea that she can still do so thrills her each and every time she picks up her bow.

Action Plan: Ask yourself the following questions, and listen carefully to your answers. Then make some changes.

- If I didn't have to work at all, how might I spend my day, my week?

- Who are the people in my life I would like to emulate and why?

- How can I seek out more people I admire?

- Who are the people in my life who most challenge me and why?

- How can I seek out more people who challenge me?

- What are the possibilities and future outcomes that scare me most and why?

- How can I make changes in my life without feeling guilt or remorse?

- How can I seek out challenges instead of run from them?

- How can I learn from the past without dwelling on the past?

- How can I find ways to value myself more or differently than I have in the past?

Learning How to Teach and Teaching How to Learn

Having been a professor for many years now, I sit in a front-row seat every day to examine what learning looks like. My students, of course, come to my class to learn, and I am still learning how to be a better teacher, class by class, semester by semester, year by year.

One thing I've noticed is that being a college student has changed dramatically in the years since I first arrived at college. As a first-generation student, I knew that graduating from college would be my first and most important success. The pressure to do well in college was of my own making, not that of the adults in my life. The decisions about my major and courses were entirely my own; I never consulted the adults in my life or other students on any such matters.

Though I might have been somewhat of an anomaly then, I certainly would be these days. Many students feel that they will have failed if they are unable to do well in the major that would have made their parents proud, even if they successfully graduate from college. Even if they do well in terms of their GPA, but they have chosen a major that did not reflect doing as well as or better than their parents did, they feel that their parents will be disappointed in them.

The American Dream of intergenerational mobility—doing better in work and income than one's parents—has become something of a nightmare. That push to succeed has caused almost unbearable stress for many of my students. It also, in my view, detracts from the beauty of learning to satiate your curiosity, to expand your horizons, to cultivate new passions. Has learning, in our modern education system, in some of the best universities in the world, lost its ability to help us flourish?

My students are so stressed about getting a grade lower than a B– that I, a professor of a class on the sociology of happiness, have had to find plenty of ways to provide them with meaningful work in which they feel they can succeed on their terms—and on everyone else's. In these circumstances, how can learning—or teaching—new things be fun or meaningful, for me or my students?

I knew I needed to change something about this teacher-student interaction, to wring some more pleasure and passion out of both me and my students, but for a long time, I wasn't sure what. I finally realized what the problem was: I had forgotten how to learn myself! As a result, I had lost some of the joy that teaching had once brought me. Was it possible that my class on happiness was mostly helping to make my stressed-out striving students a little *more* miserable?

I needed to change how I taught. I had to figure out how to make my material as immediately relevant to students' lives as possible. So I completely revamped each course. From that point on, I approached every topic from the perspective of how my students—the young adults sitting in front of me—could use the material in their lives right now or in the not-too-distant future. I reduced the amount of reading to no more than two articles a week; often the articles we read were from mainstream magazines such as *Scientific American, The Economist, Vanity Fair,* and *Rolling Stone.*

I started to show YouTube videos, and I assigned TED Talks—but even with those naturally entertaining tidbits, I carefully vetted each video to ensure that it offered inspirational and emotional appeal. Soon enough, each semester there were moments in each class when the material and discussion brought tears to the students' eyes. There were deeply touching moments of emotion about all sorts of topics we covered: dying a meaningful death in hospice care, feeling anxiety about not measuring up to your parents' expectations, not loving yourself, the moments when you think you can no longer endure life.

My students were listening to those lessons, of course, and taking notes—they were still striving students, of course—but they were also *living* those moments in their own lives. They were worrying about parental disappointment, they were mourning their lost grandparents, they were suffering the painful fear of never finding love. Even the simple but profoundly important act of writing and sharing a letter of gratitude could bring the class to a standstill.

I had finally figured out how to make my lessons apply to my students' lives, not just those of the people in the textbook. My students were feeling something! Just as exciting to me was when I realized that making learning relevant to them made teaching relevant to me. I was shocked and gratified when my classes, no kidding, would fill up within five minutes of being opened. Students would have to wait until they were seniors before they could even get into my classes, because seniors always got first dibs on courses. My students regularly wrote reviews and comments stating that in my course they had learned material they could apply in their own lives.

The changes I made in how I taught changed me for the better, that's for sure. But I also got the impression that it might be—dare I say—changing some of my students' lives? At least that's what they reported to me in the weeks, months, and even years after they had completed the course. For many students, my new approach to teaching, to learning, was giving them the opportunity to think about how the choices they were making on a daily basis were affecting them.

I had stopped teaching as if they needed to learn about my discipline and started teaching as if they needed to learn something about *themselves.*

Self-Change Is the Only Change

When I was working with a cognitive behavioral therapist, she told me quite honestly that she expected to help with, at most, 20 percent of any improvement I would experience. The rest, 80 percent, is entirely up to me. She told me that she can lead me, but she cannot do the work for me. For me to make the internal changes to stop negative thoughts from ruining my life, I had to do the homework myself. I had to practice, practice, practice until I could stop my negative automatic thoughts in their tracks and replace them with more positive, realistic thoughts.

When I found myself being triggered by unexpected or undesirable situations and people, I got better at working past my negative thoughts. But I also had to learn to embrace some unpleasant realities in the process. Sometimes, in a tough moment, I was forced to admit that it was difficult experiences from my past that were heightening my emotions, not the person in front of me I was currently furious with. I had to embrace the fact that I'll never be able to control how other people behave, but I—and only I—can choose the way I react, from the meaning I assign to an upsetting event or interaction to the boundaries I choose to set (or not set).

I don't mean to take anything away from the very real and profound suffering people are enduring. People all around us—perhaps even you—have lived through injustice and pain in their past and their present. But many of our problems, our responses to our difficulties, are ingrained into us as habitual ways of thinking, feeling, and behaving. They exist inside us; hence, we are the only people who can access them and, hopefully, change them.

I also had to embrace another important lesson I learned from a Zen Buddhist who said, "Corey, whatever is happening to you at any given moment is the best possible thing that could be happening to you." At first I was like "Wait, that's cool when things are going well and I'm getting what I want. But how can that be true when things are going horribly in my life? How can we possibly apply that lesson to people who have experienced abuse, neglect, trauma, death? How can those things ever be the best things that could happen to me?" What bullshit, I thought.

But he softened his words to help me understand his point. The Buddhist philosophy is that we should sit with whatever is happening to us with complete awareness and try to accept it—and our response to it—without judgment. That awareness will slowly grow into an understanding that we're united to the rest of the living world by suffering.

As I discussed in Part I of this book, building tolerance to negative emotions gives us more agency over how we choose to respond. I still don't buy into the fact that people suffering very real traumas are enduring "the best thing" that could possibly happen to them—but I can get on board with the idea that bringing complete awareness to our very real pain is something to strive for. Perhaps "Whatever is happening to you at any given moment is the *only* possible thing that could be happening to you" would be more accurate. Once it's happened, it's happened.

In her book *When Things Fall Apart: Heart Advice for Difficult Times*, Pema Chödrön, a Buddhist nun, wrote that we can "step into uncharted territory and relax with the groundlessness of our situation . . . dissolving the dualistic tension between us and them, this and that, good and bad, by inviting in what we usually avoid."

Chödrön's teacher called this "leaning into the sharp points." My Zen Buddhist friend clearly agreed; he told me that when disaster strikes, when things go wrong, when the world delivers humble pie, I need to learn from, rather than run from, the negative and tragic experiences in my life. I have to take the attitude that this is the only thing I have in my life now, no matter how much I might wish it away. I have to face it and make better choices. At first, I practiced choosing responses that didn't make things worse. With more practice, I could choose to act in ways that made me and the situations better, even when my negative feelings tried their hardest to pull me in the opposite direction.

But as much as I believed in the merits of such a conviction, that I needed to work with and through the pain rather than avoid it, I needed examples of virtuous people who are capable of doing such an impossible thing. I wanted mentors, ideally, or at least people I could admire who would inspire me to move in the same direction.

Comparison Versus Admiration

We all have people we truly admire because they are people who have gone through a lot but have remained good, perhaps even become better over time. To admire someone is to know that their good qualities are genuine and that they deserve the praise and rewards they receive from others, their workplace, their family, and their communities. But what happens when we start to compare ourselves to those people instead of simply admiring them?

What holds many of us back from making improvements in ourselves is the kind of discouragement that results from social comparison. It's not just the glam selfies posted on Instagram—LinkedIn is full of postings of people attending important conferences, giving talks, getting their degrees. TikTok is built of people pushing for visibility and recognition—for their dance skills, cute pets, cooking skills, and plenty of worse things. Families and friends used to be the sole recipients of our joy during important moments in our lives. Now we post about them, we push them out into a vast, uncaring world, like throwing confetti into the air, with no control over where it lands.

Comparison can trap us in negative feelings. Inferiority or exhaustion—how can we ever find the time or money to take an advanced cooking class? Anger—secretly thinking our colleague didn't deserve the promotion and accompanying praise from the boss. Envy—seeing success as a zero-sum game, a hypercompetitive capitalist culture reminding us that someone else's good fortune is inevitably paving the path of our own failure. Socrates believed that envy is the ulcer of the soul. Recurring thoughts about how we're not keeping up, that we're not good enough and never will be, stop personal growth in its tracks.

Admiration works by a completely different logic. It turns our attention inward because others we admire have inspired us to become a better person. Greater admiration of others is associated with two elements of flourishing—a greater sense of purpose in life and a higher level of personal growth—both of which nudge us closer to flourishing.

Researchers found that envy is negatively correlated with all sorts of measures of well-being. People with less envy have better relationships, more purpose, and more of a sense of personal growth; even more, people with less envy are much more accepting of themselves (self-acceptance), take more responsibility for and are able to manage their own lives (environmental mastery), and are much more confident in thinking and expressing their ideas and opinions (autonomy). As we turn the volume down on envy and turn the volume up on admiration, our personal growth increases.

The Process of Self-Change

For most people, moving away from languishing will require a greater focus on functioning better in life, in making changes, especially changes that lead us to feel we have improved who we are and how we function in life. We tend to think that if we engage in the project of self-improvement, the results of this change, the improvements we see in ourselves, will be rewarding in and of themselves.

Well, maybe not. A few years ago, I set out to measure just how much people enjoy self-improvement. I was surprised to discover that when people are offered the option to stay the same or make changes, most respondents chose to stay the same, regardless of how well they saw themselves functioning at the time. This is why so many people can't escape the gravitational pull of the patterns of thought and behavior they've been in for so long. Others yank themselves out of the cycle only to watch themselves slipping back to where they began, sometimes before they even realize they've relapsed.

Even stranger was that our research found that, compared with staying the same, making *more* improvements in being a spouse, an employee, or as a parent created *more* negative emotions. Moreover, making more improvements resulted in fewer positive emotions than staying the same. At the same time, people who saw themselves as making more improvements reported higher levels of personal growth than those who were staying the same. Making improvements might not be comfortable, but it means you can *see* that you are becoming a better person.

A Note on the Role of Willpower and Privilege in the Process of Personal Change

We all have limited mental and emotional resources, and sometimes there's not enough energy left to create the changes we want to. If you're contending with a mental illness, functional barriers, or systemic oppression, simply "putting in the effort" may not, in fact, be so simple.

As the therapist K. C. Davis wrote in *How to Keep House While Drowning*:

> Many self-help gurus over-attribute their success to their own hard work without any regard to the physical, mental, or economic privileges they hold. You can see this when a twenty-year-old fitness influencer says, "We all have the same twenty-four hours!" to a single mom of three. The fitness influencer only needed to add effort to see drastic changes in her health and so assumes that's all anyone is missing. The single mom of three, however, is experiencing very different demands and limitations on her time. For her, she needs not only effort, but also childcare, money for exercise classes, and extra time and energy at the end of the day, when she has worked nine hours and then spent an additional five caring for kids and cleaning house.

Why would positive change be so uncomfortable? Do these results mean that we should never try to improve ourselves? That aspiring to become better partners, friends, parents, and workers will lead only to negativity?

The research on perceived improvement suggests one answer: that our desire for self-consistency holds us back. Many people who make improvements go only so far, almost never as far as they wished to or was necessary. But you can envision a better self in your future. You can even

Davis added that "different people struggle differently—and privilege isn't the only difference." A life hack that works brilliantly for someone on one part of the neurodiversity spectrum may only frustrate someone whose brain functions another way. Our individual strengths, interests, and personalities mean that personal growth is not a one-size-fits-all process. Let's be honest: Many of us probably feel that we're just too busy to make real changes in our lives. For God's sake, most of the time we can barely get through our days as it is, let alone add to our to-do list: 6:00–9:00 P.M.: Work on improving self. Enough already, right?

So when setting goals for personal growth and figuring out how to reach them, remember that it's okay to go at your own pace.

Every single day, you can try to do one thing differently from the day before. Maybe it will work; maybe it won't. No one is judging your tiny successes and tiny do-overs but you. Just remember that the next day, you will have a brand-new opportunity to try again—and that you can lean into what feels easiest and most motivating to *you*.

Try aiming small, like reading one book on a topic that interests you every month. Perhaps, as you try to attain that goal, you'll need to keep tweaking your approach to better suit your needs, temperament, and personality: Maybe trying to read for thirty minutes before bed next to a burning candle isn't working. What if instead you were to listen to that same book on your headphones while you are running around doing your daily tasks?

---

tell yourself that the path forward to improvement is an absolute necessity. In some cases, it's a matter of life or death.

Anybody trying to become a better person, to change and grow from languishing to flourishing, will be tempted to move through the pain and difficulty of growth more quickly than might be desirable or useful. We don't like pain; we are motivated to medicate it, run from it, move through it as quickly as possible. But so often, we find we are capable of so much more than we imagined.

Stressors and Challenges

In fact, it seems that humans can be held back from the very things they want—such as flourishing—if they are not challenged. We sociologists have a rather antiseptic word for such challenges: *stressors.* Stress is a physiological reaction inside our bodies that marshals resources to handle danger or adversity, whether perceived or real. A stressor is a real adversity, in that it is external to you; it is an event or situation that represents change in your life or your circumstances, and it demands that you adjust yourself to the change.

There is a term in both stress and aging research that is relevant here: "manageable difficulties." When stressors arrive that are "just right," we believe that the changes and challenges can be met or overcome even if they exceed our capacity for coping but seem manageable. We have to *feel* that things are within reach even if they are out of reach; challenges that exceed but do not overwhelm our capacity to learn and cope feel as though they can be endured or overcome. A friend of mine calls them "stretch assignments"—the challenges you handle or hand off to those around you that are achievable but not necessarily easy. That, to him, is what good growth looks like.

Getting married is, for most people, a positive event, one that is eagerly anticipated—but when it happens, it is a stressor. There is a wedding to throw, for one. Then you have to confront actually *being* married, a real change in your life that demands adjustments by both parties. As I've covered, a lot of positive changes require us to adjust our lives and can cause stress reactions inside us.

Throwing a big wedding, celebrating a marriage—an undeniably positive event that causes stress is one thing, but what about an event that creates a less positive but still manageable level of adversity, such as failing a class, moving to a new town, or losing the bid for a new project at work? All of these slightly negative but definitely survivable occurrences have the potential to lead to personal growth if you allow them to. Instead of focusing on the very negative recent past, try to focus on the potential for growth on the other side of the challenge. This goes back to the Buddhist teaching earlier in the book: that fighting against a current is difficult, if not dangerous, but swimming with the flow of the river can sometimes lead you to calmer waters.

The most damaging kinds of stressors are negative or unexpected; the more prolonged or chronic they are, the worse damage they can do. The next study I discuss focused on those unexpected and undesirable stressors and investigated whether such stress had uniformly negative consequences.

The study asked people if they or a loved one had experienced a serious stressor in their lifetime, which they defined as illness or injury, various forms of violence (e.g., assault, rape, physical or verbal aggression), death and bereavement, economic or psychosocial events (e.g., loss of employment, living in dangerous housing), relationship stress (e.g., divorce), and disaster (e.g., major fire, flood, earthquake, or other community disaster). The researchers then had a count of the total amount of lifetime adversity each study participant had accumulated up until that point. They then measured participants' satisfaction with life, which is a component of emotional well-being used to measure flourishing.

The study found that life satisfaction was *highest* among participants who'd experienced just above, or just below, the average number of total lifetime stressors. By comparison, participants who had the highest level of lifetime stressors or, oddly, the lowest—those who had suffered no adversity or very little of it—were *less* satisfied with their lives.

In other words, the study shows that there is a Goldilocks relationship between adversity and life satisfaction. Both too much and too little adversity leads to much lower satisfaction with life; the "just right amount" of adversity leads to people having the highest life satisfaction.

The study also measured participants' global distress, where higher scores meant that someone felt more somatic aches and pains, more depressionlike symptoms, and more anxietylike symptoms. A higher distress score does not mean that someone has clinical depression or anxiety, just more symptoms such as sadness and fear. Participants with low to no lifetime adversity scores and those with very high adversity scores had much higher levels of mental distress than those with a moderate amount of lifetime adversity.

God knows, I'm not going to wax poetic or romantic about accumulating adversity in life; too much pain is no gain at all. After all, studies show that high levels of adversity create cumulative wear and tear on internal bodily organ systems that eventually result in physical disease and premature death. But remember that the adversities that damage the body do not *have* to do equivalent damage to our psychological or emotional systems.

Experiencing, enduring, or overcoming adversity means that people no longer have to struggle with their fear of the unknown. *Been there, done that.* We fear what we do not know—and when adversity comes into our lives, we learn more about ourselves and our lives. We learn about our own strength and capacity for endurance, and we learn about the people and things we can count on.

Suffering One's Way to Success

Without experience with adversity, your first setbacks in life may feel overwhelming. With experience, new adversities may seem more manageable. Our mindset about adversity matters, and so does our mindset about what stress experiences might do to us if and when we encounter them.

Several years ago, I had a wonderful student, Nicole. She'd been trying to get into my class for most of her undergraduate career, and finally, when she was a senior, I was able to get her off the waiting list. When we caught up recently, she reminded me that before she and I had met, when she had been in her sophomore year, she had gotten very ill. Meningitis, encephalitis—she had been in really bad shape. Eventually, she had started to recover, but it was a very slow process. Previously, her passion had been dance, and she'd looked forward to pursuing it throughout her college career, maybe even beyond. But her doctors told her that dance was no longer an option for her—her body just physically wouldn't be able to handle it. It, and she, needed rest in order to properly recover. She was devastated.

Nicole was at a loss. Everything she thought she knew and loved seemed as if it had vanished in an instant. She floundered about, not knowing where to put her attention, her energy, her displaced passion. Not far from her dorm at Emory, there was a law library where she began to go to study, mainly because it was calm and peaceful. One evening, as she sat down to study, she noticed a sign announcing a meeting of the Feminism and Legal Theory Project. Curious, and with a smidge of extra time on her hands for the first time in a long time, she researched it and was intrigued by what she read. She contacted the professor who was running the project and asked if she could be involved somehow.

That chance encounter started an informal mentoring relationship that would prove vital for Nicole at that critical juncture in her life. If dance wasn't an option anymore, maybe law could be? Law school suddenly seemed like an avenue worth pursuing. Whether she realized it in the moment or not, she was forced to let go of her preconceived expectations of how her life was supposed to unfold. If she had languished for months, even years, wallowing in the disappointment of her inability to pursue dance, just imagine what she might have missed out on. That new passion of hers would never have ignited.

From that moment onward, she never lost the spark. After graduation, she went on to Duke for law school, moved to New York City to work at a big law firm, and had just recently, when we spoke, accepted a visiting professorship at a law school in North Carolina. She told me that this is the career—teaching law to law students—she wants to be involved in for the rest of her life.

What was undoubtedly a period of terrible loss and isolation—getting so sick while being away from home, giving up on her love of dance—turned into a period of growth and learning for her. She experienced adversity—likely more than at any other point in her life up until then—and man, did she find it unpleasant, even painful. But instead of succumbing to the stress of it, she allowed it to change her life.

Action Plan: Allow your curiosity to triumph over your disappointment. And don't let fear of the unknown—a new subject, a new skill, an entire new life plan—scare you away from investigating something new. Next time you're at the library and see a sign for a new group forming, maybe sign up instead of walking back to your dorm room. Pick up that violin that your child abandoned years ago and decide it would be worth doing something a little embarrassing, if only to fill that space in your heart that your now-grown children once filled. Let curiosity win.

Perception Is Everything

When we think of adversity and what accompanies it—stress, discomfort, pain—we may be making things worse by ruminating on the discomfort. If we could approach adversity from what I'll call the Nicole point of view—accepting manageable adversity and seeing it as an opportunity to let go of our previously held expectations—we would all be better off.

A study of how people view stress and how their perception of stress affects their risk of premature death brings this point home in a powerful way. Participants who reported having a lot of stressors in their life and also reported that they believed that stress affected one's health "a lot" were more likely to report mental distress and had a substantially increased (43 percent) risk of premature death. But adults who experienced lots of stressors but who thought that stress affected their health hardly or not at all reduced their chance of premature death by 17 percent and reported the lowest levels of mental distress.

Now, there are tolerable stressors—facing a tough opponent on the basketball court, an extremely tight work deadline, or your teenager having a meltdown—though everyone has a different "window" of tolerance. Then, there are truly serious ones: assault, abuse, systemic racism, childhood trauma. They are not the same, and I will never tell someone who has experienced one or more of the latter to simply buck up and change their mindset. Those more serious stressors can undeniably affect your health each and every day. But as someone who has experienced many of those traumas myself, I encourage you to work at separating out the serious stressors you've endured and continue to endure from the ones that are more manageable.

Action Plan: Work on the manageable stuff. Fix what can be fixed. Remind yourself that although some things cannot be undone, other more manageable stressors in life can be reframed in your own mind as opportunities for growth.

When a coach is preparing a team for a game against a really tough opponent, they don't just throw up their hands and say, "I give up; this seems too hard." Instead, the coach breaks the game plan down into manageable pieces, figuring out ways to neutralize the opponent's strengths and compensate for their own team's weaknesses. A good coach sees the challenge ahead as an opportunity for positive change and finds a way to approach it as a set of just-manageable difficulties.

Think of a barrier in your life right now. Maybe it's a course you need to take in order to get to the next level in your job. Perhaps it's a meeting you need to set up in order to kick-start an important project on your to-do list. Maybe it is a family member you need to call in order to plan the next get-together or smooth out a misunderstanding.

Now, instead of thinking of it as a barrier, think of it as a speed bump you're going to encounter as you head down a new road. Even if the call with your family member goes sideways, you can learn a lot about how you—and others—respond to conflict. Think of it as an opportunity for growth—for you as a loved one, an employee, or simply a person trying to better understand themselves and the world around them. Think of it as a just-manageable challenge that you can, indeed, overcome.

Growth After Adversity

In his poem "The Guest House," the Sufi poet Rumi wrote about how
adversity arrives on our doorstep again and again over the course of our
lives; our job is to welcome the sorrow, dark thoughts, shame, and
anger and to treat them with the respect they deserve. They are our
guests; eventually they will depart.

Adversity can be useful; it helps us clear out what no longer serves
us well. To paraphrase Rumi, adversity, like all guests, will eventually
leave when we have experienced it, listened to it, facing whatever it's
stirred up inside of us. Then, and only then, that guest will have served
its purpose. If it visits again, it is no longer something to fear. It is
known. You will have grown.

None of us sets out to screw up in life. But the fear of failure has
proven to be misplaced. The obsession with perfection is just as great a
folly. The only thing that remains perfect is something that is never
used—like the good china my wife and I received as a wedding gift
that has yet to be touched by food in our thirty-five-plus years of marriage. But humans don't sit in a cabinet, untouched and unblemished.
People who hide their mistakes from others end up hiding their very
humanity. As we've seen, the only path toward flourishing is one that
encompasses change (which is uncomfortable), failures (which can be
painful), effort (which can be exhausting), and improvement (which
feels impossible sometimes).

What about mistakes that endanger the lives of others? Like all of
us, doctors fall prey to negligence and errors in judgment leading to
misdiagnoses, drug dosage miscalculations, treatment delays, hospital-
acquired infections, avoidable surgical mistakes, and more, with serious repercussions for patients and their families, the doctors themselves,
and their colleagues and institutions. Medical errors may cause between a hundred thousand and two hundred thousand deaths per year
in the United States.

Many of these errors are due to system failure rather than human failure, from inadequate staffing and resources to crumbling communication infrastructure that allows critical patient information to slip through the cracks between staff, departments, and facilities. Researchers at the Stanford University School of Medicine found that physicians suffering from burnout were twice as likely to report making mistakes. It's sometimes difficult to separate out "preventable" mistakes from the casualties of broken processes and grueling conditions.

But there are instances where responsibility does fall on the shoulders of individual clinicians. Do doctors grow from such mistakes? The answer is yes, but only if they have the courage to face their mistakes—which often leave them wracked by shame, self-doubt, and fear of retaliation or even losing their jobs. One study found that 34 percent of doctors don't believe they ought to disclose significant medical errors to patients, and 20 percent of doctors admitted to not fully disclosing an error due to fear of being sued. But research on doctors who chose to disclose their mistakes has yielded universal lessons on responding to disappointment or defeat.

The first step those doctors took was to accept what could not be undone or changed, resisting the urge to pin blame elsewhere or rewrite the narrative. This was both an internal act, requiring them to face shame, fear, and psychological turmoil head-on, and an external one, summoning the integrity to be transparent. Doctors who maintained their careers after serious mistakes not only took responsibility for their actions, but they also "played back the tape" to figure out what had gone wrong and why. As one doctor put it, "First off, I knew what I had done. . . . I knew what I should have done, and so it became, well, how did you miss it in this case?"

Many of the doctors saw, upon reflection, that they used to practice as if they had all the answers. Postadversity, however, they regularly sought out more input, questions, and critiques. Others reported having developed an enhanced ability to tolerate disagreement as a way to move toward the best possible decision for a patient.

We may want our doctors to act as if they are invincible, but that would be as detrimental to us as it would be for them.

Action Plan: Self-change may bring us closer to perfection, but only if we embrace our own and life's imperfections. Embrace your imperfections. Invite humility into your life. Give yourself space to screw up (preferably not in a medical setting) and accept the inevitability of failure. Give the grace of that same space to those in your life, too—I've learned a huge amount about being a good human from watching those around me show me what the opposite looks like.

Rather than sitting mired in regret about something we've done until it becomes too much and we pack the memory away, can we "mine our mistakes" to unearth insights about ourselves, our deepest motivations, our coping mechanisms, and our behavioral patterns? This kind of introspection yields not only self-awareness but self-compassion.

Be like Rumi—accept that guest of adversity in your house as an opportunity, not an opponent, and learn the lesson it leaves behind. Or, as one doctor put it as she tried to recover from a tragic mistake, "I haven't gotten very wise from anything that went right the first time."

[6]

Connect: Building Warm and Trusting Relationships

When Carl and his husband, Aaron, moved from a big city to a small town with their young child during the height of the pandemic, they were eager to get started on the next stage of their lives. They didn't have to upend their lives completely—neither had to change jobs, as they could both commute from their new house or work from home. As relatively new parents, they were excited for their son to begin making friends. They started taking long walks around the neighborhood with their child in the stroller—and after a few weeks, they started to notice something.

People were crossing the street when they saw them coming. They joked—gosh, people really don't like gay people here, do they? But, thinking it through together, they began to suspect that in this pretty liberal, open-minded town, everyone was just so scared of this new disease, they were steering clear of anyone new in their path, literally and figuratively.

Still, they were lonely. They were confused. They were, frankly, getting a little tired of their core family unit. They felt, you guessed it, empty. Had they made a mistake moving there, leaving all their loved ones behind?

Luckily, they had some close acquaintances left over from their city days who had moved out to the suburbs a few years earlier, and from those connections, they started to stitch together a life in their new town. Carl, the more extroverted of the two, joined the PTA and a few other local boards once the schools opened up again. Soon he started feeling more like himself again. Aaron, with his quiet chuckle and gentle sarcasm, began making friends with neighbors and parents of their son's new preschool friends—not as much of a man about town, but beloved by those who knew him. Fast-forward a few years, and now they are surrounded by people they could easily ask to watch their son if they needed a night out together as a couple or to care for their older, sick dog when they take a trip out of state—people who, suffice it to say, never cross the road when they see them coming.

Meaningful connections took a while for them to develop, but when they finally found them, everything changed. Despite the fact that they are both far from their families, they feel cared for, sewn into the fabric of their community.

Friends Versus Friendships

What is a friend? What makes any relationship warm and trusting? And in the age of growing interconnectivity, where we can have Facebook friends and Snapchat buddies and Instagram connections and TikTok followers, why are so many of us having trouble making meaningful connections? Does our increasing number of online touch points serve mainly to decrease the number of real-life connections we make every day? A lot of people are explaining the phenomenon with some version of the following: We are all mistaking friends for friendships. Though the former feels good, it's the latter we can't live without.

In C. S. Lewis's book *The Four Loves,* he made the somewhat surprising case for friendship as the rarest and most profound of human bonds, above natural affection, like the fondness that springs up between a dog and its owner; *eros,* the most passionate and often unstable of relationships; and *agape,* the unconditional love often seen between family members and others we choose to love selflessly. He wrote, "In each of my friends there is something that only some other friend can fully bring out. By myself I am not large enough to call the whole man into activity; I want other lights than my own to show all his facets."

Social connections need to answer quite specific needs—and shared interests, hobbies, and values might matter less than you think. Though fangirling over a book series helps grease the wheels of conversation, easy conversation starters aren't the best predictors of the quality of a friendship, and, as it turns out, having too much in common makes it harder to learn from each other.

A true friendship hinges on reciprocity, with both sides giving and receiving freely (and without scorekeeping). For some of us, being there for others comes more naturally than allowing them to be there for you. It can take more effort to share your deepest needs and struggles than to be a supportive listener—but for real intimacy to form, it has to be a two-way street. As Lewis wrote, friendship "is born at the moment when one man says to another 'What! You too? I thought that no one but myself . . .'"

To enable flourishing, social connections must have a mutual sense of equality. True, many of our relationships have social status differences. Parents and children are not equal (and some would say that being best friends with your parents isn't the healthiest goal, even when you're all adults); employees are not equal with their bosses or managers; and we all have differing degrees of power and status in different realms of our lives. These inequalities give us the opportunity to send the message to others that *you don't belong here* or *I have the upper hand*. But the message could also be "I see you, you belong here, we are the same."

From that foundation of equality and reciprocity, true friendships hinge on the willingness—and in some cases, the skills and ability—to empathize, understand, collaborate, and compromise, even when there's conflict. When you're struggling, someone who knows you well will know you need more than a quick hit of sympathy or an easy-button solution—and if they're not sure what kind of support would be most meaningful to you, they ask. You feel at home with each other, even when you are not at home.

Needless to say, quality wins over quantity.

So what does an emotionally close and satisfying friendship look like in practice?

Friend: "Shitty day at work? Totally. Me, too. My boss actually had the nerve to say to me. . . ."

Friendship: "Shitty day at work? I'm so sorry. Me, too, actually. Want to grab a drink somewhere quiet and talk about what's going on?"

Friend: "Your son got suspended from school today? My kid got suspended a couple of times in high school, don't worry about it. He turned out fine."

Friendship: "Your son got suspended from school today? Wow, that must be so stressful for you and for him. Do you want to talk about it?"

Friend: "Your mother went to the hospital after a fall today? God, that's awful. Is she doing okay?"

Friendship: "Your mother went to the hospital after a fall today? God, that's awful. Can I drive you to go see her? Can I dog sit for you while you're busy? Can I bring some food to the hospital for your family?"

There's nothing wrong with good, fun friends—we all need them. And there's nothing wrong with the first set of answers above—sometimes that's just what we need to hear in the moment. But we, as humans, also need friends in our lives who offer more—who see us fully and support us in the ways we crave most.

Action Plan: Focus on quality, not quantity. Life provides many slings and arrows that remind us that we can't do it on our own, but with so much time spent on "the daily grind," meaningful relationships sometimes fall far down on our list of priorities. Many of us do have close friendships—or ones with the potential to be close—but don't fully appreciate them until something shifts our time perspective. As our elders teach us, when our time perspective shifts from abundant to compressed, we see how precious these relationships really are. This shift toward prioritizing meaningful connection also happens when we get very ill and when we're about to leave a place where we cultivated good neighbors, good friends, good colleagues, and so on.

There are all kinds of valid reasons and motivations for having more casual connections, from professional networking to having a good laugh about a Twitter thread. But the goal of social contact cannot simply be wanting to *feel* busy and popular. And we have to carve out the space and time—and mental energy—that emotionally satisfying relationships require in order to move toward flourishing.

Belonging and Dignity

About ten years ago, I gave a talk in the United Kingdom on flourishing. During the question-and-answer period, I was asked a jarring question: "Dr. Keyes, do you think members of the Hell's Angels are flourishing?"

The Hell's Angels call themselves a motorcycle "club," but really, it functions as more of a gang. The group is known to engage in a number of illegal activities, everything from drug smuggling to assassination. The person asking the question was getting at a question I found fascinating: Is it possible to find flourishing through unconventional forms of community that sometimes involve illegal activities?

Social connection is far from a given in life for so many of us—not just for mothers of newborns, socially anxious teenagers, and isolated older folks, but for so many others in between. Warm and trusting relationships are so important that some people who don't have them readily available will go to great lengths to find some semblance of connection, even if that means violating social norms—or even breaking the law—to feel as though they belong, that they have something to contribute to this world, that they feel protected, and that they are no longer alone.

Gangs—of all different kinds, from Hell's Angels to the yakuza, from MS-13 to the Mafia—remain a significant presence in a number of towns and cities around the world, even in the richest countries, causing what seem like intractable problems for both the communities and the members themselves. But if that's the case, why do many young people join a gang, by whatever name you might call it?

A gang is a group of teenagers and young adults, predominantly male, that adopt symbols and special ways to communicate and often engage in illegal activities. Gangs exist and operate over a period of time in a neighborhood or specific geographical location. Defined this way, other than the illegal part, it is hard to distinguish a gang from a Little League baseball team or a Boy Scout troop, isn't it? We, as humans, are deeply wired to crave human connection; perhaps it is not all that surprising how far we'll go to find it. Perhaps the only true difference separating a neighborhood Little League baseball team and a gang is that the latter routinely engages in criminal behavior and uses intimidation or violence to further its ends.

We belong to social units—families, neighborhoods, social groups— that provide us with not merely a sense of belonging but also safety and protection. It is pretty hard to flourish in a world where you do not feel protected and safe. Physical safety is a precondition for healthy attachments and true connection; although many of us take that for granted, not everyone can. There is a reason that safety and security are basic needs.

But other kinds of safety are just as important as physical safety. Psychological safety allows us to feel a sense of belonging and acceptance. Emotional safety gives us the peace of mind to freely share our feelings with others. And social safety, which can only follow these other types, is where we finally feel we can contribute.

Throughout human evolution, the survival of our ancestors over millions of years depended on their finding these various kinds of safety; historically, a sense of physical and psychological safety has come from being a useful, valued member of a hunting and gathering unit, a unit Sebastian Junger discussed at length in his book *Tribe: On Homecoming and Belonging*. Our tribal nature as hunters and gatherers remains part of our physical and social DNA, teaching us the most basic lesson of the necessity of social connections that comes from being a member of something—and yes, this means everything from church choirs to gangs. It doesn't have to be an organized group, necessarily; the same benefits accrue to a close, connected group of friends, whether they are young mothers in Brooklyn, retirees in a fifty-five-plus living community in Arizona, or, yes, members of Hell's Angels.

Lots of people have been obtaining social status, power, and money through questionable and illegal means for years. One could argue that individuals who are denied access and opportunities to find flourishing through legitimate social means, such as good schools, good neighborhoods, and so on, still have the human will to persevere. People who don't have close, safe (in every sense) relationships are more likely to join a gang of some sort, which simply shows how deeply wired we are for connection. Membership in a community, of whatever sort, is a vital ingredient in the struggle for human dignity.

The Desire to Belong

We all have at one point struggled to belong. We too often have trouble believing that we are equal to those around us, who may all seem smarter, stronger, faster, better, or more effective at being alive than we are, which hinders our ability to feel as if we belong.

This struggle starts early. Infants of all races and cultures exhibit what psychologists call *effectance motivation,* which is the need to have an effect on one's surroundings. This desire develops into a need to develop competence and useful skills that can, as adults, lead to our making social contributions. Racism, sexism, homophobia, abuse, and countless other lived traumas deny and suppress the development of the competence to act on our inherent motivation for effectance.

That certainly rings true for me. When I was young, I lived through a horribly dysfunctional childhood of abandonment, addiction, physical abuse, and emotional abuse, which led to my struggling mightily in school. I was, on a weekly basis, in detention or failing my classes. Once I was adopted by my paternal grandparents at the age of twelve, my life changed 180 degrees.

Suddenly, I lived in a peaceful, safe environment where my grandparents showered me with love and guidance. I blossomed, almost overnight, into an honor roll student who was active in the choir, quarterback of the football team, and a member of the homecoming court. I had friends—real friendship—for the first time in my life. I had love, I had a home I felt safe in—I was not alone in this world anymore.

As I look at the sentences I just typed, I reflect that perhaps it should come as no surprise that I became a sociologist, a scientist who believes that if we change the environment we live in, we can change, for the better, the people we are and the people we can be. Sometimes we flourish where we are "planted," and sometimes we need to be re-planted somewhere better, where we can flourish. Never assume that because someone is languishing, it is their own fault.

By the time I graduated from high school, I was one of only three students out of a class of fifty-three who decided to go on to college. I would be the first person from the Keyes family to attend university—what is now known as a first-generation student. But I struggled to internalize a sense of equality—basically, the sense I belonged—and have continued to do so for most of my life.

My high school just hadn't prepared me for college, because rarely did anybody from Three Lakes, Wisconsin, go on to college. My first year of college was a disaster; I was a decimal point (my GPA was 2.01, a C average) from being put on academic probation my sophomore year. I couldn't write a basic essay, and nothing I did to revise my English 101 essays, having sought the help of a tutor, satisfied my professor.

At the end of that year, I received the lowest grade I ever received in college for English 101: a D minus. My professor of English sought me out at the end of the semester to give me what must have felt like sage advice: "Corey, I don't think you belong here." Without knowing it, he had struck at a core belief that my childhood trauma had instilled in me: You do not belong, you are not wanted here, you are not equal. His denial of my competence cut me to the bone.

The other thing my trauma instilled in me was a chip on my shoulder. What was activated at the very moment the professor told me that I didn't belong was a desire to prove to him—and the entire world, for that matter—that they were wrong about me. That motivation has persisted throughout my entire life. I was not going to let trauma defeat me. It is a mantra I have said many times: "You will not defeat me, you will not win."

That chip on my shoulder served me well. Despite my very rough start, I graduated from college summa (almost magna) cum laude and was accepted into what was at that time the world's leading graduate program in sociology, at the University of Wisconsin–Madison. I received my PhD within five years and published a dissertation on social well-being.

That chip—that sense that I wasn't equal, that no one would ever see me as equal—pushed me in my studies, my research. I wanted to know whether other people struggled and yearned for the same things I did: feeling more socially integrated, being more accepting of other people, wanting to make a meaningful contribution to society, trying to better understand or make sense of what's going on around us in the social world. I was studying what I wanted more of in my own life.

Succeeding as a first-generation student puts you into a strange place of social dislocation. You're gratified—perhaps even surprised—by your success, but now you feel stuck between worlds. There is the world you came from and can never really return to without feeling that others think you have changed so much that you are no longer the person they grew up with. You can't go home, so to speak, without showing that you have moved up the social hierarchy; you might now be the target of resentment. You no longer feel accepted where you came from.

At the same time, you never quite feel that you belong in the new social hierarchy you have moved up into. You can talk the others' talk and walk their walk. But as the saying goes, you never forget where you came from. In subtle ways, no matter how hard you work, how hard you try, you will keep getting the message that you don't quite fit in where you now live, either.

Fighting Dislocation with Connection

This feeling of being caught between social worlds makes social connection more difficult for so many people today. Part of the challenge comes from the creeping collapse of the small towns of rural America. Today, the majority of the world's population resides in densely populated urban areas—cities. Not that long ago, the population was more equally distributed into rural and urban areas. The urbanization of people and life had begun while I was a child, and the kind of life I led as a child, in my small hometown of Three Lakes, Wisconsin, is slowly disappearing. Three Lakes, luckily, is a vacation mecca, home to the largest chain of freshwater lakes in the world. Wealthy families from Chicago, Milwaukee, and Madison have second homes on the lakes, so my town is likely to survive and thrive. But not all small towns are as lucky to have such natural resources to sustain them; many are instead witness to their own slow demise.

Years after my grandmother passed away, I was on a vacation trip with my wife and her parents in northern Wisconsin. I asked if they wanted to see where I had grown up. We decided to change course and go to Three Lakes and visit Lake Terrace, the mobile home park where I had grown up. To my surprise and shock, my grandparents' mobile home was gone. All that remained was the hole in the ground, the empty foundation into which they'd placed their mobile home. Most of the trees, bushes, and flowers that my grandparents had lovingly cultivated over the years had died.

Perhaps it seems silly to you—a mobile home, by its very definition, is about as far from a permanent fixture as you can get. But still, I felt so lost, disconnected, cut loose from the world. Without a home I could lay eyes on, my hometown no longer felt the same. To this day,

I wish I had never seen that sight; it would have been better living with the memory and belief that someone else is now caring for and growing up in that home that I considered the best part of my childhood.

Waiting for Permission to Belong

I have spent an entire lifetime trying to forget that, to most people, I was considered trash. We have countless other terms for people we believe are "less than"—I won't list them here and give them any more power than they already hold. These "terms of destruction," as I call them, can affect our sense of self-respect and dignity. They make us feel as if we don't belong—not here, not there, not anywhere—and leave us subconsciously waiting for permission to belong. We can't let others win by internalizing those external messages.

I can't imagine how much harder my childhood would have been if my grandparents hadn't showed me that I mattered. Then, years later, in terms of my career, I was lucky enough to experience something similar. A grad school mentor of mine, a professor whose work I deeply admired, told me he saw himself in me. I was floored. At my best moments, I felt I could see myself in him as well—that despite our vast differences in background, accomplishments, and public accolades, perhaps someday I could become like him. And perhaps I, too, could change the lives of students like myself, simply by making them feel equal and fully seen. It was life-changing.

Getting the message that you're an outsider, especially early in life, can warp the self-narrative you carry through adulthood. When we believe that we'll never belong, our brains unwittingly search for evidence to support it—for example, reading negativity into an unusually short text from a friend—and it can become nearly impossible to trust that people will accept us if we let our guards down. As Brené Brown wrote in her book *Braving the Wilderness: The Quest for True Belonging and the Courage to Stand Alone*, "I don't think there's anything lonelier than being with people and feeling alone." If we're lucky, someone like my professor might break through a wall and shift something within us. For most of us, it takes deep inner work to challenge the false belief that we're not worthy of dignity or respect, to begin practicing unconditional love and acceptance toward ourselves, and to build a self-narrative around our fundamental worthiness and equality.

Action Plan: Take the time to truly listen to your internal dialogue, and separate out the external messages that need to be flushed out of your system. Remind yourself as often as you can that the people in your life who tell you they love you—and back up their words by their actions—mean it. Try to relax in the knowledge that they'll accept you in good times and bad and that you don't have to socially "perform" to be interesting or lovable. And when you're hurting, don't wait for your friends to read your mind. Start by asking for help and offering your help in return.

Send Out Messages of Equality

Any of us with seniority and power can send out messages of equality in our interactions with people who weren't always told by the world that they belonged—a privilege we too often take for granted—or who are operating with less social and economic status, education, work experience, and so on. The sheer dumb luck of being born in the right place or the misfortune of being born in the wrong one can profoundly influence the ease with which we form meaningful connections and the time, learning, and effort required to do so.

I have a friend who spends a great deal of time in Sweden, and she often returns from trips struck by dramatic societal differences. Over there, children call their teachers by their first names, and young people greet their parents' friends quite casually, without the sort of cautious, age-related respect we often expect in this country. At first, she found it startling—do they not revere their elders over there?

But soon she came to see that as one of the reasons the Swedes have such holistic, egalitarian lifestyles and social policies reinforcing the message that everyone is equal. For example, lunch is a very popular meal during the week, and in any given stylish downtown restaurant, you'll see nearly every table full: men and women in posh business attire at one table, a retired couple in casual outfits next to them, and a construction crew in reflector vests just across, all frequenting the same establishment with similar expectations for their midday meal. This cross-pollination of humans—from different backgrounds, working different jobs, at different life stages—exists everywhere there. It appears that the Swedes have figured out that the expectation of equality is a form of respect that they are unwilling to compromise on. Their social connections reflect that assumption, and according to my friend, they all seem to be benefiting from it.

Action Plan: SEE: Work on your vision; see people clearly, even those who look or behave differently from you or who come from a very different place than you do. THINK: What can I do to make someone's day better, even if someone else's needs seem very different from my own? How can I make them feel I am present, that we are equals, that I understand them in this moment? DO: Then just do it. Imagine what you might have needed from a true friend in your darkest moment and try to offer that, whatever it is. It might be a casserole delivered in a time of sadness, but it also might be the offer of a quiet evening walk, where few words are spoken but the feeling of support shared is incalculable.

Mattering

That grad school professor-mentor of mine changed my life when he told me he saw himself in me. His words—his kind attention—showed me that I mattered, not just to him, but perhaps eventually to our shared profession as well. Mattering—well, it matters.

From a sociological perspective, "mattering" is a vital ingredient in the "social contribution" component of flourishing. To *matter* is to be able to live a life in which you can contribute things of worth or value to others and the world. All social creatures, from the ant colony to the beehive, from the wolf pack to the elephant herd, have specific roles in which they are useful, contributing members of society, whatever their society is.

The scale to measure mattering consists of only five questions, each of which strikes at the heart of what it means to be truly connected to other people.

1. Do people depend on you?

2. Do people listen to what you have to say?

3. Do you feel that people pay attention to you?

4. Do you feel you are an important part of others' lives?

5. Would you be missed if you were suddenly gone?

The researchers who created the scale of mattering point out that two groups of individuals in particular tend to bask in the glow of mattering: children and older, preretirement adults. Kids feel they matter because they are the center of the universe—or at least they think they are! The midlife adult, who is likely to be a parent, spouse, and employee, feels responsible for others and for making things—in their own lives and others'—function well.

The result of this, though, is that it sets up young adults and older adults for a shock of sorts. When adolescents enter into the world of the young adult, they no longer feel like the center of any universe. Likewise, when older adults retire, they must either find new ways to matter to the world beyond their work, or they might face the unsettling fact that the part of their life during which they mattered is—well—over.

Family and work—being the center of attention of the family or being in charge of making things function at home or at work—may be primary sources of mattering to many people. But the opposite scenario can also unfold, in which families and work can make us feel insignificant, unimportant, devalued, and invisible.

When the world doesn't treat you as though you matter—when you've suffered prolonged emotional neglect or you're part of a marginalized group, such as the growing population experiencing homelessness—you're left vulnerable to what York University psychology professor Gordon Flett calls the "'double jeopardy' of feeling alone and unimportant." Flett has spent much of his career studying, along with his colleagues, the role of a sense of "antimattering" in health and well-being, finding links not only to low self-esteem but also to low extroversion, a decreased sense of competence, an inability or unwillingness to engage in self-care, and higher rates of neuroticism and insecure attachment styles.

In a 2021 study, Flett found that people prone to feelings of not mattering may "internalize thoughts such as 'I am not worth paying attention to' and 'I am not worth listening to'" and "will be vulnerable and potentially hypersensitive to negative responses and reactions from other people directed toward the self," leading to "a defensive motivational orientation and desire for protection from adverse interactions."

In other words, a lack of mattering can lead to isolation; this sense of aloneness can compound on itself. Our walls go up when they most need to go down. If we feel we don't matter, we withdraw from the activities that give us a sense of social contribution; when we aren't being useful to others, we feel we don't matter. The correlations in that study between levels of mattering and loneliness were strong; as your sense of mattering increases, your feelings of loneliness tend to decrease.

There is perhaps no greater pain than the sense that we have nothing more to give. And every time we allow someone to feel that way—or make them feel that way—we are failing them. Everyone—everyone in the world—can be important and useful. For far too long, we have relegated the work of caring to women. Not only is that an unjust burden, but it impoverishes the rest of us. The heart and soul of connection is doing for others what they cannot or will not do for themselves in a moment of pain, failure, or loss. In those moments, we can be kind, caring, supportive, and helpful and take our place in the intricate web of interdependence.

Action Plan: Many of us suffer from the belief that we need permission, we need to be asked or invited, in order to participate and help. But that isn't true. When you see someone or something that may need our help, reach out. See them, and be seen in turn.

A friend told me about a great piece of life advice her mom had given her when she was young. She told my friend to stop asking if there was anything she could do to help in the kitchen as everyone was getting dinner on the table. Just walk to the sink, pick up a dish brush, she told her, and start scrubbing. Basically, she was telling her that asking how you can help is a waste of everyone's time. Just step right up and jump in. Join in, she said, and you will always be contributing—and hence, you will feel you are part of something bigger.

For some reason, such exhortations always bring back the memory of junior high school dances for me. The girls and boys stood on opposite sides of the gymnasium. The music would come on, but nobody would dance. As we nervously eyed one another across the room, we secretly wished for someone to come over and ask us to dance. Worried about rejection, most of us waited, and waited, and waited. Suddenly, a lone person would walk across the gym toward someone. Their eyes would lock, smiles would emerge, and she or he would ask the other to dance.

I remember the first time I read about the "liking gap"—the assumption that other people like us less than they actually do. Wait—so all this time I've spent worrying that no one wants to hang out with me but it turns out they might? So try asking someone to dance—literally or metaphorically. We all want so badly to receive that invitation.

My Wall of Love

In my office, I've put together a "wall of love" collage over the years—a collection of pictures of all the people who have been loving, caring, and important parts of my life. Recently, I emailed a picture of it to that beloved old college professor of mine you met earlier in the chapter. He was then and remains to this day like a father to me and shows up in not one but two of the pictures on my wall of love. His nickname is "T-Bird" (Thunderbird) Brown, and I love him as though he were my father.

Sent: Friday, July 1, 2022 6:43 AM
To: Brown, William T.
Subject: Some important pictures

Hey you,

I made a picture collage of all the people who were so important to me and my life and had to share the two pictures that feature you.

Happy fourth weekend. I love and miss you. If you ever need anything, and I mean it, you or Joan should let me know and I'll be there in a heartbeat.

Corey

Sent: Friday, July 1, 2022 4:03 PM
To: Keyes, Corey L.
Subject: Re: Some important pictures

I am genuinely touched, moved, pleased and, as I think about it, teary eyed at your generous expression of love and concern for Joan and me.

I have long referred to you as my "all time" favorite student, and told and retold my story of threatening to adopt you while I bragged on your distinguished career and success.

This, however, goes beyond all that. This says that something about you touched something in me that made me a better person and allowed me to experience life more richly and to do and to be more than I would have otherwise been.

So I love you too Corey Keyes, just like you were and are—we both got a pretty good deal out of what could have been "nothing special." A few classroom hours, a scribble on a transcript . . . maybe a letter of recommendation . . . but we got lucky, we found each other and it turned out way-good for us and because of that probably for some others along the way. You can't buy that in stores or order it from Amazon!

Thank you for putting me up on your wall of people who have been "important" in your life. You're on mine too. Thank you as well for your offer to "help if/when" because I know you mean it.

Keep on keepin' on my man, and don't ever look back because something may be gaining on you (that's from Satchel Paige).

Old T-bird and Joan too

Action Plan: My beloved professor is closing in on his ninth decade on this planet. It is only a matter of time until I will not be able to tell him that he mattered so much to my life. So don't ever waste the chance to reflect on how others matter in your life—and let them know it. Try writing a gratitude list, perhaps once a week, of the people who've enriched your life in large or small ways. Maybe tell them so.

Then write a list of gratitude for yourself. Remind yourself of all the ways you made people feel seen, cared for, and supported. Don't wait or put it off.

The Struggles of a New Mother

When Denise was twenty-seven years old, she and her new husband moved from Austin, Texas, to a quieter suburb in the Hill Country. They were both able to work remotely and commute occasionally, and they had just found out they were expecting a baby, so the timing seemed perfect. They would have a little more space and a little more peace and quiet, and their modest salaries would go much further outside the city limits. They both agreed that it was time to leave the city for a new, different stage of their lives.

But after the baby was born—beautiful, healthy, wonderful—and her husband headed back to his job after an all-too-short paternity leave, Denise started feeling drained. Not just the to-be-expected, mom-of-a-newborn crisis-levels of exhaustion—though she had that, too—but also that she couldn't really see a moment in the future where things might start to look up.

She had pictured maternity leave to be filled with enjoying her time away from work, perhaps going on long walks with other new moms, chatting about diapers and feeding schedules. But she was mostly alone with her baby, for hours and hours on end every day. She hadn't quite been able to connect with other new moms in her town yet. "Mommy and Me" yoga seemed far too pricey. The free story hour at the tiny local public library was filled with people, but everyone already seemed as though they knew one another and always rushed off afterward without her.

Her family lived a few hours' drive away and couldn't come visit much. Her closest friends were still back in Austin, and none of them were having kids yet, so connecting with them felt close to impossible. By the time they got home from work and postwork outings, she was ready for bed. When she wanted to chat during her morning walk or her son's afternoon nap, they were busy at the office. Was everyone else having a better time than she was? Where were the new magical mom friends who would give her the sense of community she craved? Why was she not content just finding joy in this gorgeous new family she and her husband had created?

Denise is very open about this time in her life. She talked to her doctor, who agreed that she didn't fit the criteria for postpartum depression. She adored the baby and had no worries that she might harm him. She did not cry uncontrollably, she wasn't having panic attacks, and she felt perfectly capable of carrying out her duties as a new mother. But she felt enervated and empty. She was disconnected, unsure of herself, feeling as if she didn't belong anywhere anymore—not back in Austin with her old, busy friends, and not out here in the outskirts, isolated in her new house, alone with her baby for hours on end.

In my view, we have missed an opportunity to name what Denise was going through, what so many new mothers go through: postpartum languishing. A sense of disappointment, as well as self-judgment, characterize PPL. Why *aren't* I feeling happy, joyful, and fulfilled with this new baby in my life? Do I not love my baby enough? What am I doing wrong? Early research on PPL suggests that we must do far more to help mothers through a vulnerable time of transition—a time when cultural scripts suggest that they should feel overjoyed.

We all have a deep need to feel we belong to a larger community, to have warm and trusting relationships, and to believe we're able to contribute to our larger social worlds. Many new mothers have these core needs yanked away by circumstances, and they suffer for it.

Denise had been more than eager to meet other new moms like her, and certainly, that would have helped her. But such friendships just didn't materialize in the right way, at the right moment, as she'd expected they would. Instead of giving up hope of any sense of connection, she might have thought to look elsewhere. She might have felt seen in an entirely different way had she found ways to connect with people whose life was entirely different from hers: a young woman just starting out on her career path in her office she might offer to mentor while she was out on maternity leave, a retired executive who volunteers at the local library, whose own children are long grown. They're looking for new, special connections, too.

Looking for Someone Different

We so often restrict our social circle to people who are doing the exact same things as we are. But doesn't that limit our learning? Recently I was speaking to a man in his late seventies who told me a story I found surprising. He had grown up in a mostly white, upper-middle-class neighborhood in Cleveland, Ohio. After graduating from high school, he had gone off to college on the East Coast, followed immediately thereafter by heading to Harvard Business School. When he arrived on campus, he was a twenty-two-year-old kid, directly out of college. He peeked tentatively around the door of his dorm room, carrying his bags. His roommate was already in their room, lying on the bed, wearing a dashiki. My friend said, "I think this is my room." The man on the bed scowled. "I asked for a single."

The man lying on the bed was Franklin Delano Roosevelt, a thirty-two-year-old self-proclaimed Black nationalist, also from Cleveland. He was the deputy director of Hough Development Corporation, a nonprofit working to provide support to those who lived in the Hough Avenue neighborhood, which was then by far the roughest in Cleveland. Frank had finished only two years at San Francisco State, but because of his work experience, he had been accepted into the MBA program.

Though the two seemed to have little in common, other than their city of origin, Frank had hopes that his new roommate, having already spent some time on the East Coast, might know something about how to meet women. They headed off to dinner together, where, it turned out, my seventy-six-year-old friend did indeed meet his future—and current—wife. Frank was, of course, invited to their wedding a year later, in 1970; he'd be the only Black person in attendance. Their connection was not an obvious one to those around them but would turn out to be, to both of them, a cherished friendship.

A colleague of mine told me a similar story recently. A few years ago, she had a standing weekly lunch date with her boss from work at a local restaurant around the corner from their office. After a few weeks, she noticed that she kept seeing the same person at the bar, hunched over a laptop, nodding her head to the same music my colleague was nodding her head to.

It turned out that the woman was the manager of the establishment, and it was her playlist that was always on, and it was always excellent. They were introduced and within minutes knew that they were pretty much kindred spirits. One had grown up in Greenwich, Connecticut, going to boarding schools and spending summers on Nantucket. The other had grown up in Elizabeth, New Jersey, in a very poor neighborhood, in an incredibly difficult family situation, faced with almost un-imaginable hardships throughout her life. Yet there they both were, humming along to the same music over lunch in the same place every week. They were on different sides of the bar, quite literally, and had different viewpoints on almost every single issue, political, social, and otherwise. But they agreed on music and, it turned out, on so much else.

My colleague told me that the woman is still one of her closest friends in the world, many years later. They have traveled together, shared their joy and pain, and offered surprisingly different perspectives on problems they are facing. Why? Because they both examine most subjects from two entirely different lenses. She says that they would have been tempted to judge each other—for the other's life-style choices, career decisions, solutions to problems, or conclusions in arguments that are diametrically opposed to the ones the other might have come to herself. But because they have such a deep, abiding respect and love for each other, instead, they listen. They learn. Every time they talk—or argue or cry together—they take on new perspectives and look at the world in an entirely different light, because they have learned to see it through each other's eyes.

The joy these two friends found in a new sense of shared under-standing bears up in the research. Having friends from different backgrounds helps us not only learn more about each other but can also change how we interact with the wider world, helping us foster a better understanding of people different from us, remove biases, and develop perspectives that are completely outside our experience. Studies have shown that workplace diversity training, which helps people under-stand and appreciate other people's points of view, also known as "perspective taking," is key to fostering workplaces that are more inclusive, more aware of inequalities, and more avoidant of stereotyping.

Action Plan: Keep your eyes open to people who don't look the same as you or haven't lived the same kind of life as you. Befriend that older woman in your pottery class. Chat with that young man at the dog park. Strike up a conversation with the person down the bar from you. You might feel awkward. You won't understand everything about them at first. Try taking the word *should* out of your vocabulary: how the interaction *should* go, what you *should've* said, what you *should* be doing with your hands. It's exhausting to think you have to present a carefully curated personality to the world. Remember that it's good for us to be thrown off balance every so often. Just be present, be open, and *listen*.

Emotional Support

Listening is everything—and too few of us practice this skill as much as we should. But as we get older, this actually starts to change. My research has found that although the *quantity* of emotional support we give and receive declines as we get older, the *quality* of emotional support increases. We're less likely to respond to a friend in crisis by inundating them with unsolicited advice, or by sharing a similar story to foster a shared sense of suffering—which mostly just serves to bring the attention back to us. Sometimes just asking questions and listening carefully to the answers—without interrupting or passing judgment—is the best balm you could offer. Same for holding someone's hand while they call a therapist or giving a warm hug, with no words exchanged. Active listening, perspective-taking, patience, and unconditional acceptance are all skills we learn or traits we develop. This kind of support lies at the heart of close, intimate, caring connections.

Friendships also have to feel balanced to allow for true closeness. The more equitable the exchange of support, the better *both* parties feel about the relationship. As we age, the exchange of emotional support becomes more balanced—especially after the age of fifty-five, when adults report a greater sense of equity and satisfaction in their relationships.

Like a beautiful, long rally between two tennis players, we give and we get, back and forth, over and over. As we receive and provide emotional support, we give and we get more comfort, joy, belonging, purpose, contribution, worth, solidarity, and ultimately fairness in our interpersonal connections. We no longer confuse quantity with quality. We live out, in our social connections and exchanges, the truth that sometimes less is more.

Friendships in a Distrusting World

Like the atoms that form the foundation of matter in the universe, trust forms the foundation of our social fabric. We live, work, and play together more peacefully—and form connections more easily.

But in the United States, it seems as if our sense of fairness and trust is slowly eroding, and it isn't just a collapse of civil political discourse and a lack of trust in institutions—it's the rapid growth of income inequality. The science could not be more clear: As income inequality increased in the United States over the last several decades, we as a nation became unhappier.

The research points clearly to two ingredients that explain how growing inequality decreases our happiness. Growing income inequality causes fairness and trust to decline; conversely, when income equality increases, so do trust and the sense that life is fair.

Years ago, I spent quite a bit of time lecturing and touring in newly postapartheid South Africa. When I walked through the richest neighborhoods in Pretoria, I was shocked by the extremely high fences, topped with barbed wire and guarded by vicious guard dogs, that surrounded the wealthiest homes. I read in the newspaper about the carjackings that happened almost weekly in Johannesburg and Pretoria—and the cars that were targeted for hijacking were, of course, always the most ostentatiously expensive cars.

The United States isn't all that different. Here, the wealthier you are, the more likely you are to live in a gated, fenced, armed, and/or surveilled neighborhood; Patrick Sharkey, a sociology professor at Princeton University, has done fascinating research on this topic. The price and cost of income inequality are softened by a false sense of protection and security. It is the same sense of protection that the gang members you met earlier in this chapter sought when they joined up. Rich people are seeking this same sort of protection, but, like the gang members, they can never find safety, because what they are really seeking is belonging.

We need to start rebuilding the atoms of our societies by learning to trust one another once again. When we prioritize satisfying and meaningful social connections, not just for ourselves and not just when life is telling us it is nearly over, we create the conditions for more people to flourish.

[7]

Transcend: Accepting the Inevitable Plot Twists of Life

Our next flourishing vitamin involves practicing religion or spirituality. "Oh, boy," you may be saying to yourself, "I'm not religious and don't wish to be," or, "I'm not spiritual and couldn't care less about such things." Okay, I understand that, and you shouldn't commit to anyone else's belief system if it doesn't serve you.

Kind attention, acceptance, and a reverence for mystery are three ideals I chase; all of them guide me and many others toward becoming more comfortable with being small. How? By understanding that we are part of something much bigger than we realize. We need practices that root us in these ideals, that help us constantly come back to them and recenter ourselves in them, whether we label them as "spiritual" or not. We must also learn the right vocabulary to understand our place in the larger story.

Our universe is so mysterious that even the greatest thinkers, including Stephen Hawking and Albert Einstein, could not fathom its innermost workings. Einstein was, however, convinced by his study of gravity and electromagnetism that humans are essentially connected to something infinite.

In a poignant exchange with a devastated New York father whose eleven-year-old son had just died of polio, he wrote, "A human being is a part of the whole, called by us 'Universe,' a part limited in time and space. He experiences himself, his thoughts and feelings as something separate from the rest—a kind of optical delusion of his consciousness. The striving to free oneself from this delusion is . . . the way to reach the attainable measure of peace of mind."

The realization that we're mere specks in this universe can destabilize our egos and make them scream out for attention—unless this realization also forces us to see that we're inextricably connected to a great web of living things, united by both our suffering and our essential worthiness.

Believing in something bigger than yourself doesn't necessarily require attendance at religious services or a daily contemplative practice—though if that's what works for you, by all means, get thee to the closest place of worship or join an ashram. Personally, Buddhist teachings have always resonated with me, but I haven't attended church since I was a young boy.

If you seek something greater, start paying attention to the right things—right attention, the Buddhists would call it, or kind attention. Accept the world around you and learn to live in it in peace. Direct loving kindness and acceptance to those around you and, perhaps most important, to yourself.

The Serenity to Accept the Things We Cannot Change

What practices can we lean on when things go differently than we'd planned or hoped? When expectations and reality diverge, how can we accept, rather than resist, the inevitable plot twists life throws at us so that we're more at peace and better equipped to adapt to our circumstances?

A friend told me a story of a recent Alcoholics Anonymous meeting he attended during which a regular member, Eric, collected his thirty-year medallion, having relied on his "higher power" to stay on the path of sobriety. Although AA does have religious roots, its language around believing in a higher power is deliberately vague, and doesn't necessarily have spiritual or supernatural connotations. Some members prefer the phrase "a power greater than ourselves." In this case, Eric was talking about his first sponsor, who had passed away many years ago, in a beautifully reverent way.

As Eric felt the weight of the anniversary coin in his palm, he recounted attending a meeting years earlier in which another person shared their recovery story. They'd never forgotten the sponsor who'd helped them feel visible and valued, telling them repeatedly that "we're going to love you until you learn to love yourself." Eric had felt a jolt. Those exact words had saved his life. The saying wasn't original to his first sponsor, but he felt their presence in the room, as if they were standing behind his shoulder. Afterward, when it emerged that he and the speaker had, incredibly, shared the same sponsor, Eric was both surprised and not at all surprised. Their wise voice lives on to this day.

One of the founders of AA was Bill Wilson, who often said that honesty had started him on his journey of sobriety but acceptance was what had kept him sober. At every AA meeting, participants begin with a moment of silence, because silence is sacred. They pray for the alcoholics who are still out there drinking; then they recite together— because a shared prayer, uttered out loud, creates sacredness—the serenity prayer: "God, grant me the serenity to accept the things I cannot change, the courage to change the things I can, and the wisdom to know the difference."

What are the things you can change? The only thing you have power over is yourself. Only you can change how you think, feel, and behave. We are powerless over pretty much everything else. We can try persuasion, coercion, invitations, requests, or desperate pleas. We can try making demands verbally, or even physically, to change other people or situations in the world. But mostly, we have to live our lives on our own terms, and we have very little control over how everyone else lives theirs. We hope to get our way and have our expectations met, but that's not always how things go.

Action Plan: Work on your ability to accept what life throws at you. Better yet, remember that no one is actually throwing anything at you. You are traveling your path, and you will pass all sorts of bumps in the road. They continue to exist whether you drive that road or not; no one put them there to slow you down or nudge you off your path.

Every single day, we have to figure out how to be a good person in whatever situation life puts on our plate. We can respond to life's surprises based on our most deeply held values and principles rather than react out of fear, anger, resentment, or frustration.

I once sat down in the middle seat on an airplane, and the woman in the window seat next to me looked aghast as a young mother and her baby sat down in the aisle seat of our row. I chuckled and made a light joke that we'd better be ready to sing songs and make silly faces for the next few hours. She responded with an eye roll, "This *always* happens to me. I always have a screaming kid next to me on every single flight I take. I mean, I don't know what I did to deserve this."

That crying child in her aisle—that challenge, that trial, that speed bump—was happening *to* her? No—it wasn't happening *to* her, it was just happening *near* her, and God knows, it wasn't personal. If we can learn to accept the things life throws at us (especially those that are far more trying than a sleep-deprived toddler wailing nearby), with equanimity and grace, to trust in a higher power that we are capable of doing so, we will be able to take on all sorts of challenges.

Acceptance is where we begin the journey into spirituality, into accepting that we are often at the mercy of something greater than ourselves.

Acceptance Begins with Ourselves

Among the many divine or sacred qualities that we can exhibit, we know that acceptance is one of the most virtuous ones. But without acceptance of most parts of yourself, how can you be accepting of other people? Much as with compassion—without compassion for yourself it is harder to be compassionate toward others—acceptance needs to start with you.

You want to know one important reason why people who are flourishing are less likely to become depressed or anxious? It has everything to do with acceptance, and we can see that in two distinct but related data points. We have found that people who are flourishing have a higher disposition to apologize. Moreover, people who are flourishing have higher levels of self-compassion.

Who here, dear reader, hasn't screwed up and hurt someone, especially someone we love? One response to doing such harm is often shame. But the brain on shame—which the psychologist Mary Lamia describes as "a concealed, contagious, and dangerous emotion"—does not learn or grow from mistakes; it punishes itself. A better option is to try to be kinder to yourself. None of us is perfect—far from it—but we all, to paraphrase Brené Brown, still deserve love and belonging. You can make things right—or better—and learn and grow at the same time by saying you are truly sorry, by apologizing to the other person. Admit you are wrong, admit you are imperfect, admit that you sometimes react out of your emotional state rather than choosing how to best respond to the situation.

Shame can also bubble up in moments of intense pressure in our lives and careers, along with strong feelings of hopelessness, fear, anger, or envy.

Meditation that cultivates kind awareness helps "decontaminate" our minds. The starting point is to become aware of our emotions and thoughts as they crop up without pushing them away, however uncomfortable they may be. Simply naming a feeling and allowing it to come up without resisting it can spur panicked thoughts that *it's too much* or that *I can't handle this*. When we're accustomed to letting uncomfortable thoughts simmer, unnamed and unprocessed, in the background, welcoming them to the front of our minds can bring up a wave of resistance.

Kind attention helps us stop perceiving difficult emotions as threats or personal failures, but rather as temporary sources of discomfort—often having less to do with the present moment than the past—that we can treat with tenderness. It brings what feels overwhelming down to size. By focusing on our in-breaths and out-breaths to ground ourselves, we can let pain and compassion coexist. Our default responses to stress are deeply embedded through years of practice, so it may take a regular, if not daily, meditation practice to undo all that lived experience.

As neuroscientists have found, what we practice grows stronger in our brains. If we practice shame, we hide and do not learn from our errors. If we practice self-compassion, that kindness toward ourselves allows us to be vulnerable, to be imperfect, and to do what we all should practice more of: to apologize and grow from our mistakes. This in turn allows us to build new patterns of response, become more observant and less reactive, and be more forgiving of others for their own imperfections.

Shauna Shapiro, a psychologist who studies compassion toward the self and others, described her own struggle with shame and self-doubt in a TEDx Talk and a subsequent book. She found that simply trying to be more compassionate may not be enough. She, like all of us, can be judgmental about her failings at compassion.

Shapiro's meditation teacher at the time encouraged her to do the following each morning as she awoke to the gift of one more day of life. Look herself in the mirror, place her hand on her heart, and say, "Good morning, Shauna, I love you." She said she balked at the idea, finding it a bit too cringe inducing. Rather than doing nothing, though, she chose to start small by simply saying, "Good morning, Shauna." To her surprise, it began to work; she felt more tender and caring toward herself. She also began to become more courageous, and toward the end of her TEDx Talk, she turned to the audience and proudly said those difficult words out loud: "Good morning, Shauna, I love you."

The Silence Inside

I was on the phone with a surgeon and colleague of mine the other day when she told me a story that stopped me in my tracks. One of her mentors happens to be one of the most renowned female transplant surgeons in the world. She is getting close to retirement now, but throughout her career, she was notorious for her intense style in the operating room. In stressful moments, she would regularly bark at the residents, nurses, and techs in the operating room, and she was known to have very little patience for anyone else's opinions but her own.

Her lack of interpersonal skills didn't go over so well, my colleague said with a chuckle. She was feared as much as she was revered. Despite her obvious skill and incredible depth of knowledge in her field, she wasn't capable of bringing a team together in such a way that they would all perform better together. Even she knew that she wasn't serving her colleagues or her patients as well as she could.

Interestingly enough, her husband, who is also a transplant surgeon, often worked side by side with her. They would do live donors together—she would take part of the liver out of the living person, then hand it to him, and he would put it inside the person with the bad liver.

One day about a year ago, he asked her a strange question: "Hey, what are you doing differently?"

"What do you mean?" she asked.

"Well, you know, you're the best and always have been," he responded like a smart husband. "But for the last year, every liver you've been giving me has been perfect. Like literally, unbelievably, noticeably perfect. What changed?"

As she thought about it, the only thing that had changed in recent months was that she had been meditating consistently before every surgery, partly in the hope of improving her relationships with others in the operating room, and partly, perhaps, to improve her relationship with herself. As a result, she'd learned not only to quiet her emotions and choose her words more intentionally in the face of chaos but also to slow her mind, to calm her hands, and to breathe through difficulty—skills we could all use, whether we are holding a scalpel or not.

Meditation taught her to exist inside a moment—without allowing mistakes from the past or concerns about the future to intrude. The form of meditation she practiced also guided her to bring kind attention to all the sounds, sensations, thoughts, and feelings that arose in the moment. She met them all with tenderness, even the voices of negative self-evaluation and worry, which gradually quieted as a result. That ability to pay kind attention to the task at hand—and nothing else—translated into noticeable, measurable improvements in the health and safety of her patients and increased performance on a level she had never achieved before.

In other words—yes, something had indeed shifted.

Flexing Your Mind

Much like that transplant surgeon and like Shauna, I, too, struggle with self-compassion, with acceptance. I never feel as if I'm deserving of any praise or success; as you readers know, I can't help but think I still need to prove to others, indeed to the world, that I belong. Despite my years of work in this field, I am still struggling with accepting myself.

Some of my good friends and colleagues in the Netherlands have developed and tested a public health approach to promoting mental health. The program is based on acceptance and commitment therapy (ACT), the point of which is to increase mental flexibility. This kind of flexibility is a competence that includes two interdependent processes: (1) the acceptance of negative experiences and (2) the choice of how to respond based on values or principles.

A person who is mentally flexible is willing to remain in contact with rather than avoid negative, undesirable personal experiences. Remember my seatmate on the airplane when faced with the arrival of a toddler in her row? Most of us try to control or avoid such unwanted experiences. Rather than reacting emotionally to negative experiences, the ACT program encourages us to consciously make choices toward unwanted experiences based on our values and goals for creating a good life. A flexible mind thinks of all the ways that the baby sitting next to you on this long flight could be fun or, if not that, could at least be an opportunity for growth or generosity, could be a learning experience, could be an opportunity to practice being mindful, present, and without judgment.

Here's an example. When coming to the end of a very difficult quarter at work, you have a big report due to your higher-ups based on results you've been collecting for months. A group of colleagues has worked on the project with you, and you are just putting the final touches on the report. With just a few days to go, your boss's boss changes the reporting structure. Although the results will stay the same, the entire report will need to be rewritten to fit into the new format. In short, you've got a few miserable days ahead.

Most of us would either yell or cry or probably both, and then call a sympathetic friend or colleague to rant and rage. That's totally understandable. But what would you do *next*?

Inflexible reaction: Refuse. Go to your boss and tell her the request is impossible, it's too late, and there's no time to meet the new parameters she's given you.

Flexible reaction: Call a meeting of your colleagues. Allow everyone in the room to vent their frustration. Then, once the air has cleared, start making a new plan of attack collectively. One person gets to work on this part of the revision process, the next person rewrites the next, the third pulls together the numbers still needed, and so on. You are still furious and still exhausted, but you are choosing acceptance rather than avoidance. You accept what has changed, and you work together with your colleagues to solve the problem.

The same flexible-versus-inflexible reaction can be applied in countless situations, from serious to silly ones. A mutual friend's wedding where your ex-husband insists on bringing his new girlfriend. A weekend ski trip with your buddies when they choose a mountain you and your middling athletic skills have no business skiing down. Your book club picks an author you dislike and is meeting at a person's house who has been unkind to you in the past. Your favorite coffee shop stops taking credit cards and insists on cash only. Your longtime bridge partner ghosts you, and you find out he has been playing with a new partner on the side.

In the ACT program my colleagues in the Netherlands put together, participants are encouraged to discover their values in multiple domains of life and taught how to respond to negativity and adversity based on their own deeply held commitments and values. The course also teaches them to be open and nonjudgmental toward personal experiences. The goal is to have them learn to consistently choose effective responses in any, but especially difficult, situations to build behavior repertoires that are flexible and value driven.

The whole idea is actually reminiscent of the Buddhist strategy for living better lives: the Buddhist eightfold path. Adversity and negativity are natural—suffering exists!—but we can live in a way that mitigates the problems caused by avoidance or repression of negative experiences. We must learn to respond to adversity and negative emotions based on personal values.

In two experimental trials, one that included mindfulness training, my colleagues found that the program led to moderate to large effects for promoting flourishing. They were also able to test whether the program enhanced mental flexibility and if the enhancement of mental flexibility was the reason for the increases in flourishing. In both studies, mental flexibility explained how the program enhanced flourishing, and I was thrilled to hear that the effects of the program were maintained three months later.

Action Plan: Be flexible. Commit to your values. Choose acceptance. In order to flourish, we must train our minds to focus on what matters, to make conscious choices about how to best respond to the challenges and trials of life, to achieve a better balance of prioritizing feeling good with functioning well, and to be compassionate, both toward others and also toward ourselves.

Sometimes, when I'm caught in a cycle of rumination where I repeatedly run the same set of negative thoughts about something I've done—or something someone else has done—through my head end-

lessly, I tell myself out loud to stop. Sometimes I even hold out my
hand as a physical gesture: No more! Then I replace the thought—or
try to—with something else.

If you are angry at yourself for breaking your no-sugar pact or for
not having finished a work assignment by the deadline, let yourself feel
the worry and anger. Take a little time to let it roll over you, your guilt
or shame or fury, then *press stop*. Focus instead on what you can
control—what you will do tomorrow—the vegetables you will eat, the
head start you'll get on the group project due next month—not the
things in your past that you can no longer control. Accept your failures. Forgive yourself. Practice kind compassion on yourself first and
foremost.

Move Closer to the Divine Inside You

What do spiritual practices such as meditation have in common with
religious belief systems and rituals such as prayer? Healthy religions
provide stories and practices that reduce our ego and its self-centeredness
and replace them with the opposite—kindness, generosity, acceptance,
and so on—and answer weighty questions about the world. They teach
us what to do with our pain and suffering and remind us how to live
in a way that matters to others and the universe. You might not agree
with the answers given by various belief systems, but those answers
have been a balm for questioning minds throughout human history. If
you are a religious person, it is likely that you have found that your
worship of whatever god or gods you believe in brings great meaning
to your life.

When we use the word *meaning*, we are usually referring to the sense
that people feel their lives have value or significance. Study after study
supports the conclusion that there is an inarguable connection between religious belief and having a sense of meaning in life.

I think often of a study I read recently that compared levels of religiosity in wealthy nations versus poorer nations. Now, the researchers

were scientists, not rabbis or imams or monks or priests, so the conclusions they reached seem all the more surprising. The study found that *satisfaction* with life was higher in wealthy nations than in poor nations, while *meaning* in life was higher in poor nations than in wealthy nations.

The italics are mine, because I want to emphasize the difference. Why would satisfaction be higher but meaning be lower for residents of wealthier nations? Perhaps more baffling, why would residents of poorer nations consistently find more meaning in life? I suspect that when the respondents defined "life satisfaction," they took it to mean "Do I have access to the markers of success I feel are necessary for me to survive and thrive?" But if they then also grade their level of "meaning" as lower than those of the residents of poorer nations, are they truly more satisfied with their lives in the true sense of the word? My guess is that they are not. A loss of, or lack of, meaning in one's life means that true well-being—not the markers of success of achievement, but the sense of a life well lived, well-being as I might call it—is likely not present.

In that study, the researchers found that a lack of meaning was at least in part attributable to a disconnection from religion. According to their data, they could see that as a nation's GDP goes up, fewer of its citizens say that religion is an important part of their daily life. Meaning in life was higher in poor nations because people in those nations view religion as important in their daily life. It appears that economic success erodes religiosity, and the loss of religion in daily life diminishes meaning in life. Readers of this book might not be surprised to hear that their data showed that the decline in living a meaningful life increases the risk of suicide.

Other studies have come to the same conclusion, one stating that "Religiousness may foster a sense of significance, importance, or mattering—either to others (social mattering) or in the grand scheme of the universe (cosmic mattering)—which, in turn, support perceived meaning." I found it interesting that the same study found that social mattering, which I discussed at length in the last chapter, was important but cosmic mattering was the real game changer in terms of the link between religiousness and perceived meaning.

One study I have been involved with all my career, the National Survey of Midlife Development in the United States, has examined in part how important religion was in participants' households while growing up. The researchers wanted to determine if there was a link between the level and consistency of religious importance in childhood and adulthood and whether this adherence to religion was critical to flourishing in adulthood. The results showed that only high religiosity, meaning religion was very important, was predictive of flourishing. If religion was somewhat important or less, religion was unrelated to flourishing in adulthood.

Consistency also mattered. When religion had been very important during childhood and remained so during adulthood, participants were much more likely to be flourishing. However, another group of adults was almost more likely to flourish if religion had become very important to them over time, even if it hadn't been important in their life when they were children.

My conclusion? You have to be "all in" for religion to contribute to flourishing. Believing in belief—if you choose that path—is vital to flourishing.

Languages of Spirit and Spirituality

We are born with the potential to become kind, generous, accepting, self-aware, and socially conscious. His Holiness the Fourteenth Dalai Lama often says that each person on this planet is Buddha, has Buddha nature, and is capable of becoming just like Buddha. The catch is that we must practice, practice, and then practice some more. Spiritual and religious practices and activities are exercise; we aren't just born with bulging moral and ethical muscles—they need training to grow bigger and stronger.

Practicing spirituality can come in forms besides meditation or worship. Cultural practices can be a form of spirituality, too. Language is considered to be among the most concrete symbols of a culture—it describes things seen and unseen, the material and the spiritual worlds. It sustains the past and connects it to the present and the future—just like the practice of spirituality does.

We talk about species extinction, but we rarely extend the concept to language extinction, even though the extinction of indigenous or aboriginal languages is happening at an alarmingly rapid rate. The Indigenous Language Institute estimates that barely half of the more than three hundred indigenous languages once spoken in the United States are alive today and at the current rate of language loss only twenty will still be spoken by the year 2050.

A culture can die when its language dies; language is the breath and heartbeat that keeps cultures alive. The death of native languages among native indigenous people represents a threat to the health and well-being of those people, especially its youths. Canadian researchers have introduced a concept of cultural continuity in First Nations cultures, the loss of which has been strongly related to suicide rates within specific communities. In their research, they discovered that the rates of school dropout and youth suicide increased and far exceeded the national averages in Canada as the number of markers of cultural continuity declined.

They also found that First Nations communities in which more than half of the members had a conversational or better knowledge of their aboriginal language had very low to no youth suicides. Where less than half the members had a conversational knowledge of their aboriginal language, youth suicide rates were six times as great.

What makes indigenous First Nations languages so powerful, so conducive to sustaining life?

In many First Nations and Native American cultures, spirituality is central to views of health and well-being, alongside mental, emotional, and physical health. Language permits indigenous people to continue to engage in spiritual traditions, rituals, and ceremonies. Through their native language and spirituality, indigenous people pay respect to, honor, and supplicate nature—its elements, seasons, and inhabitants and the cycle of life—and maintain contact with ancestors who have died and exist only in the spirit world. The sense of continuity, from the past to the present to the future and beyond, is a balm for the stresses and anxieties of modern life. Perhaps the knowledge that we can forge connections over time, throughout history, with loved ones past and present builds a level of faith that we exist for a reason, to bridge the past and the future with our vital and necessary presence.

To me, this is a beautiful example of the kind of reverence for mystery that we should be striving for. When we lose someone close to us, we mourn them forever in one way or another. Cultural continuity, in this case created by indigenous languages, and a belief in something bigger, allow us to keep our ancestors with us forever. We don't need to know where they are to know that they are still with us.

When Belief Wanes

When I stopped relying on my once deeply spiritual approach to life about eight years ago, anger, resentment, and a hunger for apologies once again took over my life. My wife and I moved into a smaller, one-story home to age in place. I left behind my beloved yoga studio where I had been practicing yoga for twenty years, and suddenly I lost my spiritual community. Instead of trying to find a replacement for that loss, I stopped doing yoga. Soon enough, I felt increasingly unappreciated at work. I traveled the world giving invited talks and had thousands of citations—the currency of intellectuals. Yet my university gave me only a temporary, three-year endowed professorship. I felt damned by faint praise. I became self-centered.

As my ego expanded, my spiritual life shrank. That change happens gradually; you don't realize you are falling down on the dimensions of divinity until it is almost too late. It pushed away my capacity to live, to be kind, to give rather than seek forgiveness. Our minds can lead us, but they can also be led. Our thoughts and attention can be taken over by forces that are more powerful than others.

We know the research about negative versus positive emotions—our negativity bias—and we understand too well the conclusion: that bad is often stronger than good. In a game of one-on-one, a negative emotion will "win" over a positive one—it will be more influential in our memory and in terms of motivation. But believe it or not, we can change this. We can work to negate the unfair advantage that the negative has over the positive. Spiritual and religious practices, when done regularly, strengthen our mind's capacity to lead rather than be led. We can teach ourselves to slow things down; we can choose, again and again, to pay attention to our values and principles.

When we strengthen our good intentions, we act in better ways that honor the sacred and divine inside us. The importance of cultivating what Buddhists call "right attention" cannot be overstated; right attention leads to right intention. When we honor the best inside us, we honor our higher power, whether that higher power be God, nature, or anything else that is inherently good, bigger and stronger than you are when you are at your weakest.

Peace Is Not an External Condition

I have spent many years working to overcome the belief that peace is an external condition that is created for me, not a quality that I can create for myself and others. I also realize that the dual-continua model is everywhere: The absence of violence, chaos, anger, and so on does not mean the presence of peace and serenity.

The Saint Francis prayer speaks to this point beautifully. It begins by making the point that you are an "instrument," meaning that you are not supposed to act in this world like a passive audience, merely listening; you must create the music you wish to hear. Mahatma Gandhi made that point famous when he asked us to be the change we seek in this world.

The prayer then turns immediately to using right attention to create right intention. It isn't about avoiding negative emotions but instead leaning into those emotions to find something positive on the other side. When you feel hate, sow love; when you are injured, pardon others; when you are in doubt, focus on hope. The prayer then turns our attention to doing for others what we usually seek only for ourselves: to understand rather than be understood, to love rather than be loved. When we give, we receive.

What we rehearse in our minds grows larger and stronger, and where we place our attention determines what we let inside to influence us. If you rehearse being rejected or agonize over the many ways you feel disconnected, those ways of thinking—excellent ways to encourage languishing, by the way—will become neurologically stronger.

I recently read a study in which researchers looked at two groups of musicians rehearsing a certain piece of music. One group physically rehearsed a piece of piano music, whereas the other group rehearsed the same music for the same amount of time but in their minds. The group that only imagined rehearsing the piece of music had substantial neuron growth in the brain's motor cortex. What you rehearse in your mind creates the neuronal pathways that enable your behavior. What you do shapes your brain, but what you think also shapes your behavior.

Every day we have a choice as to what we rehearse and where we spend our attention. When you practice for a play or a recital in school, you rehearse again and again, over and over, to be ready for performance night. Over the course of many rehearsals, you increase your intention to act a certain way when the time comes. Most religious and spiritual practices are just that: rehearsals. You rehearse in the acceptance and commitment program, you rehearse when in prayer, you rehearse in meditation, and you rehearse in yoga poses. All of this rehearsal stimulates the neuronal growth needed to increase your intention to act in ways that are good rather than bad. All of this presupposes the deliberate use of attention, because you are choosing to pay attention to something spiritual even when faced with so many other distractions. Attention is a gatekeeper. Intention is the gateway.

Action Plan: Be a better gatekeeper. We are the mental gatekeepers of what we want to let inside ourselves. Our attention is our doorman, our security detail. What we choose to pay attention to is what we allow inside us and therefore what we allow to influence our brains and behavior.

You cannot always choose who comes into your home, but you usually get to decide who gets to stay. If you focus on the rain clouds on the horizon, you might miss the sunshine overhead. If you cannot get over your fury that the coffee you ordered at the deli arrived cold, you might not notice how kindly the shopkeeper smiled at you when he handed it to you. If you are too busy yelling at the driver who just switched lanes in front of you without using their blinker, you might forget to sing along to your favorite song playing on the radio.

Search for a Spirituality That Serves You

I have heard meditation described by Buddhist monks as creating the base camp necessary for the hardest stage of a climb—that is, summiting the mountain. Nobody goes to Mount Everest to sit at the base camp and say they accomplished something worthy of their time, effort, and life. They all want to summit.

Building a base camp is vital, but we shouldn't be content with hanging out at base camp. Life spent at base camp is a life spent languishing. But life is not for languishing. We live in order to try to reach our own summit. We are meant to aim higher—to flourish.

According to contemplative spiritual traditions, where we should begin is by trying to see ourselves and our life more clearly and honestly. We must begin with our mind. Our base camp is a quiet mind, one that remains laser focused and under control during duress, a place we can always return to in order to recover and regain our strength when the climb becomes too difficult.

My base camp happens to be yoga—that is where my mind quiets. The sutras, written thousands of years ago by Patanjali to codify the principles and teachings of yoga, are to yoga practitioners what the Bible is to Christians, the Torah is to Jews, the Koran is to Muslims, and the teaching of the Buddha is to Buddhists. In them, Patanjali framed yoga as a means of spiritual development that is necessary if one is to overcome many of life's obstacles and adversities.

Action Plan: Find your base camp, whatever it might be. Seek out a state of relaxed awareness wherever and whenever you can. For me, after a session of yoga, I feel as if I am a wet rag, completely wrung out in the best possible way. I am absolutely relaxed in both my body and my mind. This is not anything like the relaxed feeling you have after that first bourbon you drink after coming home from work—that's relaxed oblivion. Yoga makes you feel relaxed yet alert and very aware. Relaxed awareness is how I describe a truly quiet mind.

Relaxed awareness is the place where learning dwells. It is the state of mind in which learning can occur, the kind of learning that inspires us to take the next steps toward becoming a better person. It's base camp. From there, we all have a better chance of summiting.

Quiet Your Mind

In addition to the cessation of a chaotic mind, the sutras of yoga promise changes in one's interpersonal relationships. Yoga practice leads to more than just relaxed awareness; it can lead to a mind that is quieter and less judgmental, not just of others but also of yourself. Some sutras promise just that—that yoga practice will lead to a personal transformation: "Through cultivation of friendliness, compassion, joy, and indifference to pleasure and pain . . . the consciousness becomes favorably disposed, serene, and benevolent." When we are at peace and kinder to ourselves, we in turn bring peace and are kind to others.

With that quieter mind, you act in better ways toward others and behave differently in tough situations. Difficult situations and people bring up difficult emotions in us. Without thinking, we tend to focus outwardly on what we think is the problem rather than inwardly on what we can control. A quiet mind does not fuse with negative emotions.

Action Plan: Sometimes when I notice myself getting upset over someone else's behavior, I stop myself and think about my reaction. Why is my reaction automatically to blame and judge someone else for their behavior? I try to take a beat to quiet my mind. After all, my reaction speaks far more to something happening in me than the behavior I'm reacting to. Take a moment to examine what is happening inside you—without blame or judgment. Quiet your inner critic, and work, in that moment, to accept yourself without judgment. From there, it is far easier to accept others as well.

Instead of reacting to a negative situation with negativity, a quiet mind looks outward to do right by others rather than instinctively protecting itself. Cultivating the habit of doing right by others also fosters our serenity—a self-sustaining circle of positivity.

There's No Magic Pill

Is yoga really this magical? Can it fix us all and make us all flourish? Sadly, no—it's not quite that simple. A national study of people who are regularly attending members of yoga studios found that flourishing was no more common among people who practice yoga than among college students. Encouraging you to get into yoga might be no more useful than nudging you to go off to college, at least when it comes to moving from languishing to flourishing.

One large national study of yoga found that a "fuller practice" of yoga produces more benefits than does a practice devoted only to the poses. People who studied the philosophy of yoga and practiced yoga more regularly reported higher levels of mindfulness, had a healthier diet (meaning that they ate more fruits and vegetables), slept better, and were more likely to be flourishing. A full yoga practice done consistently over time leads to a greater chance of flourishing.

In other words, as in most things, you must devote yourself to the practice; continued practice will strengthen your devotion to the path.

The philosophy of yoga, meditation, or any other spiritual practice is much like the Buddhist eightfold path: it is studying and then practicing ways to be more ethical, a better person, in your everyday life. The peace you feel at the end of yoga or meditation is a preparation, a beginning, for working on becoming a better person. A quiet mind is a mind that is ready to learn about itself. A quiet mind allows you to feel comfortable going inside yourself to learn about yourself—that is the essence of the internal path to flourishing.

Yoga, just like other forms of mindfulness that are practiced fully, can lead to transcendence. Transcendence can be described in a lot of ways; it can mean you no longer feel that you are a separate, disconnected self; the boundaries between you and something larger than you—nature, the world, your spiritual practice, your god—have melted away.

A friend told me a story about a trip to New Orleans she had taken many years ago with friends. The group had spent their evening joyfully seeking out the most packed venues they could find, ones that had music spilling out the front doors. If it's loud and crowded, it must be the place to be, right? One of their chosen stops was quiet, though—almost too quiet. They entered to find a still, almost reverent crowd. There were two white-haired gentlemen up front, seated near each other in chairs, playing their instruments with their eyes closed. They looked as if they'd been jamming together in New Orleans for fifty years.

The two men were playing a slow, mournful version of "Time After Time"—such a stunning rendition that in the pauses between notes, my friend said you could've heard a pin drop in that room. She told me she had stood alone in the middle of that crowded room, not just hearing the music but feeling it, listening in on that musical conversation between two old friends that had probably been going on for decades.

Tears slipped almost unnoticed down her cheeks. That, she told me, was the closest she'd ever felt to transcendence.

Action Plan: I'm not going to make you do yoga—unless you want to. It has brought me a great deal of fulfillment and joy, but it's not for everyone. When you take on something, take it on in a big way. That doesn't mean you need to devote twenty hours a week to your new hobby or commitment. It just means that you should allow your heart into it—believe in it deeply.

If you have time to take an adult beginning painting class, don't hide your work when the teacher comes around. Don't skip the second session because you found the first one embarrassing. Embrace the awkward; push past the hesitation.

Open your heart and your head to the possibilities of finding meaning and beauty in all sorts of places. Perhaps it'll be in a classic jazz venue in the Tremé neighborhood of New Orleans. Or maybe in the modern art wing of your local museum on free admission day. It might be while bird-watching in the woods near your house or watching gulls swoop down for their dinner on the beach at sunset. It might be while reading a piece of poetry printed on the walls of the subway and feeling your breath catch in your throat. Beauty is everywhere if you allow yourself to stop and look for it.

Believe that an emotional connection to something new or different or special or rare is a worthy thing to chase. That sense of connection with something bigger, of being one with something larger than yourself, is incredibly powerful.

Spiritual Connections

Connections with the world around us, but also with one another— are more powerful than we can imagine. We know from the extensive research that I touched on earlier that our loneliness level as we age is a big determinant of our health. Studies have shown that an increased involvement in religion can help protect against loneliness.

In one study I examined, the researchers found that "religious attendance is associated with higher levels of social integration and social support and that social integration and social support are associated with lower levels of loneliness." As the data from this study shows, "involvement in religious institutions may protect against loneliness in later life by integrating older adults into larger and more supportive social networks."

Connecting to something bigger makes us feel less alone. When we feel most alone, we get the sense that we are a single cell or atom floating alone without purpose, questioning our life. Being alone breeds fear and a sense of danger, which makes the world seem more dangerous and less hospitable. We become more reactive and likely to act negatively toward others. It becomes a self-defeating cycle that feeds on itself and, if unchecked, leads to destructive behavior.

Alcoholics describe this self-defeating cycle of fear, the one that causes disconnection, which serves to create more fear, as the downward spiral that led many to their "bottom." The end of that cycle is self-destruction that leads either to death or to rebirth. For some, it takes facing down the ultimate and imminent choice between death and life to turn that cycle around.

I sense this downward spiral happening in small ways around the world, not only in so many people's lives but also in a big way—in societies, in this country. I believe that people are feeling increasingly alone and disconnected from the spiritual nature of the universe. Climate change, a global pandemic, war, the return of nuclear threat, rampant wildfires, flooding in some areas and terrible drought in others, hotter temperatures worldwide, and more and increasingly violent storms are all making us feel as though we live in an angry, vengeful universe, not one that celebrates life.

It's hard to connect with a universe that seems bent on destruction—perhaps even our destruction. If we don't take care of it, it cannot take care of us; charity and kindness are the oldest religious and spiritual—nay, human—lessons known to humankind. Let's keep them in mind.

For me, it all starts with mystery. My fundamental belief that the universe celebrates life and love makes me want to connect to its mysteries. Even when I'm not in my spiritual state of mind and working in that place, something that happens that sparks a sense of life's mystery in me will take me there. So I would counsel you to invite more mystery into your life—mystery about yourself, mystery about other people, mystery about all the ideas and questions and life that's out there.

When I am presented with something about life and the universe we live in that piques my sense of mysteriousness, I become curious. I want to know more, I want to explore. We are built to be learning machines; our bodies have an amazing aerobic capacity for endurance, combined with limbs that carry a mind with them everywhere they go. You can't truly learn about something that you hate and destroy; you need to start from a standpoint of care, of concern.

That care goes both ways. When I feel connected to the universe, I don't feel alone because I sense that I'm walking with a higher power—a universe that is nurtured, healthy, and remains a place where I am secure and safe, and therefore a place I belong.

Over the course of my spiritual searching, I have increasingly come to agree with teachings that say that we are created with the spark of the divine, the sacred, already inside us. We are born with the potential to be good, to become better people. When I practice self-compassion and acceptance—when I adhere to the values I believe in—I honor myself. As I honor myself, I treat other people with the honor they deserve because they, too, have divinity in them.

I always thought God had to come into me, that I had to invite that higher power in. I now feel as if it is the other way around; I was trying to let God in when I think the key is that the hard work of becoming a better person is letting the God inside us out.

Doing the Work

There is so much more to spirituality than the physical practice of it—yoga poses or a short stint with a meditation app—just as there is so much more to religion than attending services, though thousands of studies show that these practices do reduce stress. But the point of religious worship—in my view—is to remind us, through stories and parables, of the work we have yet to do and realize in ourselves. So much more is added to life if we observe the call to ethical work and action behind religious and spiritual practices.

Action Plan: Seek out activities that ask you to put yourself aside; then commit to them with an open mind and open heart. Check yourself—what can you gain from the group you are joining or the task you are embarking on? What's in it for you? Spend at least some of your time on activities with no particular end game in mind—ones that simply call for you to pay more attention to the world around you, the feelings that flow through you.

A friend of mine told me a story recently about when she was lucky enough to do a semester abroad in Paris during college. As a full-time student there, she could go to almost any museum she wanted for free. She lived not too far from the Louvre, so at least once a month, she put her headphones on, walked over to the museum, and picked just one wing to spend an hour or two in. She didn't want to stand in line for the *Mona Lisa,* nor did she want to rush through the entire museum in a day so she could check a box on her "been there, done that" list.

She wanted to feel something. She wanted to experience reverence, find a moment to live inside, by herself, for a moment, in silence and awe and joy. She'd pick, say, Egyptian artifacts or French sculpture, and she would wander slowly through the halls, listening to music, looking at the beautiful art, and feeling the feelings that rolled through her.

Transcendence is a slow walker. If you don't slow down, it might never catch up with you and you'll miss it entirely. As my friend who was brought to tears while standing still in a New Orleans jazz club discovered, if you take a moment to slow down—maybe even stop in your tracks—transcendence will sometimes have a chance to catch up with you. Now, *that* feels like succumbing to something bigger.

Open Your Eyes to the Path in Front of You

Religious teachings and spiritual philosophies direct us toward the sacred but difficult task of working on becoming more godlike in terms of the qualities of our character. If working on becoming a better person were so easy, wouldn't most of the world be kind, generous, honest, and so on?

I will warn you, I have not come across a religious or spiritual path that someone walked alone, and no one has ever walked such a path by standing still. Nobody has made it to the top of the spiritual equivalent of Mount Everest alone, unaided, without a guide, without a community. And no one who sought enlightenment stayed in base camp.

Every Buddhist place of spiritual development has what is called a *sangha,* a community of others seeking the same end, wanting to practice the same means, knowing they will need help to continue the work and stay on the path, to learn from leaders who have been on that path much longer and whose character exemplifies the teachings. Find the people who will help you stay on the path, to keep looking to see what's around the next corner.

As we all know, walking that path isn't just about the destination you will get to; it's about what you experience along the way. In my seminar on happiness, one of my favorite things to show my class is a wonderful TEDx Talk on gratitude by the time-lapse photographer Louie Schwartzberg. His photographs are stunning—unforgettable, even—but another moment in the talk has stuck with me even longer. In the video he introduces a little girl who talks at some length about, basically, learning to turn off the TV. What she is describing is essentially wonder: "When I watch TV, it's just some shows that you just, that are just pretend. But when you explore, you get more imagination than you already had. And, umm, when you get imagination, it makes you want to go deeper in so you can get more and see beautifuller things. Like the path, if it's a path, it can lead to a beach or something. And it could be beautiful."

Is there any greater metaphor for life than that? That little girl—a budding Buddha, if you ask me—has cracked the code. If you follow the path—which will inevitably be bumpy, cracked, twisted, even hidden at times—and trust that there will be something beautifuller around the next turn—you could walk yourself right out of languishing and into flourishing for life.

Action Plan: Explore the beauty and wonder of life.

[8]

Help:
Finding Your Purpose
(Even in the Mundane)

n the words of the writer and theologian Frederick Buechner, your vocation, or purpose, is "the place where your deep gladness meets the world's deep need." Sometimes we confuse having a purpose with setting goals. Setting goals gives direction to our lives, it's true. The former can direct us toward success by any number of measures; the latter directs us toward significance. Unlike goals, which can be achieved, your purpose in life may never be fully achieved or resolved.

Identifying and pursuing a calling is neither easy nor a one-shot endeavor. The journalist Po Bronson, in his 2002 book *What Should I Do with My Life? The True Story of People Who Answered the Ultimate Question,* chronicled more than nine hundred interviews of adults from all walks of life who had found or were searching for a purpose in life. Bronson found some surprising self-limiting beliefs about purpose. Many of those interviewed believed that finding a purpose was selfish, that it could lead them away from rather than closer to their loved ones. Or they believed that searching for their purpose was impractical and would bankrupt them rather than enrich their lives and the lives of others. Others believed that a purpose in life is so mysterious and scarce that it would take too much time to find.

But purpose is not a luxury good. If your life revolves around keeping yourself and your loved ones safe, keeping a roof over your family's head, or paying your mortgage, you can remind yourself—often—of the significance of those acts because you're providing essential care and support and you need to recognize the meaning in them. That can be enough for right now. And for many of us, pursuing a purpose doesn't require having the freedom to completely change careers or the resources to enable us to uproot our life. Instead, pursuing a purpose is about having the willingness to do inner work, seeing how our skills and abilities might be able to fill—or perhaps already are filling—an unmet need, small or large.

But how can you figure out how to create this kind of meaning in your life? Begin with asking a couple of questions. Research shows that less than a third of people at any moment in time have a purpose in life and would say yes to the following questions.

1. Do you want to help others (make them happier or reduce their suffering) or improve some condition in the world?

2. Do you believe you have a talent, a skill, or a personal quality with which to do so?

The key—but not the only one—to finding your purpose in life is to determine when and how you can say "yes" to both of the above questions. For many if not most of us, our purpose might be waiting just around the corner—or hidden away in our very own homes. The trick is to convince yourself to go find it.

The Most Basic Question

A third important question for you may be harder to answer, but it could lead you toward your purpose:

3. Who are you?

We tend to describe ourselves in terms of the roles we occupy (parent, spouse, employee) and the kind of person we think we are, based on our successes and failures or what others think of us. Set all of that aside for a moment.

By asking "Who are you?" I want you to think about the kind of person you know you were meant to be—the very best version possible. This is the version of you that has to do with how you matter to the world, what will be your significance rather than your successes.

People who are unsure of their purpose report having lower well-being than those who have a purpose in life. Yes, the search for purpose may bring up feelings of uncertainty and maybe fear. There is even a new term for the kind of anxiety that sprouts up when people set out to find a sense of purpose: *purpose anxiety.*

Unfortunately, sitting down to make a plan to find your purpose doesn't always work. It is rare, though not unheard of, for us to find our purpose at the office, where most of us spend many of our waking hours. If you are one of the lucky few, congratulations. The rest of us might need to look in other places to find our purpose. As you look, as I keep reminding you throughout this book, contemplate your purpose with an eye toward intentions.

External path: Searching for your purpose might start by volunteering for a local charity—a noble endeavor indeed. But choosing your action out of a sense of responsibility or perhaps out of what might "look" like purpose to someone else might not achieve your greater goals.

Internal path: Instead, think about choosing your path for your own reasons, because it is closely connected to *your own* greater "why," no one else's. If you follow your own instincts rather than someone else's idea of what you should do, purpose can sometimes turn up when you least expect it. But you have to be open to it. If you put yourself into the right places, a time might come when something calls to you—this is why you've been placed here, on this earth, at this moment. Be ready when the call comes.

Purpose Is Highly Personal

Purpose for an eighteen-year-old deciding whether or not to go to college will look and feel quite different from his seventy-five-year-old grandmother figuring out where to live for the last years of her life. That eighteen-year-old's purpose might be to expand his worldview, meet people with different points of view from those of the people in the small town he grew up in, figure out what he does not yet know about the world around him.

His mother? Her purpose might be to figure out how to hold down a second full-time job in order to help him cover the costs of college so he can discover his purpose. His grandmother? Her purpose might be to feel physically and emotionally closer to her daughter and grandson as she ages, as her grandson strikes out on his own in this world, as her daughter handles her anxiety over watching her baby take flight.

I was recently chatting with an acquaintance, Meghan, who was going through a bit of a difficult time. Meghan had young kids and a very busy job, but her sister-in-law had recently called in a favor. Her daughter—Meghan's niece, Molly—was taking a gap year before college and needed a place to live. Living at home with her parents, clear across the country from Meghan, was not going well; Molly needed a change, a big one.

Taking on an eighteen-year-old—let alone finding her a bed in a house that happened to be undergoing a major renovation—was not a small ask, but Meghan knew what the answer was. Yes, it would make her life more difficult, more complicated, more emotionally fraught, but saying no was not an option. So in moved a recent high school graduate who was going through plenty of her own turmoil.

Meghan took on the challenge with only one goal in mind: not easing her own burden but figuring out how to help her niece find what she was looking for. Molly had her own car; that was a relief. She was able to get around town, so she could run an occasional errand and meet up with her favorite cousin who lived nearby. One more mouth at the dinner table was barely noticeable, and she helped out around the house when she could. But how to get her out of the house—or at the very least off the couch?

Meghan passed out her number to friends who were looking for babysitters and dog walkers, and she gave Molly the contact info of an acquaintance at a local soccer program who was looking for a volunteer coach. But nothing seemed to stick, not until she introduced her niece to a group of moms—most in their thirties, forties, and fifties—who worked out together in a local garage almost every day, under the watchful and loving eye of the toughest, kindest trainer in town.

At first, Molly was slightly mortified to be hanging out with the older, very chatty women every morning, not to mention horrified at the intensity of the workout. But her aunt kept making her go back. So Molly did. Eventually a funny thing happened—even when her aunt couldn't make it, Molly kept showing up. She had found warmth in the group of surrogate moms, she was gaining confidence in her own strengthening body, and she was learning to feel comfortable in a group of women who had not long before been complete strangers, all of whom were cheering her through that difficult time in her life. The trainer wasn't surprised at all; she had seen hundreds of people come through her garage over the years, all going through their own difficulties, all finding solace in the shared pain of a tough workout and the love and support of a group of people, all at different life stages, all sweating and suffering together.

But the part of the story that interested me the most? It wasn't that physical movement can heighten one's sense of self, though that's true. It wasn't just how formidable a strong support network can make us feel, though that's also true. I was most interested in Meghan's change, not Molly's, though that hadn't been the point of the story being told.

What I found fascinating was how the task of seeing her niece through this tough time had made *Meghan* thrive as well. She had plenty on her own plate—and she still does—but the joy of seeing her niece blossom into a new, wonderful version of herself brought a sense of purpose and wonder to Meghan's life, one she had never expected nor even realized that she might be running low on.

After all, her young tween and teen children were just old enough not to need constant care, which was a relief and a sadness all at once. Suddenly being a surrogate mother to an unexpected eighteen-year-old—and watching all her adult female friends gently mother her niece on her behalf—made her understand that her purpose as a mother wasn't over as soon as her children learned to pack their own school lunches and bike to town by themselves. A new, different version of mothering was just around the corner—just around every corner. There were, she now knew, countless corners ahead to navigate. And maybe, just maybe, she'd know how.

Having a Purpose, Living Your Purpose

Our capacity for self-reflexive thought—our human ability to take ourselves as objects of our own thinking and to reflect on not only our past but our future actions and lives—gives us the capacity to find a cognitive sense of purpose in life.

While the absence of a sense of purpose in life can lead to languishing, research has shown that developing a sense of purpose has been linked to numerous benefits. People with a strong sense of purpose in life report less stress, more positive emotions, fewer daily physical ailments and limitations, and better overall health.

I recently read a fascinating study on resilience in military veterans. The researchers found that a number of traits were predictive of resilience, including emotional stability, extraversion, gratitude, altruism, and *having purpose in life*.

The benefits go on and on, with links to improved mental and physical health, executive functioning, memory and overall cognition, and even increased use of preventive health care and fewer nights spent in hospitals.

Our increased desire to find meaning in our lives stems from the recognition that we have—in both the past and future tenses—important work to perform. When individuals find a purpose for their lives, they discover the sense of aliveness and "mattering" to the world that comes from dedicating some portion of their life to personally and socially important activities. It is this sense of purpose that reduces some of the ambiguity of the future. With a purpose, individuals' futures remain important to them precisely because they have unfinished business to accomplish.

Many scientists, myself included, have proposed and tested theoretical models of positive health that include the psychological and social dimensions of purpose in life. Conceptions of good health portray individuals as believing that there is a plan for, and thereby a meaning to, their lives.

My friend and colleague the psychologist Carol Ryff remarked that in psychology, the very definition of maturity "emphasizes a clear comprehension of life's purpose, a sense of directedness, and intentionality."

The psychiatrist Viktor Frankl, who wrote movingly about surviving the Holocaust, argued that the sense of purpose is ultimately a product of the will to meaning, a motivation to make our lives meaningful. The question is whether and to what degree individuals believe they have something worthy and valuable to give to others and society.

Ryff views purpose as individualistic, emphasizing possession of goals and a sense of direction as grounds for a positive purpose. As a sociologist, I have argued for a conception of human functioning that reflects the fact that adult lives are lived with and often *for* other people and communities. Thus, purpose is more than whether lives have direction but also whether individual lives are useful and constructive for others and our communities. This is why a sense of social contribution— the feeling that you are living a life in which you are making a useful contribution to others or your community—is a key element of the "functioning well" aspect of flourishing.

There is a difference between having a purpose in life and living a life of purpose. The latter is what I call having "authentic purpose"— a psychological sense of purpose in life combined with a sense of social contribution. Psychological purpose means having a direction in life and a wish to leave a legacy of some sort behind. Social contribution is whether one is doing anything to make a difference in the world through one's actions.

Seeking Clarity; Resolving Uncertainty

The last half of the twentieth century can be described as a process of the gradual unscripting of social life. Norms about the timing of marriage and childbirth, divorce and cohabitation, to name only a few, became more diverse and diffuse, placing greater responsibility on personal choice. As I have discussed, life expectancy increased greatly during the last century, which is a good thing. Ironically, with more life to live, we are confronted with more of a future to anticipate, and the future is inherently uncertain. Our improved life span has become a source of concern and anxiety.

I had a student who thought she had resolved some of the uncertainty of her future, but then life happened and questions started to crop up again. I have seen this happen many times in my teaching career; students are being groomed for one thing but start having doubts as their hearts pull them in another direction.

One of my beloved students decided to follow her heart. Kari joined my Sociology of Happiness class her freshman year, and within weeks of starting the class, I saw her absolutely light up. She went on to take every one of my classes and even decided to become a sociology major.

During her junior year, Kari came to me to ask for some advice. She told me she had a big decision to make: She was deciding where to study abroad. She told me she'd been offered a spot at a school in Ireland to study child behavior in the psychology department there. It would be practical, aligned with her major, and something her parents were strongly encouraging her to do.

Now, Kari had been raised with a practical, middle-class suburban mindset, in which you go to a good college; get a good, safe job; get married; have kids; and live a well-thought-through life. Her brother had just graduated from dental school, and was, as far as she knew, likely to live a nice life as a dentist, married with kids, probably settling not far from where their parents had raised them in suburban New Jersey.

But something about that safe track wasn't sitting well with her, and she knew it. She told me she'd always appreciated how tough my class was and how I'd forced my students to try to look at the world in a different way—and that there were good scientific reasons for doing so. And it's true. A lot of people think that social sciences and the study of happiness and well-being are, well, fluffy. But I have always tried to make my classes quite rigorous; I wanted my students to take the possibility of flourishing as seriously as I did. She told me the reason she loved my classes so much was that I was there week in and week out, providing scientific proof and reams of data that our commitment to our own well-being is vital and that we have some control over our fate.

She reminded me of what I had taught her over the past four years. "What is life for, after all?" she said. "It's not just to feel good, right, or to feel happy. That's part of it, of course. But what are they in service of? What is your success in service of? What is your money in service of? What are all of your life choices in service of if not some sort of growth or experience or increase in well-being?"

After several of my courses, I knew she was awash in evidence of how much well-being matters. I tried not to beam with pride. I asked her what her other option was, the one she was so tempted by but felt she couldn't responsibly choose.

It turned out that a year or so earlier, I had told my students about an upcoming visit from the Dalai Lama. That had inspired her to take a class on the Dalai Lama—which had led to her taking charge of the planning for his visit to campus. The other option she was considering? Moving to India to study Tibetan Buddhism and immerse herself in the Dalai Lama's teachings. As she talked about that other path, she sat up straight, practically glowing with excitement. I could see it. And I could tell she could feel it—that glow that meant she was onto something that stirred up really important emotions for her.

I chose my words quite carefully that afternoon; I certainly didn't want to push her into something she wouldn't be comfortable with. But to me, the choice was clear. I told her it seemed obvious to me that she really wanted to go to India. Why was she afraid to choose that path?

We talked through her options carefully, and she told me I was right. She really did want to go to India. She was sure that everything in her life was leading her there; her passions were pointing her in the right direction—toward her purpose. Sure enough, she ended up choosing to go to India, which, as she put it, changed the course of her life.

To this day, Kari remains quite obsessed with the idea that following one's passions and finding one's purpose are truly what leads to flourishing. As I write, she is working on her first book about mindset, well-being, and resilience. I am so proud of her. Kari is spreading her gospel far and wide, encouraging countless others to make better choices for their own well-being. The student has become the teacher.

Is It Ever Too Late to Find Your Purpose?

We know from research that both psychological purpose and social contribution decline in later adulthood. Those who do have some sense of direction and meaning seem unable to translate that purpose into social contributions to others.

Why is it harder to live your purpose in later life? I agree with the explanation that society lags behind aging adults in offering them outlets and opportunities for meaningful contributions to society. This is known as "structural lag." The increase in the healthy life span of adults has not, according to the gerontologist Matilda Riley, been accompanied by changes in social norms and institutions that could channel and employ aging adults' passions, talents, and interests. Society's purpose for older adults—to retire, enjoy life, be free and easy—no longer reflects older adults' search for purpose. I would argue that we, as a society, are missing a huge opportunity to benefit from the wisdom of our elders and in turn offer them vital opportunities to flourish in their later years.

But the problem doesn't start in our sixties and seventies. The graphs of authentic purpose suggest that the decline begins before the average retirement age, generally starting around ages fifty-four to sixty-four.

Once adults have exited formal education and entered the workforce, there is no other institution besides formal religion that encourages, let alone helps, them to find a purpose in life. There are life phases, such as marriage, moving upward in one's career, and volunteering opportunities, that could help contribute to our sense of purpose but in many cases, people have trouble recognizing their social contributions in these more personal life phases.

Someone recently told me a story about a good friend of hers who had, after many successful years in a big career, made a momentous decision. Tanya's job, in sports television production, had allowed her to travel all over the country, as well as overseas, to the NHL playoffs, to *Monday Night Football* games, even to the Olympics. At one point, she was traveling so much, she decided to try to run the stairs at each and every NFL stadium she visited. Although the job was fun, demanding, and certainly impressive to those around her, it was no longer fulfilling a core need of hers. It just wasn't *her* anymore, because she wasn't who she'd used to be.

Tanya's children were now grown—her youngest was just getting ready to graduate from college—and she and her husband were contemplating moving to their quiet weekend community, away from the bustling town they'd been living in for most of their adult lives. Everything around her was changing, and although her career had been very rewarding, she felt it might be time for her to change, too. So at the age of fifty-three, she decided to start her own flower business.

Tanya had always loved flowers—her much adored mother had taught her the basics of flower arrangements—and she loved bringing color, joy, and beauty to a moment with a perfect arrangement of flowers. She'd done so for family and friends for years, but now she wanted to spread her joy a little further. She started small, telling only a few friends, but her business grew. Within just a few months, she was doing weddings, graduations, birthday parties, and building arrangements for restaurant lobbies.

Her greatest joy was, as it turned out, being generous to others. Her loved ones had always known that, but she hadn't seen it in herself.

That was her purpose: spreading love and sunshine to those around her, making a moment beautiful and unforgettable in the best way she knew how. The twilight of her first career and becoming an empty nester didn't derail her; it forced her to examine what made her tick, what her true purpose was. My friend told me that she had always been a stunning, wonderful woman—but now you could see the glow around her from down the block. Whatever internal thermometer existed inside her, it was red hot. It isn't always this obvious—eureka moments are few and far between—but I believe that if you slow down and listen to your heart and figure out how you can help others with whatever it is you bring to the table, you, too, can find your purpose.

Action Plan: Take advantage of unexpected opportunities to find your glow. A perceived absence of options for meaningful challenges to grow and contribute can happen at any time in adulthood. Retirement and nearing the end of one's career appear to be the capstone of the "dumbing down" of life; society, whether it intends to or not, is sending older adults and retirees the message that they have no social relevance. But you can choose to accept the natural changes and shifts in your life, as Tanya did, as an opportunity to reassess what your inner need is; then, instead of fighting change, you can flow with it. But don't focus your thinking on how to find your own glow; instead, try to focus outward—notice the ways in which helping and contributing to others' happiness can bring out the best glow in yourself.

It's Never Too Early to Find a Purpose

What about young people? Is a formal education helping prepare them to find their vocation? Are they ready and primed at an early age to seek out and determine their authentic purpose? Are we doing a good job of launching young adults into adulthood with a clear purpose in life?

Yes and no. A study of youths ages eleven to twenty-one found that one-quarter were working on finding a purpose, meaning that they had not settled on a purpose but were actively seeking one. One in ten had a clear goal of helping others but were not acting on it, meaning that they had a purpose but a very low sense of social contribution. Middle and high school–aged youths, by and large, had no purpose in life, with only 16 percent reporting a clear sense of purpose that they were acting on.

By the time they entered college, there was a spot of good news: Four in every ten nineteen- to twenty-one-year-olds did have an authentic purpose. Those with an authentic purpose had found it and were acting on it in the arts, in community service, through spiritual endeavors, and in and through their families. Yet more than 40 percent of students had not found their purpose. What I found scary was that they were not trying to find their purpose, either.

Studies suggest that if young people are to develop a more prosocial orientation, it is important for adults to be role models of career aspirations aligned with a prosocial orientation. Would you describe your own work in terms of an aspiration to be successful—good at what you do—in order to leave some part of the universe a better place or at least with less suffering? Would you describe your work in terms of consumption or contribution?

Parents who describe their own work in terms of what they get out of it rather than what they give to others and society—how they are helped rather than how they help—may model an orientation to life that is more consumption based and selfish rather than contribution based and prosocial. The same may happen when parents respond to and talk about their children's occupational dreams and aspirations.

Action Plan: When a child becomes passionate about their path toward a future occupation, talking to them about how much money they might make, how important they would be, the kind of lifestyle they could have may simply make their orientation to their work more selfish rather than prosocial. Getting excited about your child's occupation aspiration by describing how they could help others or society, solve an important problem, or alleviate suffering in the world may help them focus more on a prosocial orientation to their future, one in which they will contribute rather than only acquire and consume things from their work.

Success at the Expense of Flourishing

How do we know if what we seek is purpose or merely success at all costs? A phenomenon I will refer to as the Asian American paradox is a great example of this conundrum. My research has shown that although Asian Americans are relatively free of mental illness, they are flourishing at very low rates. Why?

Asian American families have the highest median income ($100,572), compared with white ($75,412), Latinx ($60,566), and African American ($46,774) families. Higher-income households are usually headed by adults with higher education levels and higher-status jobs, resulting in a higher socioeconomic standing. Children's quality of life, health, and success are correlated positively with increasing socioeconomic standing of their family. Any sociologist would predict good mental health outcomes to be ranked as follows: Asian students doing best, followed by White students, with Latinx students ranking third and African American students reporting the worst mental health, that is, the highest rates of mental illness and languishing.

But this just isn't true. Asian American students are languishing at far higher rates than their indicators would have us believe. But why?

Part of the explanation is the "model minority" stereotype that both helps and hinders Asian American students. The stereotype is that Asian Americans are hardworking, self-sufficient, mentally healthy, successful academically and occupationally. Compared to other racial and ethnic groups, Asian American students have higher GPAs and achievement test scores, more of them participate in gifted academic programs, and more of them are admitted to prestigious colleges and universities.

The Asian American paradox can also be explained by the confluence of cultural values and practices. For example, achievement appears to be emphasized more in Asian cultures and in Asian families in the United States. Parents and families can and do exert pressure on their children to do well academically and to choose high-prestige jobs with high social status and pay.

Asian American youths reportedly feel more pressure to succeed academically because it honors one's family and the sacrifices they have made to help their children succeed and have more opportunities. Yet these successful young students often describe their parents' expectations as extremely high and sometimes unachievable. Their abilities and academic interests are not always reflected in their parents' career expectations, which push them toward advanced degrees and careers as doctors, lawyers, bankers, engineers, or professionals in the natural sciences. Their relentlessness is the key to success but, like a double-edged sword, it prevents young people from savoring their accomplishments and feeling good about themselves and the choices they are making as they shape their goals for the future.

Parents' expectations predict the rise in students' unmet expectations for themselves. Between the years 1990 and 2020, numerous studies were published that correlated various measures of perfectionism in youths and their perceptions of their parents' influence on their academic behavior in the United States, Canada, and the United Kingdom. Since 1990, there has been a steady increase in all three forms of parental influence in the three countries. Why?

There are a few likely culprits. Parents are more directly involved in their children's academic lives than ever before, and the rise in this involvement appears to be greater among parents with higher education and higher socioeconomic status. Parents spend less time with their children on play and leisure and more time with them on school activities. This shift has occurred more dramatically in families in which the parents have achieved success—more education and more prestigious, better-paying jobs, both of which incentivize using the same playbook that created their own initial success for their children's success. I believe, too, that the rising cost and, frankly, outrageously high expense of college is also to blame for parents' rising expectations of, involvement with, and pressure on their children to leave college with a clear path to economic success.

All of these factors can lead to maladaptive perfectionism—very high and therefore unmet expectations—which has reached proportions that are irrational, unrealistic, and punitive. This kind of perfectionism undermines the well-being that could arise from amazing academic achievements.

There is such a thing as adaptive, or healthy, perfectionism. It is the kind where you, and perhaps others who care for you, have high standards and expectations for you. You therefore work hard and put a lot of effort into moving toward your aspirations and dreams. What is missing in healthy perfectionism is self-judgment; healthy perfectionism doesn't involve beating oneself up over perceived shortcomings or failures. Healthy perfectionists are more self-compassionate.

People who are more self-compassionate are more motivated to improve themselves. They believe that their weaknesses are modifiable, and they work harder to improve their intellectual and moral weak points and failures. When their mistakes hurt others, self-compassionate people are more likely to apologize and make amends. Their sense of self is rooted in humility and the realization of a common humanity of imperfection and struggle, and they have much lower levels of narcissism and a higher and more stable sense of self-worth.

High effort and persistence—"grit"—is undeniably a good thing. But when grit is untethered to self-compassion or a purpose in life, it may set young people up to suffer without any meaning, as so many college students do. We could help young people if we could discourage maladaptive perfectionism and replace it with adaptive perfectionism, which is all about developing self-compassion.

Viktor Frankl argued that suffering per se isn't the problem; it is suffering without meaning that is the most harmful. Maladaptive perfectionism creates very high standards and achievement expectations accompanied by harsh and self-critical responses to failure. To be perfectionistic is to face the life of academic challenges and suffering without meaning.

Action Plan: Work hard on finding and achieving your purpose, but go easier on yourself. Be compassionate and curious, and most of all try to be understanding toward yourself as you make mistakes on your journey toward seeking a purpose. The practice of self-compassion creates a more balanced life when you have high standards and are working toward laudable achievements.

The Journey Toward Purpose

The last ingredient of purpose is putting it into action. How can adults help youths in this regard? Adults can help youths find their purpose by being a role model or supporting them. As a parent, you have to shuttle your child and maybe his or her friends to countless activities every week. How many of those activities are ones in which they serve others or their community, contribute to a cause, or help others in need? We—both parents and kids—can get so wrapped up in the myriad daily activities of childhood, many of which have little to do with helping others. What if you were to swap in or add an overtly prosocial activity to the list?

Once engaged in prosocial activities, young people have the chance to develop their concerns or act on issues that worry them, such as the health of the environment, gun safety, or the mental health of young people. Greta Thunberg is a famous example of a rather young person who, with the support of her family, acted on her concern to reverse the degradation of the global environment. By trying to help solve a problem of their choosing, young people have the opportunity to pull themselves a step back from the mundane details of their own life and reflect on larger issues. Such stepping back and reflecting are likely to help them clarify their future occupational aspirations and their prosocial orientation.

Action Plan: Many people feel that they cannot act on their purpose in life because that purpose requires acquiring knowledge, skills, and a position in society they have not yet achieved. That's okay. Make a "plan for a purpose." Making a plan for a purpose in life is not the same as searching for a purpose in life. Searching means that you have no idea of what you want to do to help others or the world. Having a plan for a purpose in life means that you know there is a journey ahead that you must devote yourself to, a program of apprenticeship or learning, in order to get where you need to be.

Start the journey, even if you know it might take awhile to get there. For example, getting an education or furthering the education you do have might be one of the steps in your plan to find a purpose in life and be able to act on it.

If young or older people do not have a clear purpose in life, perhaps we are asking them the wrong question. Ask them if they have a *plan for a purpose* for which, right now, they are developing some skills so they can find a way in which they can be useful or helpful to others or the world around them.

Work May Not Be Where You Find Your Significance

One acquaintance of mine was miserable in his work at a large mutual fund. He was reasonably well compensated, but his work analyzing the metals and mining industry brought him no joy. Once he finally got up the nerve to leave, he joined a small start-up fund that was investing in clean energy—wind power, solar power, batteries, carbon capture. It was still finance, which wasn't his favorite, and it paid nothing at first, but there was something about the work that captured his attention. His job in his previous company, basically trying to game the markets to make rich people richer, had felt deeply soulless, but in this iteration of his career, he felt that maybe, just maybe, he might be making a difference for the planet in some infinitesimal way. It was something to hold on to when nights got late and stress levels ran high. There was something in his spreadsheets that now felt a touch more important than it used to.

The reality is that adults spend the bulk of their lives at work. The ability to find or sustain purpose in work is essential. After family, employment institutions are the second most significant organizations in terms of time, expended effort, and resulting personal influence in our adult lives.

Research shows that people view their work in one of three ways—as a job, a career, or a calling. People who view their work as a job derive satisfaction from its *material* benefits (i.e., the salary and fringe benefits); they will change where they work or the kind of work for better pay. To them, work is a means to achieving financial security, permitting them (if it is important to them) to pursue avenues outside work for meaning and fulfillment.

Individuals who view work as a career derive satisfaction from the *prestige* of the job and professional advancement; in addition to meeting their material needs, the increased pay, prestige, and status that come with advancement are salient, because they bring higher self-esteem, increased power, and higher social standing. Thus, employees who view work as a career are more likely to change *where* they work rather than the kind of work they do.

Having a calling traditionally meant being called by a higher power, perhaps God, to do morally and socially significant work; today, it may as easily mean individuals who have reflected on the question of what life expects of them and feel called to live a spiritual life. Adults who believe that their work is a calling agree that the following best describes their employment: *My work has special meaning because I have been called to do what I'm doing, regardless of how much time it takes or how little money I earn; I was put on this earth to do what I am doing.* Studies suggest that between 15 and 30 percent of adults view their work as a calling.

Most adults (56 percent) view their work as a career and 29 percent as a job, but only 15 percent view it as a calling? My point is that you will be lucky if work is the place where you find your cause, your most authentic expression of your purpose. Unfortunately for the vast majority of us, the scientific data suggests that it is rare for work and purpose in life to merge, to be on the same page.

Why Is Purpose Lacking in the Workplace?

Labor economists point out that the U.S. job market has shifted from manufacturing to a predominantly service base. Service jobs are comparatively less stable, with lower wages and fewer benefits; they are also often part-time occupations. Without attributing causality to their results, the sociologists James Davidson and David Caddell discovered that individuals who were employed full-time, had greater job security, and received larger salaries were more likely to view their work as a calling. Part-time, less secure, lower-wage jobs were associated with viewing work as a job.

Much of the world's economy has shifted toward an occupational base that appears more conducive to employees' viewing their work as a job or a career rather than a calling. This is in no small part due to the rise of low-level service work being the only opportunity for anybody who does not get sufficient formal education. It is a shift that has been driving the rise of income inequality in this nation, and it will not abate until we find a way to ensure that more people can get a college degree.

But no matter the specific field we happen to toil in, the overarching system may be the culprit. Democratic capitalism encourages competition, choice, entrepreneurship, and investment, which form a primary, though by no means the only, purpose of organizations. Democratic capitalism generates substantial profits under conditions of significant risk of material loss. The integrity of for-profit organizations therefore depends on fiduciary fidelity.

However, the political philosopher C. B. Macpherson believed that democratic capitalism can become dominated by "possessive individualism," or the singular purpose of accumulating capital quickly through any means possible and with minimal concern for, or compunction about, the impact of companies' actions on the fiduciary system and the integrity of the institutions of democracy.

What pushes a society toward possessive individualism? It is likely to happen when trust in financial institutions and processes is weakened. That happened during the 2007 predatory mortgage lending crisis and the realization that buyers, not banks or Wall Street firms, would pay the price. When the big banks were bailed out in 2008, it became clear that the victims, rather than the perpetrators, suffered; it is no wonder that people lost their trust in financial institutions.

Loss of trust in economic institutions isn't the only place our society's seams are fraying. Possessive individualism also rises when our confidence in the future and the viability of the political process are shaken. Possessive individualism rises when it appears that the commitment of our leaders and our regulators to maintaining and protecting the structure of personal and public integrity is absent. Untethering ourselves from sources of ethical and moral guidance—whether religion or trust in our judicial system, social institutions, and political system—is the equivalent of success without any significance.

A Purpose Found Can Be a Purpose Lost

I landed in long-term—what is called "intensive outpatient"—treatment as an adult at the height of my career. At least I thought it was the height. I had just been promoted to full professor and then awarded an endowed professorship. I was now the Winship Distinguished Research Professor at Emory University. As part of the promotion to full professor, I, as is customary, received a semester-long sabbatical. I planned to sit down and write a book on flourishing. Things didn't go as planned.

Right around the same time, a friend of mine was reviewing a draft of a chapter for a book. As soon as she read it, she sent it to me in the hope of giving me, as she called it, a "heads-up." She didn't want me to be blindsided or hurt. The book, as it turned out, was to be called *Flourishing;* the subtitle suggested that the book was introducing a revolutionary new approach. But that upcoming book would be published ten years after my first article had been published in a scientific journal, and I certainly hadn't stopped writing about the topic in the intervening years; in fact, I had published a great deal since that 2002 article.

The book my friend was reviewing introduced a model of flourishing that was remarkably similar to my own in that it combined various kinds of well-being—emotional, psychological, and social. I felt as though I were a balloon, suddenly popped by a sharp pin. I was crushed. My research had long been my highest purpose in my life. If this "revolutionary new approach to flourishing" book was coming out, based on work like mine, perhaps the world no longer needed me.

I had lost my purpose. I decided I was no longer needed. I made alternative plans.

I sat one late afternoon and drank myself into oblivion to prepare myself. I planned to hang myself. That evening, my wife arrived home early from work. She found me alone in the pitch-dark living room, drunk and with tears in my eyes. She was puzzled and asked what was going on. I told her I could no longer "do this." Every fiber of my being—emotional, psychological, physical, spiritual—was exhausted, used up, gone. I had no interest in refueling my existential tank, either. Besides, I pointed out, the world didn't need me anymore.

Then she said the four words that saved my life: "But I need you." I wish I could write a book as powerful for others as those four words were for me.

I told her that if this was going to work, I would need serious help. I knew that one weekly visit to a therapist would not be enough. I needed to address the childhood traumas that I thought I had outrun: the abandonment by my biological mother, physical abuse by my stepmother, neglect by my alcoholic father. I thought I had outsmarted my past, but as it turns out, the past will define you until you face it down.

No matter how old you are, how many accomplishments you have, or how many degrees you add to your name, look over your shoulder, and there it is.

I took medical leave and started treatment right away. From the beginning, the treatment team hammered home a very difficult lesson, which was to start small with my goals. But I had spent my entire adult life working toward accomplishing rather large goals. I had no idea how to set small goals anymore. And when they said "Start small," they meant *really* small.

We started with meditation. I have long been a yoga-lover who does an hour and a half of yoga several times a week. Twenty minutes of meditation would be a breeze, I told my therapist. No, start with one minute, she told me. One minute of meditation five times a week? That's . . . pathetic. They're crazy, that will not help me, I defiantly told myself.

In my cognitive and behavioral therapy, I had to take notes on my negative emotions and keep track of what caused them and what thoughts came to mind. Keep it simple, I was told. I'm a professor, I thought to myself. I teach my students about cognitive behavioral therapy. I know this stuff already.

Oh, those egos. My ego did not want to submit to being changed. But I did as I was told. So it went with everything in my treatment plan; every time a therapist asked me to start small and keep it simple, I resisted and then relented. Resist, relent, a small step forward. Suddenly weeks had passed. Before I could see it in myself, I had made a huge amount of progress just by taking those small steps.

Others saw the positive changes in me before I could. It was hard work—almost unbelievably hard. But with the help of others, I helped me find a better me. My purpose had gotten lost, but I found it again. This book is the testament that I am once again living my purpose. As I typed those words, "living my purpose," there were tears in my eyes because I was so close to not being alive, all because I lost my purpose.

Start Small, Go Local

If you sense that you need to find a purpose but you don't know where to start, or aren't in a mental place where you are able to do deep soul-searching, start small. If you want to move from languishing toward flourishing, keep it simple. Accept that you will want to resist changing. Practice the mantra "Resist, relent; resist, relent." If you are taking your daily spiritual vitamin, you will be able to practice acceptance and self-compassion when you want to fight changing, so you can surrender and let go. Only when you do so can you truly start learning and growing. The spiritual vitamin helps support the learning and growing vitamin, which helps you take the purpose in life vitamin. See how this is all starting to come together? This is the virtuous cycle at work.

So let's start small by doing three small acts of kindness. More often than not, being kind is a surefire way to help another person. And as we know, helping others is an intrinsic part of finding your purpose.

In a recent study on kindness, participants were divided into four groups; all were contacted once a week to be reminded of their weekly assignment. In one group, the assignment was to do three acts of kindness toward other people. In a second group, the assignment was to perform three acts of kindness for the world; they didn't have to focus on other people but could direct their kindness toward other things, such as animals or nature. The third group was asked to perform three acts of kindness toward themselves. The final group was the control group, who were not asked to do anything.

The study went on for four weeks. At the end of four weeks and at the follow-up two weeks after the study ended, all those who had performed more acts of kindness experienced an increase in positive emotions. Even those who had performed acts of self-kindness felt more positive emotions; they also felt as positively as those who had performed acts of kindness for others or for the world.

But the researchers found that self-kindness did not increase flourishing the way acts of kindness for others or for the world did. This suggests that acts of kindness that are selfless do more than make you feel better; they tap into something about flourishing that has to do with functioning better—such as, perhaps, making a contribution to society or increasing one's sense of purpose in life.

Action Plan: Start small. This week, make a list of three things you can do that will reflect kindness toward other people or the world. Later in the week, make another list for next week and the following one and the one after that, too.

Set a reminder on your phone that pings you at least once a day, something to the effect of "You promised yourself and the world that you would perform an act of kindness today." Write down on a Post-it note what specific acts of kindness you intend to do today, tomorrow, and the next day. Put the note on your coffeemaker or your bathroom mirror. Maybe you can even take a moment in the morning as you wait for your coffee to brew to update that day's phone reminder with the specific act of kindness you plan to do that afternoon.

We all know how difficult it is to sustain behaviors that we have not practiced regularly or that aren't connected to a place or to a group of people to whom you feel a sense of responsibility. Indeed, the participants in the experiment on kindness did not always perform three acts of kindness; the average was about 2.5 acts of kindness per week, suggesting that some weeks, they performed only one act of kindness, but more weeks than not they performed either two or all three acts of kindness.

That's why you should set up guardrails, especially in these early weeks. The Post-it notes and pinging phone reminders will keep you honest—and focused. Consistency is key, and after a few weeks, this practice might become the best—and easiest—of your new purposeful habits.

These smaller acts of kindness will have an undeniable social impact—a small ripple effect in the world right around you. The larger sense of purpose that I've been discussing throughout this chapter, the one that lies at the intersection of personal connection to a cause, competence, as well as social impact, may begin to come into view as you weave more gestures of care into your daily life.

Giving Is Getting

As you become more mindful of these opportunities, and (when you have the time and resources) accept invitations to offer kindness and support, you'll begin to cultivate a new kind of attention toward the world around you. You'll gain a richer awareness of the diversity of human experiences and emotions—and of our shared needs for security, dignity, and compassion. This is when random acts of kindness can become the foundation for a more sustained commitment to purposeful action.

Taking on a true social role—at least as defined by a sociologist like me—means choosing to enter into an implicit or explicit agreement with an institution, a program, or a group. By making that commitment to volunteer, you can change your identity or self-image.

It's funny; I've changed my tune on this topic over the years. Early in my career, I found the concept of volunteering with any eye toward personal gain—helping others in this modern, box-checking, show-offy fashion to be part of what I called a "consumption model" of well-being. In this model of well-being, happiness depends on your resources, acquisitions, and achievements—even when it comes to something as socially beneficial as volunteering. In the consumption model, more income, more education, more social status, even more charity create a greater quality of life.

All living things must acquire and consume valuable resources in order to live. And we aren't wrong to do so; the consumption of goods does affect us in a somewhat positive way. But only to a certain extent. (Some studies indicate that gains in happiness plateau after $75,000, while others show evidence that the threshold is a bit higher, in the six figures.)

You can spend your whole adult life working, even sometimes more than one job at a time, because you don't have enough to get by. You can also spend your whole adult life working despite the fact that you already have more than enough. But most of us believe that there's just a little more happiness at the end of yet another rainbow of a new success, new acquisitions, and further increases in wealth.

We all have money to spend—some of us, not much; others, far more than we can use—and we all have to decide how best to do so. But we also have a *life* to spend. If you viewed your life as something you owned, that you could offer to the world, and you knew that by giving it, you would get all the happiness and the flourishing you crave—would you now agree to "spend it all" before you die?

Religious and spiritual texts have been trying to tell us this for millennia—that when we give away good things, such as kindness or forgiveness to others, we will receive the good things we desire: happiness, flourishing, a good life. I suggest that we explore this model more closely—rather than a consumption model, I call this a "contribution model" of well-being. An increased focus on giving, rather than getting, may help humans create a more sustainable approach to happiness and flourishing.

I found in my research that adults who identified themselves as volunteers were much more likely to be flourishing. There was a simple but important condition: They had to have been a volunteer recently, and the volunteering had to happen locally, in their neighborhood or community. Adults who had volunteered in the past twelve months were much more likely to be flourishing than adults who had been volunteers in the past and when compared with those who had never volunteered. Volunteering has to be recent, it has to be sustained, and it has to become part of the way we live our life as well as *where* we live. It also has to be one of the ways we define ourselves, not just as something we do but as the person we are.

Action Plan: Find a cause you believe in, whether large or small, and commit to contributing to it in whatever manner you can. Donating money to a charity you believe in is great, of course, but donating your time is going to benefit you—and potentially those you hope to help—far more. Also, think bigger. Or, more accurately, think smarter. Volunteering at a soup kitchen or a food drive is wonderful, but if for some reason, that isn't an option for you, open your eyes to other opportunities. Your local church or the Parent Teacher Association at your local school needs you, too.

It doesn't need to be an official charity or nonprofit institution. Do you have an elderly neighbor or a friend who is going through a tough time? Perhaps you can commit to visiting that neighbor or friend on a weekly basis, bringing groceries, doing some light yard work, providing a lift to a doctor's appointment, or just lending a kind ear. Maybe you can gather a group of friends on the first Saturday of every month to collect litter in your local woods.

Volunteering doesn't have to be official, stamped in ink, approved by the IRS, or counted by the hour. Real outreach is looking around your community and figuring out someone or something who could use your help—and then diving in and doing it. Try to establish early on what your commitment to the cause, whatever it is, might look like, so that you don't lose steam. Hopefully, as you feel yourself starting to flourish, this commitment to a cause outside yourself and your closest loved ones will start to feel not only easier but absolutely necessary.

Nothing in Nature Lives Only for Itself

In its most elemental form, purpose is the quality of being determined to achieve an end. From this perspective, purpose is everywhere, in every particle, cell, compound, mass, and form of energy in the universe. The earth and the amazing laws of nature come together in such a way that they support life—all that is born and dies on this planet.

There is a beautiful quote that is attributed to Pope Francis in which he reminds us that nothing in nature lives for itself. Rivers do not drink their own water; they give it to us so we may survive and live well. Trees do not bask in their own shade or, if food bearing, do not eat their own fruits or nuts, but we are given sustenance by eating their food. He ends by saying that it is natural that we want to be happy and it is fine to be happy. But it is better, he concludes, that someone else is happy because of you. We are part of nature; we cannot flourish if we exist only for ourselves.

It is good for you to flourish. It is better when others flourish because of you. That is why it is good to have a purpose in life, but it is even better to live your purpose.

[9]

Play:
Stepping Out of Time

have a younger friend who holds a Sunday-evening get-together (sometimes called "Sunday Funday") at least once a month with other working mothers who have young kids or teenagers at home. Everyone brings something to eat and drink and, most important, arrives with no expectations or plans. They get together simply to help stave off the usual Sunday-evening stress of heading back to school and work the next morning.

One night, though, the two youngest kids, ages six and five, insisted on a postdinner dance party. They turned on the music, queued up some of their favorite tunes, and went wild. On most Sunday Funday evenings, their mothers were accustomed to shooing the children off to a playroom to entertain themselves, while the moms sipped their glasses of wine. But not tonight. The children wanted to play with their moms. And play they did. Arms in the air, music turned up loud, they all danced in the living room—and danced and danced, until everyone, moms and kids, were sweaty and flushed and laughing out loud. They went to bed happy and exhausted, and then slept like rocks.

We know that play is essential to childhood development. We think that becoming "mature" means leaving the games behind, not realizing that unstructured fun is vital for adults, too; it shrinks our egos, lowers our stress levels, and boosts our well-being.

What Is Play?

Play is any self-directed activity in which you derive pleasure from the process rather than the outcome. If rules are involved, they should leave room for creativity. These everyday experiences of fun don't require equipment, stadiums or fields, boundaries or rule books; they require nothing but imagination. The only "rule" is that you derive joy from a moment that might have otherwise passed you by, unremarked on and unremarkable. Every time I mow my lawn, I mentally picture a new pattern I want to draw, and my lawn-mowing chore becomes a form of play. It's called "lawn striping," and it's extremely enjoyable to me, which is basically all that matters.

Play takes you out of time, even if only for a few minutes, whether you are working on your calligraphy skills, learning to make latte art, going a little crazy with a charcuterie board, experimenting with clay jewelry, driving to the next town to discover a new antiques shop, collecting stamps, re-creating a celebrity makeup look, reading tarot cards, roller skating, gardening, or writing a children's picture book. It can involve, but doesn't require, joining a sport league or putting together a weekly game night that gets weirdly competitive. (I love a board game as much as anyone, but when the rule book is longer than a Tom Clancy novel, I see work in it rather than play.) Even tackling a home improvement project or chore, when done playfully, seems to go by faster. Time isn't a factor when I mow my lawn as a lawn artist.

I recently read a touching *New York Times* article by a mother describing her young daughter's grief over the death of her oldest, closest friends: her stuffed animals, which she had played with her whole life—childhood, that is. Suddenly, at eleven years old, she had lost her imagination and those lifelong friends were no longer real to her. She'd forgotten how to play.

The child went to her mother, furious: "My imagination is gone and you never told me this would happen!" She was bereft. All the conversations and emotions, from friendship to love, that the daughter had experienced with her stuffed animals could no longer be experienced. All that remained were memories. She told her mom she was going to give away her many stuffed animals because, she said, "I don't know how to play with them anymore."

Too often, we equate play with fitness, but then we stress out about scheduling fitness, and what could have been play becomes part of our to-do checklist instead. Forget the calendars and scoreboards; playing to finish or win is taking the external path. Even in play—spontaneous, carefree, without a goal orientation—we can attempt to maintain our allegiance to the internal path. Play for the sake of seeking delight, of letting one's imagination run wild, of enjoying the freedom to roam— that is play. Perhaps play, in the end, is the most selfish of all our flour-ishing vitamins—and maybe that's why it's so hard for us to do.

Do We REALLY Have to Play?

Play researchers—yes, they exist—have been fighting an uphill battle for quite some time. The very definition of play usually includes the fact that it must be optional—not a necessary item on your daily itin-erary. Well, you might argue, if it's optional, must we do it? Doesn't the very inclusion of it on our must-do list take the benefits away?

Stuart Brown, a psychiatrist and the head of the National Institute for Play, argues that unstructured fun is essential to our flourishing as adults. Brown reviews evidence that play deprivation during the first ten years of life is linked to a host of poor outcomes in life—depression, aggression, impulsivity, inflexible thinking, emotional dysregulation, and a lack of meaningful relationships.

The full list of the benefits of play is lengthy, but I'll emphasize those that clearly counter the symptoms of languishing:

- Play reconnects us with key parts of ourselves that get lost in the responsibilities of adulthood. If you still giggle, that child is still alive inside you.

- Play reconnects us to our imagination, a muscle that gets depleted with lack of use.

- Play helps us approach life with excitement, energy, and humor.

- Plays helps us rediscover an appreciation of beauty.

- Play boosts our overall life satisfaction.

We're talking about a deeply biological need here, one that evolved in many animal species, including our own, because it contributes to our survival. (It may even help attract mating partners. A playful adult may be a more attractive suitor than an aggressive one.)

Play as Resistance

My good days begin in the amazing quiet of a very early morning. I like to wake up around 4:30 A.M., leaving my wife and my beloved dogs sleeping, and head to my office to think and write. Everything is pure and possible in the morning. I think more clearly, and writing comes easily. I brew my coffee, sit down at my computer, and start moving around ideas and words. Email is for later; mornings are sacred: It's playtime. I play by weaving together ideas, concepts, theories, and statistics in order to figure out how to tell a good story. This is how I approach my "work" as a professor, and I love it.

Work and life can become play. Play and life can become work. Having fun is a choice, not an imposition.

I have a friend who hates vacuuming. But when he figured out that his dog thought the vacuum cleaner was both his mortal enemy and his favorite playmate, his most hated chore became a time to romp around with and tease his dog.

Another friend tells me that when he takes morning walks, he makes up songs about what he's seeing around him and hums them under his breath. Anytime someone almost catches him singing to himself, he can't help but laugh.

On long car trips, a woman I know buys herself an economy-size pack of Hubba Bubba bubble gum (always grape flavor, she tells me) and practices blowing the biggest bubbles possible, just to make sure she still can.

I know an engineer who has schizophrenia who goes into his spare bedroom every morning before work. He, like me, takes time to play with ideas, and he prefers to discuss his ideas with Albert Einstein in great detail. Rather than putting a stop to it, we encourage him to continue his "meetings" with Albert. Why? Because he has fun, he describes it as play, and these "meetings" with a genius inspire him to approach his work with as much joy as purpose.

Part of the reason I love to play at thinking is because it is a way of rebelling against the workplace culture, which can suck the fun out of being a professor. We can all think of play as an act of resistance. We can use play as a way of protecting our mental health in a world where we're constantly encouraged to prioritize activities that have some sort of utilitarian purpose. Time, we are told, is money; our value can be defined in terms of billable hours, and any time wasted is a loss of opportunity to monetize every last skill we possess.

Remember how I discussed in a previous chapter the possibility that anxious feelings and joyful ones can coexist? So, too, can work and play. Take a moment to save your work, shut off your screen for a moment, and fly a paper airplane into a coworker's cubicle. Build a tiny scavenger hunt for your favorite colleague who teaches two classrooms down from you, sending her on a search for her favorite chocolate bar that you hid for her in a secret spot.

Even a midmorning trip to the coffee shop down the street for an iced mocha—yes, you want extra whipped cream—is a moment to take back for yourself. Stop thinking of it as a caffeine break to improve your afternoon productivity; think of it instead as a pause you are taking for yourself to let your mind unwind and feel free. Changing your expectations of a moment changes everything.

Action Plan: If you want to take the fun out of anything, call it work and make it something you have to do. I have seen people turn family vacations into work: the scheduling, the strict itinerary, the forced interactions, the joy-sucking determination to have the *best* time. What are some small ways you can add the spirit of play to some of the tasks you have to do on a daily basis?

Try to adopt a play mindset for everything from vacuuming, as my friend did, to mowing the lawn, as I do. Take your required daily tasks, ones that so often can feel like a slog, and flip them upside down. What about creating new, elaborate dishes to cook for the family dinner—bonus points for plating them as if you were a contestant on *Top Chef*? Or taking time to do silly decorations on the cookies you have to bake for your child's Boy Scouts bake sale. Maybe you can try practicing your nonexistent drumming skills with wooden spoons on your kitchen counter when your favorite song comes on the radio while you're doing dishes? *Change your day mindset to a play mindset.*

Play Is Protective

Play is a microcosm of childhood, a protective shell like a butterfly's chrysalis that safeguards children from the slings and arrows of life, one that allows them to grow. What happens, however, when, through no fault of your own, you are born into conditions—poverty, racism, and other adversities—that groom children for bad outcomes? Can play, if nurtured and supported in such adverse conditions, create resilience? Can increased opportunities for play encourage better-than-expected life outcomes, and possibly even provide a buffer against the odds of the cycle of poverty being perpetuated?

I think back to my own childhood; when the violence and abuse started, I think I stopped playing entirely until I managed to escape that home. For me, as for so many other children, school was no place for play, either. Once I lost the sense of safety to play at home, I had no other outlets for it.

The classrooms I was educated in throughout K–12 schooling would be familiar to most of you: rows of desks in which students sat facing the front of the classroom; very little physical movement; a lot of time spent listening to the teacher; and then too much quiet time doing the required workbook or instructional activity alone at one's desk.

The direct instruction setting was a nightmare for me but even more so for my teachers, who regularly pleaded with me to stop drumming on my desk or bouncing my legs up and down, which would rattle my desk and drive the teacher crazy. I often ended up in detention, where I wrote hundreds of sentences on the board or on sheets of paper, scrawling the same sentence over and over in my messy handwriting: "I will not. . . ."

Then one year, when I was about eight years old, we moved to a new town. There I was placed in what was called an "open classroom," and for the first time ever, I blossomed. I was not in detention, my grades were nearly perfect, and I jumped ahead two years in my reading and other skills. Then, a year later, we moved again; my father was a dry-wall finisher, and we had to move to Florida, where there was more construction happening. Once again, I was back in the direct instruction classroom and back to being the problem child.

That one blessed year in the so-called open classroom, one that was total liberation to me as a child, turned out to be a lot like an instruction model that was tested in a well-known study called the HighScope Perry Preschool Study, which was conducted in the mid-1960s. The study was a preschool instructional intervention program that focused on "at-risk" children, all of them Black youths and all living in poverty. The children were randomly assigned to either a "direct instruction" group or one of two "self-initiated" instruction conditions.

The direct instruction program focused on teaching academic skills. Teachers led children in short, planned lessons in language, math, and reading, using prepared materials such as workbooks. In the two self-initiated models, the classroom in one model was organized into distinct interest topical areas—for example, reading, writing, math. The central experience revolved around encouraging the child's initiative, creating and sustaining social relationships, promoting self-expression through creativity, music, movement, language and literacy, and basic mathematical operations such as classifying and counting objects.

The second self-initiated approach was the traditional nursery school curriculum, in which the main objective was for children to learn social skills rather than academic skills. There, teachers sometimes organized class activities, discussions, and field trips. Often, the children had the freedom to choose their activities, move from one activity to another, and interact with their peers or adults. Unlike the other two models of learning, the nursery school approach encouraged play; it was a central and welcomed activity, and the children were the initiators of various forms of play.

The results? The kids who learned—or at least tried to learn—in the direct instruction classroom fell victim to the same very bad outcomes of so many kids growing up poor in the United States. The kids who learned in the self-initiated classrooms did *not* become yet another statistic of growing up in poverty in America. Just the opposite, in fact.

In most instances, it didn't matter which self-initiated classroom the kids were placed in; it just mattered that they were in one of those two settings and not in the direct instruction classroom. And the difference was devastating. Some of the unfortunate outcomes that characterized the kids who had been instructed in the direct instruction classroom were higher school dropout rates, more drug-dealing arrests, an arrest sheet with five or more arrests, bearing children out of wedlock, living on public assistance, not owning a home, and unemployment. Even if those kids were able to stay employed in the future, they were sometimes not able to make $2,000 or more per year (equivalent to about $17,500 today, adjusted for inflation).

Those unfortunate outcomes were not written in stone. The kids in the other classrooms who were lucky enough to be instructed with a play-forward mentality, by and large, were able to become successful adults. By age twenty-seven, they were more likely to own a home and to be earning a good living; they were not, on the whole, high school dropouts, single and raising children on public assistance, convicts or ex-convicts.

Prevention worked. Giving children some self-direction and allowing them to play in an enriched environment made a world of difference in interrupting the cycle of poverty.

Joe Frost, one of the leading play researchers, has unearthed similar findings: Children who are deprived of play when they are young are shown to demonstrate reduced resilience in adverse situations, lower levels of self-control, and difficulty relating to others both socially and emotionally. Play is no laughing matter, especially when it has been shown to help build a brighter future for our kids.

Why Do We Stop Playing?

As kids grow up, they start to lose the sense that play is necessary, age appropriate, and vital. They engage less in pure play and participate more in games. Both play and games socialize children in how to cooperate and how to coordinate their activities if they want the activity to continue. Both play and games encourage empathic skills, especially taking the perspective of others and responding sympathetically to moments when you have hurt, intentionally or not, another participant. But games, like grades in school, begin the process of encouraging external motivation, doing things because of the possible desirable outcome, and discouraging internal motivation—doing something simply because you enjoy it.

Games are a microcosm of adulthood. Sometimes kids get hurt playing games, sometimes physically but also sometimes emotionally. Sometimes the pain or hurt caused by games is psychological or social, because kids can feel ashamed of their performance, especially in publicly watched games. I feel heartbroken every time I watch a kid slinking off a playing field, head held low with shame, staring at the ground, tears in their eyes. In games, children begin to understand that their self-worth is contingent. It is sometimes earned based on the quality of their performance, not their effort; their sense of self is based entirely on outcomes rather than inputs.

In a sense, games are by definition distinct from play. Games have clear outcomes and anoint winners and losers. She or he who amasses the most points or gets to the destination fastest wins. Between the beginning and ending of a game are predetermined rules.

Despite all this, games can qualify as play if they are played the "right" way; some games are designed to provide entertainment over competition, emphasizing an enjoyment of the process and more imagination-building experimentation. Certain video games, for example, are more about world building than about mission domination, making it easier to lose yourself in the little moments of beauty or amazement without having to worry about the endgame or point totals.

The philosophy professor C. Thi Nguyen, an expert on games, has written that party games such as Cards Against Humanity are designed for "arbitrariness, skill-lessness, and intentional chaos." Instead of playing with an eye toward point totals and win-loss columns, the social practice of a game like this one "requires that they be played with a spirit of levity."

In this way, play and games can overlap. I recently watched a wonderful movie called *Pinball: The Man Who Saved the Game*. I learned that pinball was once illegal in many cities because it was considered a game of chance rather than skill and therefore was considered a form of gambling targeted at children. As it turned out, pinball machines were actually created to helped Americans feel a sense of accomplishment and happiness during a very difficult period of our nation's history, the Great Depression.

One of the creators of the pinball machine was apparently decades ahead of happiness researchers, because back then, he decided to design the game around the goal of building skills, not merely accruing points and chasing wins.

In the movie, the architect of the pinball machine raised the question "What makes a game good?" His answer? A game is good when it:

- Provides people with a sense of accomplishment

- Has causes and effects, which means it requires the player to use and develop skills in order to accomplish goals

- Makes people feel that what they do matters

According to designers of successful games—from pinball machines to modern, multimillion-player video games—that is what makes people happy and makes them want to keeping coming back to the game. You need to have a sense of accomplishment, to experience being the cause of outcomes that you want to accomplish, to feel that your presence matters; in this way, games can offer you all the benefits of play. We all want to know that what we are doing matters. What a wonderful metaphor for life.

Forgetting How to Play Too Soon

As a professor, I always try to practice the philosophy that if both my students and I are not having fun at least some of the time, I'm not doing my job correctly. Working with young people is fun—maddening at times for many reasons, of course—but ultimately fun. My students—mostly young adults between the ages of eighteen and twenty-three—aren't in a position where they are considered full adults, either by society or by themselves. They still have permission, so to speak, to be kids, to have fun, to play.

But students don't seem to be having very much fun these days. And it's not just the overscheduling of everything. Before, during, and immediately after class, my students invariably jump onto their iPhones to check in with friends and family. Fun? Not really. They are checking in on what is happening, what will be happening—but mostly they are checking in on what they have missed out on. They make plans, they get help with making decisions, and sure, they schedule future fun for their evenings or weekends.

But even the concept of weekend fun has taken a darker turn. Lately my students have been talking more to me about deeply concerning topics: overdoses or risks of overdoses, not just of alcohol, but of a dizzying array of illicit and dangerous drugs, from serious binge drinking to using heroin, cocaine, OxyContin, ketamine, fentanyl, methamphetamine, hallucinogens, and a variety of other amphetamines. The days of just smoking a joint and drinking a couple of warm beers have long been eclipsed by what my students call "serious partying."

My own diagnosis was that my students were doing what they could to temporarily escape the "too muchness" of being a young college student—where their performance, if it dips below a B plus, will mean failure, a future plan—to become a doctor, lawyer, or businessperson—already evaporated. They are all just kids, scared, fearful, trying to become adults but forgetting how to have fun along the way.

When I began as a professor in the late 1990s, I had little difficulty scheduling meetings with my students. But in the last decade, trying to schedule a meeting with a student has become a nightmare, and not because of me. To get one meeting scheduled requires about five to ten emails back and forth; they are busy at 9:00, busy at 11:00, lunch is out of the question, still busy, classes are all afternoon, and then there is a window from 5:00 to maybe 7:00, at least for those not participating in sports or extracurricular activities in the afternoons. Being busy, hyperscheduled, and stressed is the badge of honor on college campuses. These students aren't adults yet, but they certainly don't act like children anymore.

How Can We Remember
What We Never Learned?

Perhaps it's no surprise that by the time we have graduated from college and officially become adults, we have forgotten how to play. When kids get in a swimming pool on a hot summer day, they chuck balls at one another's heads, race from end to end, create teams, and invent challenges. Adults—well, they dip in to cool off, or they swim laps. Then they towel off and turn the grill on to make dinner. Where's the fun in that?

I might argue that adults who are in highly creative fields—say, writing books or plays or writing or directing films—probably come very close to engaging in play through their jobs. Maybe professional athletes or LEGO engineers feel, on the best of their workdays, that their lives are filled with play. Perhaps that is as close to playing as adults can get: We play through our job, making money and entertaining others who consume the products we create through our adult form of play.

For the rest of us, the play we knew as kids becomes leisure as adults; we engage in recreation. It's an interesting word, *recreation*. In Latin, *recreare* means "to create again or renew." In Middle English and Old French, *recreation* meant to attempt "mental or spiritual consolation." To console is to comfort someone in their loss.

Leisure is a word also found in Middle English that goes back to the Latin word *licere,* which means "to be allowed." To engage in leisure is to be allowed something, perhaps freedom from work and freedom to choose to do whatever we want to do.

The Danes, who are known to prioritize a healthy lifestyle and work-life balance, call their leisure time *fritid;* it means "free time," and there are entire store sections named just that, devoted to things one might use in one's *fritid:* fishing poles, hiking boots, camping gear. In Denmark, the naming and pursuit of leisure start early—schools' after-care programs are also called *fritid,* during which kids choose the activities they wish to engage in, usually outdoors, under the distant but watchful eye of instructors—but the activities are kid led and kid centered and considered absolutely crucial to a child's development for building empathy, social skills, and self-reliance. In Scandinavia, children do not even start official school until the age of seven—not until after they have spent the first several years of their lives playing, usually outdoors, snow and rain be damned, with nary a worksheet in sight.

The German philosopher Josef Pieper, in his book *Leisure: The Basis of Culture,* argued that to reclaim leisure is to reclaim our humanity and that "Leisure stands in a perpendicular position with respect to the working process. . . . Leisure is not there for the sake of work, no matter how much new strength the one who resumes working may gain from it; leisure in our sense is not justified by providing bodily renewal or even mental refreshment to lend new vigor to further work. . . . Nobody who wants leisure merely for the sake of 'refreshment' will experience its authentic fruit, the deep refreshment that comes from a deep sleep."

Refreshment really comes only from true leisure. The first quality of true leisure is to have free time from work, household, familial, and personal obligations. With this free time comes the opportunity to choose to engage in something because you *want* to rather than because you *have* to—just like those kids in Denmark. This, like play, is a shared aspect of leisure; you determine for yourself what you will do.

Leisure can be reading a book, doing a favorite hobby—from tying trout-fishing flies to making candles, quilting, gardening, bicycling, hiking, watching TV or movies, singing in a choir, going to a play or a museum, traveling, going out to dinner, and so on. The list of leisure activities is almost endless.

What you consider leisure is not likely my form of leisure. Personally, I love fly-fishing but would find tying trout flies to be work rather than a form of recreation. The important point is that leisure, like play, is not merely chosen freely but chosen because it will lead to enjoyment for you and only you.

Not all leisure needs to be done because it is solely a source of fun. For adults, leisure activities may be chosen because they satisfy additional motivations, such as the desire for personal growth, as I discussed in chapter five. There we learned that people find contentment in getting better at doing things—not because it is outcome based but because the process of practicing something is intrinsically valuable, whether playing a musical instrument or learning to paint.

A good friend of mine who just turned eighty years old started oil painting several months ago. Despite her relatively advanced age, her painting keeps getting more beautiful. It takes concentration, hours sitting still, amazing dexterity, flexibility, arm strength, and patience to do what she is doing when she paints. It is not constantly fun, nor is it easy, and that is the point. She does it because she continues to get better at various facets of it; she loves the medium of oil painting because she can paint over and over and sometimes over again the parts of the painting that she feels needs more nuance, more depth, more color, more brightness, more energy. She does it because it brings her satisfaction, pleasure, occasionally even joy.

I have recently returned to bicycling. Getting better at bicycling is not my thing. And although it does provide me with beneficial exercise and physical benefits, that alone is hardly why I returned to biking; good physical health is merely a side benefit. For me, bicycling satisfies my desire for autonomy and exhilaration. I love the sense of freedom. I am free to come and go whenever and wherever I choose to bike, and I can go as fast and as far as I choose. It is self-chosen and self-directed, and the activity itself is more important than any outcome, so biking ticks all of the boxes of play. I like riding alone or with my wife, but especially alone for that full sense of freedom and independence from technology, from our dependence on cars and fuel, from desks, from my four walls, from everything.

My wife and I bought our first boat about four years ago and are now selling it. Why? It was fun—for a while. At one point, we liked owning it, but eventually, it started to feel as though the boat owned us. Owning it required renting a slip, getting it serviced and repaired, and worrying about it when bad weather came in. It all got too complicated. Leisure isn't enjoyable when it takes work to maintain and sustain it.

But bikes are basic things, and unlike boats and cars, which are now increasingly made mostly of computers and parts that can be serviced only by a dealer-approved mechanic, I can learn everything I need to know about bikes from my local and online community. The equipment to repair bikes is still affordable, and I have found that I love being able to fix and maintain my own things.

So just as when we were children playing, as adults we freely choose to engage in activities that bring us some form of positive or beneficial feelings, experiences, or outcomes. Unlike play, which has no preset rules, a lot of leisure has what I would call preexisting rules and structure. There are sometimes right and wrong ways—easier or harder, more straightforward or more difficult—to do a leisure activity. There are commonsense rules and laws that guide the safety of participants in a lot of leisure pursuits. Injuries and fatalities are a sad reality of some forms of leisure, especially boating (and, yes, often because of drunk boat driving), motorcycling, and even my beloved bicycling. So leisure has structure, yes, but it is still designed by us, for our pleasure, for us to actively participate in, and that matters.

The Rise of Passive Leisure

A recent change in leisure has been the rise of passive leisure. For anyone who has watched the HBO show *White Lotus* in recent years, you will understand far too well the stifling desperation with which the wealthiest among us now approach their free time. Too often, even our nonluxury vacations feel like work: planning the trip, finding the Airbnb, enduring the soul-sucking nature of air travel, booking the waterfall hike, let alone setting one's alarm early enough to make it there. There is a real need at the heart of this trend; too many of us are overworked and underinspired, exhausted, and searching for something that will fulfill us. But this kind of passive leisure—even that magical afternoon we wanted to spend scuba diving only to be chased away by a jellyfish swarm—is increasingly unlikely to bring us the joy we seek.

Just over a century ago, there was literally no such thing as "couch potato" or passive leisure; most leisure, out of necessity, was active. By active, I mean that the person engaging in the leisure had to make the activity happen for him- or herself and for others who may have been watching or listening to the activity. Singing, playing a musical instrument, telling stories, fishing, taking nature walks (what we call hiking today) are examples of what were considered the staples of many leisure activities for our ancestors. The leisure was created locally as well as in, and by members of, the community or a family. Consider that nearly all traditional leisure activities were done standing up.

That all started to change around the turn of the last century. Four new pieces of technology—the radio, the phonograph (record player), the cinema, and the car—helped to create a more passive form of leisure, where participants consumed the leisure rather than creating it.

As a result of these new inventions and subsequent societal shifts, families started to retreat from their communities, where they had once grouped together to make music and share stories—to instead gather in their homes around their radios and record players. Communities lamented what was already the feeling that the family, long the primary unit of leisure, was being replaced and eroded by popular culture and influences from outside the family. Most tellingly, being in cars, listening to radios or phonographs, and watching movies created a form of leisure that was done sitting down. Real leisure was sitting back and listening, not creating and making the leisure yourself.

You continue to see this form of deactivated leisure every summer in our national parks, with an endless line of cars traveling through such majestic places as Yellowstone National Park. Where we used to walk in our national parks to see their wild inhabitants, today we observe the beauty and animals in our parks from our cars (with an occasional story of someone wishing for a more active form of national park leisure by walking toward the bison). But play cannot be passive.

It isn't just our leisure that has changed; the amount of time we have for "leisure" seems to have changed as well. I mentioned earlier in the book that we are actually working *less* now than we ever have before. A century ago, but also in just the last fifty years, people worked *more* hours annually than they do today—a fact that might surprise a lot of you. Of course, some, if not many, of the people reading this book may be genuinely working more hours than the average American. Furthermore, when both parents in a household are employed, which is more common now than fifty years ago, there is dramatically less spare time for domestic and childcare tasks.

Obviously, as our forebears worked more, they had less free time to engage in leisure. But what leisure they engaged in was active, not passive. There has been a slow and steady decline in the total average hours worked each year and an increase in the amount of time spent in leisure—yes, we spend less time working and more time in leisure today than ever before. Yet more people feel more stressed and overworked. Why?

This feeling of being overworked is real, but it is also relative and important to put into context. The first reality is something I touched on earlier—that there are two different versions of the service economy. The low-level service sector is where people cannot, with a single job, make ends meet, so they are stressed because they cannot get enough hours or have to work two jobs to make enough. Then there is the higher-level service sector, where one job requires putting in an average of fifty or more hours of work per week.

People in the latter sector, those with more education and higher incomes, engage in fewer total hours of leisure than those with less education and income. What really matters, however, is the quality rather than quantity of leisure. Studies have shown that people with more income and education spend more time doing active leisure, whereas those with lower incomes and education do more passive leisure. And we know that passive leisure does not count as play. We also know that people feel more satisfied with their lives when they engage in more active leisure.

Passive leisure makes you feel less satisfied with your life—think of our friend Taral watching YouTube alone in his dorm room for hours. Passive leisure is like junk food; spending more time, whether you are richer or poorer, doing passive leisure decreases life satisfaction.

So it's not *how much* leisure you do, it is the *kind* of leisure you do and how you engage in it that will matter for improving your life. Leisure that you actually enjoy, that fulfills you? It's called play.

The Consumption of Leisure

How much enjoyment are your leisure activities bringing you these days? Did you once truly enjoy walking your dog, but now you distractedly scroll through the list of podcasts you've gotten behind on, and then rush through the walk with your podcast playing at 1.5× speed? Did you used to meet your girlfriends for a casual Friday-night tennis game, but now you've gotten yourself stuck in a three-times-a-week USTA league, where the opponent across the way seems intent on stuffing the ball down your throat? Do you think we might all be doing it wrong?

If you are thinking that it takes more money to engage in active leisure, let me call you out on that distortion immediately. A four-star hotel in Hawaii sounds lovelier than a Motel 6 in coastal South Carolina, but if your teenager is driving you crazy, you'll be miserable in both places, I guarantee.

Need I remind you that more than a hundred years ago, with little wealth and much less time for leisure because they spent so many more hours having to work on the farm to get by, our ancestors had only active leisure as an option. And most of the active leisure they engaged in didn't cost much at all.

Furthermore, what money you have and how you choose to spend it has been a focus of a ton of happiness research. The lesson from that research is clear. It is not how much money you have that counts, it is what you spend it on that matters. People who spend their money to acquire things—clothes, jewelry, cars, second homes—are less happy. People who spend their money on experiences are far happier.

Experiences, in reality, don't necessarily require a lot of money. But money sure can help when it comes to one of the most obvious forms of collecting experiences: traveling and going away on vacation. If that isn't an option for you, what does that leave you with?

What does it mean to have an experience? I think an experience is something that is meaningful to you; there is something valuable you learn, and therefore there is something you wish to bring back with you and remember. Perhaps people can acquire experiences from passive and not just active forms of leisure—say, getting a group of friends together to watch a movie rather than watching it alone on the couch. But for the most part, I'd encourage experiences that have a more active focus.

Every day, I see people chasing experiences. But lately, I lament when I see people taking what could be an experience, and then turning it into a commodity, into something to consume. With our devices, we can be the subject of our own report—the source of news and the news reporter rolled into one. It is my belief that as soon as you take a photo of an amazing experience and post it on social media, it is no longer an experience but a thing, an object, an acquisition. This is the death sentence of the happiness that can come from a genuine, meaningful experience.

Before the advent of cameras, we had to rely entirely on memory and remembering our experiences through retelling stories. Then there were the days when we took pictures on film. We took photos of the experiences we wished to remember, but the fact that we would have to be judicious about how many photos we took—film was expensive!—and then take the time and spend the money to have the film developed—all that required us to remember those experiences by being present for them, not to quantify the impressive details of the event for someone else's jealous consumption.

Then came the Polaroid camera. We could take a picture and immediately have it processed. Now we have our "smart" phone, which enables us to take thousands upon thousands of pictures that pollute the "cloud" and rarely if ever are reviewed or reseen.

True, a meaningful experience is something you want to share. But in the past, our experiences were told and retold through stories, during gatherings of friends and families, at reunions, birthday parties, and other occasions. Experiences make our lives meaningful when we share them in a way that gives them genuine respect, through storytelling, not posting carefully posed photos and waiting to see how many people "like" them.

A friend of mine was recently at a birthday party that exemplified this shift. She told me that a group of friends, old and new, had traveled to a beautiful destination to celebrate a beloved friend's thirtieth birthday party. But the weekend—which was filled with amazing experiences designed to bring everyone joy—had turned into a seventy-

two-hour-long influencer event as several of the attendees tried to
capture every aspect of the event in the most beautiful "shareable"
way.

Without realizing it, the would-be influencers ruined some of
the joy of the weekend for everyone else, who wished to engage with
one another in a meaningful way, face-to-face, in person, not manage
their images back home with endless carefully curated photo shoots of
an enviable event. It was, she told me, a tragic loss, turning a happy
reunion into a commodity designed for social media consumption,
rather than meaning and joy and connection and—dare I say it—
play.

It is not as though you cannot record your experiences without
losing their meaning. But the way we consume our leisure now makes
me think we have forgotten why we are participating in activities in
the first place. Is it to tell the world, most of whom don't care a bit,
what we are doing at that moment? Or is it to have an experience
that is so meaningful that you alone must remember it, because then
you are cherishing it for what it is, a gift? Only you can retain the
memory of that experience, and you alone can tell it to others to
whom it might mean something and who might benefit from your
story.

Engaging in an experience in our leisure time can bring untold joy
and happiness if we are participating in it with a mind to being present
and engaged. I recently watched a young boy fish in a glassy lake. He'd
woken his mom up early that day, begging and begging for her to take
him fishing, his all-time favorite activity. Over the hours I witnessed
his efforts, he didn't catch a single fish. He threw out his line again and
again. (His dad joked to me that they don't call it fishing in their family, they call it "casting.") But his joy was apparent on his face and
completely untethered from the number of fish he came home with
(zero). He was entirely present. No camera, no counting.

Take a lesson from him. Don't let your smartphone and your obsession with social media likes remove all the joy from your joy, okay?

Play and Work, Fun and Responsibilities Need One Another

After my grandparents adopted me, I played as a child, and I played because it was fun. I wanted to have fun. What I didn't realize was how much I learned about myself, others, and nature through play. Play helped me grow up into a better person. As an adult, I want to have fun, but I also want to enjoy life. As a child, I didn't understand some important lessons I learned later on. Without cloudy days, we do not appreciate the sunny ones. It's the same with play and fun. Without work and responsibilities, we do not appreciate the fun and freedom of unadulterated play. You can't have the good without the bad.

As adults, no matter how much we do leisure, how good it makes us feel, it is a reminder in and of itself that it is ephemeral. We are seeking an escape from the most dominating forces in our lives: work and responsibilities. But in taking time for ourselves, we are reminded of what many of us do not get from our work: fun, autonomy, a sense of personal growth, curiosity, exploration, discovery, and the sense of contributing to something larger than ourselves.

When it comes to leisure, we are trying to re-create the feelings, the unbridled joy, the sense of discovery, the enviable autonomy we felt when we played as kids. But the fact is that, as adults, we can never play—truly play, wildly and freely and imaginatively—without being seen as acting odd. This sense of boundaries or restrictions reminds us that we can no longer go back to what was a once-in-a-lifetime thing: being a child.

Leisure, in this sense, is a respite not merely from work but from what lurks in all adults' minds—our sense of our own mortality. But this respite is a reminder, indeed a siren call, for us to awaken to our chance to flourish if we only listen to what the moments that seem difficult and dark—the sense of no freedom, no fun, no growth, no autonomy—are trying to illuminate.

Let's remind ourselves as adults that, despite our sense of our own mortality, play is not dead to us. We may not get to play—indeed, we may not want to play—as we did as children. Play, with its make-believe fantasy, no outcomes, and no winners or losers, is pretty hard to recapture. But we can re-create and reclaim some of the most important parts of play as an adult as well.

Action Plan: Here are some things to do to get the most out of your leisure.

1. *Increase your active leisure and decrease your passive leisure.*

   Don't watch golf on TV; go find a local public course and try your hand at it yourself. If there's a movie you're dying to watch, don't do it solo. Instead, invite friends over and make an event of it—with themed snacks, maybe a costume requirement, and a designated time to discuss the film afterward as a group. Go for a hike in the woods, not because you think you should exercise more but because you want to bask in the glory of unbound nature. Join a pickleball league, not because you want to win every game but because you want to laugh at yourself and your new friends as you try. Follow a local band and invite friends to their next free outdoor gig, and then dance under the setting sun while feeling the music course through you.

2. *Collect experiences rather than things, unless the things mean something to you.*

   Things that remind you of your journey through life, that are so important that they take a prominent place in your home, are worth acquiring; they're for you and often are an experience in and of themselves. If you find yourself saving up for a bigger TV, a fancy handbag, or a luxury car, try to think if there might be a better way to spend that cash. Instead of buying a bigger TV, can you set aside money for a movie-theater date night once a month with a friend or loved one, popcorn included? Instead of buying that handbag, can you spend a weekend away with some friends and catch up face-to-face with your phones stashed in your backpacks instead of the palms of your hands? Instead of buying that luxury car, can you take a vacation to a place that will fill you with awe, with amazement, with joy?

3. *Enjoyment is not the same as fun, not even close.*

Have more fun. Laugh more. Go find other people who make you laugh more. Let your giggles turn into a full-blown laughing fit. Be silly. Have dance parties. Jump off a rope swing into a lake and scream when you hit the cold water. Throw a Frisbee. Join a trivia team at the local pub. Sing loudly in the shower. Start a food fight (not at school!). Point at rainbows. Write a funny poem and send it to a friend. Wear obnoxiously colorful socks to your next big work meeting. Go rock climbing. Chase a butterfly. Say yes next time you're invited to karaoke. Then get up on stage and sing. Ride a roller coaster. Do cartwheels.

In my class on happiness, I tell my students to listen to a wonderful episode of the *This American Life* podcast called "The Show of Delights." The show description states the following: "In these dark, combative times, we attempt the most radical counterprogramming we could imagine: a show made up entirely of stories about delight."

In it, they quote a wonderful line from the poet and professor Ross Gay: "To achieve humanity, we must share delight." When I heard that, I thought of mirror neurons. Mirror neurons are the amazing neurons that enable us to mirror someone else's feelings—if they're doing something and we're watching, we can essentially feel what they are feeling.

In Gay's book *The Book of Delights: Essays,* he shared some of those sometimes mundane, sometimes rare, moments of jewellike delight, the kinds I wanted my students to contemplate: listening to oatmeal bubble in a pot; spotting a deer's hoofprint in a field of green clover; watching bees cluster around the butterscotch sauce dropped from a kid's ice cream sundae.

His moments of delight make me think of some of my own: a bright red umbrella unfurled on a gray, rainy street corner; the first bite of a perfectly ripe, unblemished pink peach; the smell of the air slowly shifting to ocean saltiness as I drive toward the shore.

Building a Community of Flourishers

One of the best ways to learn to flourish—and continue flourishing—is to build a community of flourishers around you. Do you remember Scott, the prison guard you met in chapter two? When he and I talked, one of the questions I really wanted to know the answer to was: How did he know he had changed? He laughed and told me that it was pretty obvious to everyone around him how much he had changed.

He told me a story about how one day he had been putting something into his teenage son's backpack and had found some marijuana hidden inside. The old Scott? He would've absolutely lost it, he told me. He'd have immediately stormed into his son's bedroom, yelling his head off, furious. He'd have thrown down every punishment he could think of, restricted his son's access to friends and fun, told him he'd lost his trust in him, and then gone downstairs and simmered with rage for hours longer.

The new Scott? He didn't do any of those things. He removed the weed from the backpack and sat down to think. Later that day, when he was calm and felt ready, he approached his son. Now, his teenager knew his stash was missing, and man, did he know his dad. He held his breath, waiting for the explosion he was sure would come. But Scott didn't explode. He sat down with his son and asked what was going on with him. Was he okay? Was he making decisions that didn't serve him? Was his friend group a problem?

His son broke down. He knew he was floundering—hanging with the wrong crowd, skipping his workouts, letting his schoolwork slip. He'd felt things splintering; he felt out of control but didn't know how to handle it. He and his father sat for a long time, talking everything through. At the end of their chat, they hugged. His son told him he'd been expecting to be screamed at—that this new father was a welcome relief.

Soon enough, Scott's son was back to making regular trips to the gym, studying more, and hanging out with friends who were making the same kinds of good decisions he was making. You might even say he was starting to flourish.

The best part? That big conversation with his dad, that moment of shared understanding, of trust, of alliance, of us together against the world, was the first, but it wouldn't be the last. Both he and Scott started to treasure their newly forged bond, and father-son conversations like that one continue to this day.

So Scott did it. The shift in his own outlook made him understand how finding the path to flourishing can utterly change your life. His newfound commitment to his own flourishing led to his making a vocation out of helping other people flourish also. His entire approach to parenting and family life changed, which helped them start to flourish. His approach to his job changed too; his mentality shifted from a job in which he was charged with restricting his inmates' freedom to helping them find the freedom to flourish. His ability to flourish led to his finding ways to make sure everyone else around him flourished as well.

* * *

Remember Nicole, my former student, who was just starting a new career as a visiting law professor in North Carolina? When we talked, she told me that before she had accepted this job, she had received several offers—tenure-track offers—from quite prestigious colleges and universities. But she didn't want to leave the town she'd settled in shortly before the pandemic. Why?

She told me that she had actually gotten pregnant during those first early, frightening months of the covid shutdown. When the lockdown had started, she began walking around the neighborhood a lot, thinking it was the only safe place for a pregnant woman to be. Sure enough, she started meeting other people and families in her neighborhood. When she gave birth, despite being far away from both her family and her husband's, instead of feeling isolated, she felt almost overwhelmed by support. Her neighbors brought over meals for months, offering advice, support, and assistance with whatever the young couple needed. They felt the warmth, trust, and belonging of good relationships and integration into their community.

When we talked, she told me that perhaps something she'd learned in my class several years before had helped her make a decision. Before, she might've taken the most prestigious offer that landed on her desk. She'd have uprooted her family and left her community to pursue the kind of glory she—and her family and friends—thought was the marker of success. Indeed, her brother told her she was crazy to turn down the offers.

But something inside her knew that chasing that kind of external success would never make her happy. Her new employer had gotten the sense that she was feeling undervalued and underappreciated in her job and suspected she might be looking around for other opportunities—so they offered her 50 percent more money and a flexible work schedule so she could spend as much time as possible with her baby while he's little. She continues to thrive in her small town near Durham, North Carolina, happily married, enjoying being a new mother, cherishing having an employer who values her, and surrounded by people who support and love her. She found a community of flourishers, if you will, perhaps in no small part due to the decisions she made to pursue flourishing herself. And that's not something you leave behind.

Ending with Your Beginning in Mind

Everything passes away, suffering, pain, blood, hunger, pesti-
lence. The sword will pass away too, but the stars still remain
when the shadows of our presence and our deeds have vanished
from the earth. There is no man who does not know that. Why,
then, will we not turn our eyes toward the stars? Why?

—Mikhail Bulgakov, *The White Guard*

Sometimes you begin a project with the end in mind. I want to end
this book with *your* beginning in mind.

A friend once told me that the job of being a parent is mostly to
nudge our children back to center. If they stray off the path or get too
close to the edge—literally or metaphorically—we gently guide them
back closer to the middle. If they make a bad choice or waver, we remind them where the path is, even if we can't always walk alongside
them.

I love this metaphor because I have always felt that my calling is to
nudge people down the path toward flourishing. Why not look to the
stars? Flourishing has become for me, both personally and intellectu-
ally, my life's work, the North Star that is guiding me home. Clouds
might obscure it occasionally, and it might be hard to spot. But I know
where it is in my sky, and I know I must always keep aiming toward it.

Sometimes the path ahead seems more obscure than ever. So many
of us have spent years feeling directionless, unable to break out of our
limiting behavioral and emotional patterns, maybe even feeling invisible. Like me, you, too, can be found; I promise you. You are not a
ghost. I see you.

I know what it feels like to be invisible. The research that ultimately
formed this book was a form of "me search." I wanted to turn my own
emptiness and invisibility into something of substance that was meaning-

ful, that would help others like me. This book, and the years of my research included in it, are the culmination of a decision I made as a child: I decided at a very young age that one day I would be seen, fully seen.

At a very early age, I became invisible, the first time almost literally. My grandmother who adopted me told me that when I was an infant, she had found me nearly dead in my baby crib. My mother, barely a week after giving birth to me, had disappeared and never come back. My grandmother called and called our home, then, after days of not getting an answer, finally drove to our home. There she found me and my two-year-old sister; we had been left alone for several days.

My grandmother took me to the hospital, where I was diagnosed with pneumonia—not a condition that bodes well for a malnourished newborn. I was told the story of my fight to survive because my grandmother wanted me to know that I was a fighter and survivor. It was when I was mourning the loss of my grandfather and having trouble figuring out how to get past my grief. My grandmother told me that nothing will stop me in this life but me.

My second early life experience with languishing and its invisibility came when I met my biological mother for the first time around the age of sixteen. My sister wanted to meet our mother, but I did not. My grandmother arranged the visit nonetheless. I remember the car pulling up to our home carrying my biological mother with her husband and three children. I was in shock. I'd had no idea that she had started another family after abandoning my sister and me.

I met my two half brothers and my half sister that day and chatted with my mother. I don't remember what was said that day or what we did. What I do recall is feeling a strong longing, a yearning, an aching hunger that overcame me then and occasionally overcomes me to this day. It was a longing for something I would never have: my mother, her love, her praise, her attention. To long for something that important to being human is to create a deep well of emptiness that cannot be filled by any substitute. Unrequited longing is the very essence of emptiness and languishing.

My third experience with invisibility came from what therapists antiseptically call "complex PTSD." My father, with whom we then lived, remarried; for a short time, all was well with my stepmother. But as soon as she had her own children with my father, something inside her snapped. Perhaps it was related to our move from her hometown in Wisconsin to Florida so that my father, a drywall finisher and construction worker, could work year round. She was isolated, with two stepchildren, and was now caring for her own two young children.

My father was an alcoholic who worked very hard and drank very hard; he was rarely home in time for dinner each night. At that point in our lives my stepmother became very physically abusive to me and my sister, though she never ever abused or even talked harshly to her children. I will save you the horrific ways in which we were beaten every day, but it went on for many years until her brother visited us. My sister and I never talked—we shut down and dissociated when we were at home—but my stepuncle noticed our odd behavior. He went home to Wisconsin, looked up my paternal grandparents, and told them that something was terribly wrong, that we needed to be taken out of that house and adopted into a loving home.

The thing with adverse childhood experiences (ACEs)—the name the Centers for Disease Control and Prevention gives the experiences that my sister and I endured for years—is that they make you feel as though the world is trying to blot you out, make you disappear, make you invisible. Such experiences take almost everything good you have as a child in order for you to survive. I am a story of resilience, but not always the pretty kind the media loves to tell. My resilience, born of the hunger of an empty belly, born of languishing, was the hunger that drove my determination to one day be seen, fully seen.

I am a first-generation college graduate who went on to get a PhD in five years from the Department of Sociology at the University of Wisconsin–Madison, the number one department of sociology in the world at the time. I received a grant from the MacArthur Foundation to begin my graduate-level research to map out the nature and causes of social well-being that would complete the vision I had of the ingredients of what constitutes a flourishing life.

Before me, nobody studied mental health. Mental health was considered the absence of mental illness, and what serious scholars studied was mental illness. Mental health was an empty, invisible category. Everything I have done as a scholar has been to make visible what was previously invisible—not just the subject of mental health but myself as well.

Flourishing has been a North Star and a gift for me that I now give to you. Let us always cherish that in all things broken, there is the possibility for healing, growth, discovery, and gifts. This book traces my story from languishing to flourishing, from invisible to fully seen. May you find and follow the path to flourishing, as I did.

We Need Mental Healthcare Transformation, and Now

This book is also about a new way of measuring, thinking about, and approaching mental health. Quite simply, flourishing means the presence of good mental health. The absence of good mental health is languishing.

Here is the challenge of mental health in America that lies ahead for those who care: There is too much mental illness and not enough flourishing in the world. Too much funding goes to study the biological and neurological bases of mental illness and not enough to the study of mental health. My dual-continua model makes it clear that this is a grave mistake.

This dichotomy between what we as humans and as a society prioritize always reminds me of one of my favorite folk tales. There is a Native American story of an elder explaining to a young boy about the two sides of human nature. "Son," the elder says, "we are made up of two wolves. One is the aggressive, angry wolf. The other is the kind, friendly wolf. They are constantly battling each other, inside each of us, all the time."

The young boy puzzles over this, picturing his own two wolves. Then he looks up at the elder and asks, "Which one wins?"

The elder replies, "Always the one you feed."

We, as a nation, are feeding the wolf of illness and death, not the wolf of health and life. We, as individuals, are prioritizing the wrong things.

If we could cure all mental illness tomorrow, it would not put us where we need to be. There is no there there. The absence of mental illness does not mean the presence of good mental health.

Good mental health is not a null category; it is filled with the ingredients of flourishing: purpose in life, belonging, contribution to society, acceptance of oneself, acceptance of others, warm and trusting relationships, autonomy, personal growth, and more. Flourishing is filled with the things that make life worth living, that bring quality to whatever quantity of life we are granted.

I now know why I was put here on this earth. This book is just another beginning. The next steps and decisions are up to each of us. So I end here with your challenge; it is based on one of my favorite quotes from Robert F. Kennedy:

> *Some [people] see things as they are and say why?*
> *I dream things that never were and say, why not?*

Do not be satisfied with the way things are if you are languishing. Don't just content yourself with reading these pages and learning why. That's a good start, but it is not enough. I want you to dream of things that could be and ask, "Why not?" Fight for your flourishing. Work past your pain, your loneliness, your emptiness. Let the light in. Believe in the path forward, and try to take steps to get there every day. Trust that there is something beautifuller and beautifuller around every corner ahead. Flourishing, and no less, is what you deserve.

Acknowledgments

Nothing worth accomplishing happens alone or is done on our own. I owe so much to an ever-expanding tribe that has made my life more beautiful. I have heard a tribe described as the people you would share your last bit of anything valuable if they needed it to survive. The following is my tribe. These are the people who fed me with whatever I needed at a vulnerable point in my life, giving me the courage and will to continue the journey, to do the science that needed doing—and then to write this book.

At the top of that list is my wife. The thought of ever getting married never crossed my mind until I saw Lisa Janovy. We met at the end of our junior (undergraduate) college year when we were inducted into the honor society called Mortar Board. We were married within a year of meeting each other. Five days after our wedding, we left to spend part of our senior year, 1986, at Jagiellonian University in Kraków, Poland. Lisa, your happiness and well-being have been my main concern throughout our life together, and I know my happiness and well-being have been the same concern for you. In addition to my grandparents, Lisa gave to me a life that inspired the idea of flourishing.

Two professors I met on my intellectual journey became part of my tribe. Professor Bill Brown taught me Personality Psychology as an undergraduate. More important, we became a special duo, like father and son, that continues to this day. He "threatened" to adopt me as his son so many times. We don't need that piece of paper, Bill, because your love, and the love I have for you, already made it happen.

Professor Carol Ryff has been my teacher, mentor, collaborator, and friend ever since my graduate school days at the University of Wisconsin. It is no exaggeration to say that the research in this book would not have happened without her. She gave me the opportunity of a lifetime—to be part of the MacArthur Foundation Successful Midlife Study—that has provided so much scientific data on well-being for so many people throughout the world. Carol is the rare intellectual giant with a heart of gold. Our profession needs more people like her in it.

Adam Grant became part of this story when he wrote a story about languishing being the dominant condition of how people throughout the world were feeling in the midst (2021) of the covid pandemic. I met Adam when he was a graduate student at the University of Michigan in Psychology when I was invited to give a lecture there. What is most amazing about Adam is that he could have easily omitted any credit for the ideas about languishing in his *New York Times* piece. Instead, he gave credit where credit was due, something that not a lot of scholars do enough of these days. Adam is a really good scholar who happens to be a really good person.

The person who would become my agent, Albert Lee (United Talent Agency), read Adam's article about languishing. Albert told me after we started working together that he was struggling during the pandemic and didn't know why or what was going on—that is, until he read about languishing and went down the rabbit hole of reading a lot of my research articles. The more of my work he read, he told me, the better he felt. So, he contacted me out of the blue. Albert plucked me out of the obscurity of the universe and said I needed to write this book. The way this all came to happen made me feel like I had guardian angels looking out for me. I told Albert that, as an agent, he has the chance to operate like an angel. He certainly was and is one of my angels.

Leah Trouwborst is my editor. She took me and my book with her when she moved from one publishing house to another—to Crown, my ultimate home. Little did I know going into this project that books can be orphaned as well, not just humans. You didn't abandon us, Leah; you believed in me and this book and took care of both of us. A book is as much a living entity as the author writing it. I knew Leah knew that, and that is why I wanted her as my editor. She has the amazing ability to remain supportive and nurturing even when a writer's artistic temperament becomes brittle or frazzled. She is a member of my tribe.

Jane Fleming Fransson was my collaborator throughout this process. We each were doing our jobs, but it never felt like work. You will never know how much you mean to me, Jane, because you made my story come to life. Something else came to life as we worked together—a friendship. Jane always gave me her last bit of patience, attention, kindness, and encouragement when I had none of those things left in my tank. From here on out, you are in my tribe. When I mailed you the gift of Ross Gay's book I meant it—you are one of my delights.

Thank you, my tribe. May this book honor your generosity. I count you all as my blessings.

Notes

Introduction

x **About a year into:** Adam Grant, "There's a Name for the Blah You're Feeling: It's Called Languishing," *The New York Times,* April 19, 2021, https://www.nytimes.com/2021/04/19/well/mind/covid-mental-health-languishing.html.

xiv **He wrote an opinion article:** Eric Reinhart, "Doctors Aren't Burned Out from Overwork. We're Demoralized by Our Health System," *The New York Times,* February 5, 2023, https://www.nytimes.com/2023/02/05/opinion/doctors-universal-health-care.html. Teachers are also feeling demoralized rather than burned out by overwork. For more information, see Doris A. Santoro, *Demoralized: Why Teachers Leave the Profession They Love and How They Can Stay* (Cambridge, MA: Harvard Education Press, 2018).

xv **My research:** Corey L. M. Keyes, "The Mental Health Continuum: From Languishing to Flourishing in Life," *Journal of Health and Social Behavior* 43, no. 2 (June 2002): 207–22, https://doi.org/10.2307/3090197.

xv **But they also found:** Marta Bassi et al., "The Relationship Between Post-Traumatic Stress and Positive Mental Health Symptoms Among Health Workers During COVID-19 Pandemic in Lombardy, Italy," *Journal of Affective Disorders* 280, Part B (2021): 1–6, https://doi.org/10.1016/j.jad.2020.11.065.

xvii **And after billions:** Ben Singh, Timothy Olds, Rachel Curtis, et al., "Effectiveness of Physical Activity Interventions for Improving Depression, Anxiety and Distress: An Overview of Systematic Reviews," *British Journal of Sports Medicine* (February 2023), https://doi.org/10.1136/bjsports-2022-106195.

xvii **is also a gateway:** Corey L. M. Keyes and Eduardo J. Simoes, "To Flourish or Not: Positive Mental Health and All-Cause Mortality," *American Journal of Public Health* 102, no. 11 (November 2012): 2164–72, https://doi.org/10.2105/AJPH.2012.300918; Esme Fuller-Thomson et al., "Suboptimal Baseline Mental Health Associated with 4-Month Premature All-Cause Mortality: Findings from 18 Years of Follow-Up of the Canadian National Population Health Survey," *Journal of Psychosomatic Research* 136 (September 2020): 110176, https://doi.org/10.1016/j.jpsychores.2020.110176; Jeff Levin, "Human Flourishing: A New Concept for Preventive Medicine," *American Journal of Preventive Medicine* 61, no. 5 (November 2021): 761–64, https://doi.org/10.1016/j.amepre.2021.04.018.

xvii **About half of the entire population:** Ronald C. Kessler et al., "Lifetime Prevalence and Age-of-Onset Distributions of DSM-IV Disorders in the National

Comorbidity Survey Replication," *Archives of General Psychiatry* 62, no. 6 (2005): 593–602, https://pubmed.ncbi.nlm.nih.gov/15939837/.

xviii **A recent study of patients:** Randolph C. H. Chan et al., "Flourishing with Psychosis: A Prospective Examination on the Interactions Between Clinical, Functional, and Personal Recovery Processes on Well-Being Among Individuals with Schizophrenia Spectrum Disorders," *Schizophrenia Bulletin* 44, no. 4 (2018): 778–86, https://pubmed.ncbi.nlm.nih.gov/28981851/.

xxii **The number of high school girls:** Centers for Disease Control and Prevention, "Youth Risk Behavior Survey: Data Summary & Trends Report: 2011–2021," 2023, https://www.cdc.gov/healthyyouth/data/yrbs/pdf/YRBS _Data-Summary-Trends_Report2023_508.pdf.

xviii **languishing is more common:** Faren Grant, Constance Guille, and Srijan Sen, "Well-Being and the Risk of Depression Under Stress," *PLOS One* 8, no. 7 (July 2013): e67395, https://doi.org/10.1371/journal.pone.0067395; Sanne M. A. Lamers et al., "The Bidirectional Relation Between Positive Mental Health and Psychopathology in a Longitudinal Representative Panel Study," *The Journal of Positive Psychology* 10, no. 6 (2015): 553–60, https://doi.org/10.1080/17439760.2015.1015156; Marijke Schotanus-Dijkstra et al., "The Longitudinal Relationship Between Flourishing Mental Health and Incident Mood, Anxiety and Substance Use Disorders," *The European Journal of Public Health* 27, no. 3 (June 2017): 563–68, https://doi.org/10.1093 /eurpub/ckw202; Corey L. M. Keyes, Satvinder S. Dhingra, and Eduardo J. Simoes, "Change in Level of Positive Mental Health as a Predictor of Future Risk of Mental Illness," *American Journal of Public Health* 100, no. 12 (December 2010): 2366–71, https://doi.org/10.2105/AJPH.2010.192245; Corey L. M. Keyes et al., "Are Changes in Positive Mental Health Associated with Increased Likelihood of Depression over a Two Year Period? A Test of the Mental Health Promotion and Protection Hypotheses," *Journal of Affective Disorders* 270 (June 2020): 136–42, https://doi.org/10.1016/j.jad .2020.03.056.

xxii **As the Harvard University historian:** Niall Ferguson, "US Teens Feel Down, but the Adults Aren't All Right Either," *The Washington Post*, February 26, 2023, https://www.washingtonpost.com/business/us-teens-feel-down-but -the-adults-arent-all-right-either/2023/02/26/54447a9e-b595-11ed-94a0-51 2954d75716_story.html.

Chapter One:
What Languishing Looks Like

6 **A 2022 study of more than eighteen thousand:** Deborah E. Linares, Veni Kandasamy, and Catherine J. Vladutiu, "Lifecourse Factors Associated with Flourishing Among US Children Aged 1–5 Years," *Child: Care, Health and Development* 48, no. 2 (March 2022): 298–310, https://doi.org/10.1111 /cch.12930.

6 **food insufficiency or sleep insufficiency:** Clara E. Busse et al., "Household Food Insufficiency and Flourishing in a Nationally Representative Sample of Young Children in the US," *Annals of Epidemiology* 76 (December 2022): 91–97, https://doi.org/10.1016/j.annepidem.2022.10.011.

7 **In the United States:** Linares, Kandasamy, and Vladutiu, "Lifecourse Factors Associated with Flourishing Among US Children Aged 1–5 Years"; L. M. Keyes, "Mental Health in Adolescence: Is America's Youth Flourishing?," *American Journal of Orthopsychiatry* 76, no. 3 (July 2006): 395-402, https://doi.org/10.1037/0002-9432.76.3.395; Ashley N. Palmer et al., "Changes in Flourishing from Adolescence to Young Adulthood: An 8-Year Follow-Up," *Child and Family Social Work* 28, no. 1 (2023): 194–209, https://doi.org/10.1111/cfs.12953; Chantie C. Luijten et al., "Evaluating the Psychometric Properties of the Mental Health Continuum-Short Form (MHC-SF) in Dutch Adolescents," *Health and Quality of Life Outcomes* 17, no. 1 (October 2019): 157, https://doi.org/10.1186/s12955-019-1221-y; Heidi Witten, Shazly Savahl, and Sabirah Adams, "Adolescent Flourishing: A Systematic Review," *Cogent Psychology* 6, no. 1 (July 2019): 1640341, https://doi.org/10.1080/23311908.2019.1640341; Corey L. M. Keyes et al., "The Relationship of Level of Positive Mental Health with Current Mental Disorders in Predicting Suicidal Behavior and Academic Impairment in College Students," *Journal of American College Health* 60, no. 2 (February 2012): 126–33, https://doi.org/10.1080/07448481.2011.608393.

8 **A recent study of Hungarian youths:** Melinda Reinhardt et al., "A Person-Centered Approach to Adolescent Nonsuicidal Self-Injury: Predictors and Correlates in a Community Sample," *Journal of Youth and Adolescence* 51, no. 9 (September 2022): 1760–73, https://doi.org/10.1007/s10964-022-01628-y.

9 **PBS aired a documentary:** "The Lost Children of Rockdale County," *Frontline,* October 19, 1999, https://www.pbs.org/wgbh/pages/frontline/shows/georgia/etc/synopsis.html.

10 **A recent study of more than thirty-seven thousand:** Robert C. Whitaker et al., "Family Connection and Flourishing Among Adolescents in 26 Countries," *Pediatrics* 149, no. 6 (June 2022), https://doi.org/10.1542/peds.2021-055263.

10 **On the flip side, positive relationships with parents:** Philip Jefferies et al., "Analysis of Protective Factors in Schoolchildren in England Using the Dual-Factor Model of Mental Health," *Research on Child and Adolescent Psychopathology* (February 2023): 1–14, https://pubmed.ncbi.nlm.nih.gov/36786892/.

12 **What happens when a parent's:** "Rising Parental Expectations Linked to Perfectionism in College Students," APA.org., American Psychological Association, March 31, 2022, American Psychological Association, https://www.apa.org/news/press/releases/2022/03/parental-expectations-perfectionism.

12 **Between 2013 and 2021:** Daniel Eisenberg, Sarah Ketchen Lipson, and Justin Heinze, "The Healthy Minds Study: 2021 Winter/Spring Data Report,"

Healthy Minds Network, January 5, 2021, https://healthymindsnetwork.org/wp-content/uploads/2022/01/HMS_nationalwinter2021_-update1.5.21.pdf.

12 **Indeed, the overall number:** Jessica Colarossi, "Mental Health of College Students Is Getting Worse," Boston University School of Public Health, April 21, 2022, https://www.bu.edu/articles/2022/mental-health-of-college-students-is-getting-worse/.

12 **Only 38 percent met:** Eisenberg, Lipson, and Heinze, "The Healthy Minds Study."

17 **Worldwide, the estimate of PPD:** Su Rou Low, Suzanna Awang Bono, and Zaireeni Azmi, "The Effect of Emotional Support on Postpartum Depression Among Postpartum Mothers in Asia: A Systematic Review," *Asia-Pacific Psychiatry* (April 2023): e12528, https://doi.org/10.1111/appy.12528.

18 **The percentage of people working:** Kathleen Gerson and Jerry A. Jacobs, "The Work-Home Crunch," *Contexts* 3, no. 4 (2004): 29–37, https://journals.sagepub.com/doi/pdf/10.1525/ctx.2004.3.4.29. For more recent estimates that corroborate the Gerson and Jacobs article, see Statista Research Department, "Annual Average Working Hours per Week of All Employees in the United States from 2007 to 2022," Statista, February 14, 2023, https://www.statista.com/statistics/261802/annual-change-of-the-average-working-week-of-all-employees-in-the-us/.

19 **Internationally, it's a slightly different:** Ruben Berge Mathisen, "Charted: The Working Hours of Americans at Different Income Levels," Visual Capitalist, September 20, 2022, https://www.visualcapitalist.com/cp/charted-actual-working-hours-of-different-income-levels/.

19 **The strongest evidence:** Kathryn M. Page et al., "Workplace Stress: What Is the Role of Positive Mental Health?," *Journal of Occupational and Environmental Medicine* 56, no. 8 (August 2014): 814–19, https://doi.org/10.1097/JOM.0000000000000230.

20 **working in a high-demand:** Carter C. Lebares et al., "Flourishing as a Measure of Global Well-Being in First Year Residents: A Pilot Longitudinal Cohort Study," *Journal of Medical Education and Curricular Development* 8 (May 2021), https://doi.org/10.1177/23821205211020758.

22 **If you live long enough:** Mark Snowden et al., "Changes in Mental Well-Being in the Transition to Late Life: Findings from MIDUS I and II," *American Journal of Public Health* 100, no. 12 (December 2010): 2385–88, https://doi.org/10.2105/AJPH.2010.193391.

22 **My research on languishing:** Ibid.

23 **Couples learn to discuss:** Laura L. Carstensen and Megan E. Reynolds, "Age Differences in Preferences Through the Lens of Socioemotional Selectivity Theory," *The Journal of the Economics of Ageing* 24 (February 2023): 100440, https://doi.org/10.1016/j.jeoa.2022.100440; Maria Wirth, Andreas Voss, and Klaus Rothermund, "Age Differences in Everyday Emotional Experience: Testing Core Predictions of Socioemotional Selectivity Theory with the MIVA Model," *The Journals of Gerontology: Series B* (February 2023): gbad033, https://doi.org/10.1093/geronb/gbad033.

24 **The influential early Christian monk:** Mary Margaret Funk, *Thoughts Matter: The Practice of the Spiritual Life* (New York: Continuum International Publishing Group, 1998); Placide Deseille, "Acedia According to the Monastic Tradition," *Cistercian Studies Quarterly* 37, no. 3 (2002): 297–301.

24 **Early Syrian writers:** John Cassian, "The Institutes of John Cassian," in *The Works of John Cassian: A Select Library of the Nicene and Post-Nicene Fathers of the Christian Church,* second series, Book 11, ed. Philip Schaff and Henry Wace (Grand Rapids, MI: William B. Eerdmans, 2000).

24 **Whatever you call it:** Corey L. M. Keyes and Jonathan Haidt, eds., *Flourishing: Positive Psychology and the Life Well-Lived* (Washington, DC: American Psychological Association, 2003).

Chapter Two:
How Did We Get Here?

30 **In a 2021 study:** Richard Weissbourd et al., "Loneliness in America: How the Pandemic Has Deepened an Epidemic of Loneliness and What We Can Do About It," Harvard Graduate School of Education, February 2021, https:// mcc.gse.harvard.edu/reports/loneliness-in-america.

30 **In August 2020:** "Time Spent Alone Increased by an Hour per Day in 2020," U.S. Bureau of Labor Statistics, August 27, 2021, https://www.bls.gov/opub /ted/2021/time-spent-alone-increased-by-an-hour-per-day-in-2020.htm.

30 **People tend to meet:** "The Friendship Report," Snap Inc., 2019, https:// downloads.ctfassets.net/inb32lme5009/7BkRT92AEhVU51EIzXXUHB /37749c3cf976dd10524021b8592636d4/The_Friendship_Report.pdf.

31 **loneliness increases as we age:** Nancy J. Donovan and Dan Blazer, "Social Isolation and Loneliness in Older Adults: Review and Commentary of a National Academies Report," *The American Journal of Geriatric Psychiatry* 28, no. 12 (December 2020): 1233–44, https://doi.org/10.1016/j.jagp .2020.08.005; Mark Snowden et al., "Changes in Mental Well-Being in the Transition to Late Life: Findings from MIDUS I and II," *American Journal of Public Health* 100, no. 12 (December 2010): 2385–88, https://doi.org/10 .2105/AJPH.2010.193391.

31 **Close relationships disappear:** Susanne Buecker et al., "Is Loneliness in Emerging Adults Increasing over Time? A Preregistered Cross-Temporal Meta-Analysis and Systematic Review," *Psychological Bulletin* 147, no. 8 (August 2021): 787–805, https://doi.org/10.1037/bul0000332; Ashley N. Palmer et al., "Changes in Flourishing from Adolescence to Young Adulthood: An 8-Year Follow-Up," *Child and Family Social Work* 28, no. 1 (July 2022): 194–209, https://doi.org/10.1111/cfs.12953.

31 **as much as 60 percent:** Keith David Malcolm Snell, "The Rise of Living Alone and Loneliness in History," *Social History* 42, no. 1 (January 2017): 2–28, https://doi.org/10.1080/03071022.2017.1256093.

31 **People already living alone:** Viji Diane Kannan and Peter J. Veazie, "US Trends in Social Isolation, Social Engagement, and Companionship—

Nationally and by Age, Sex, Race/Ethnicity, Family Income, and Work Hours, 2003–2020," *SSM-Population Health* 21 (March 2023): 101331, https://doi.org/10.1016/j.ssmph.2022.101331.

31 **The truth is that:** Caitlin E. Coyle and Elizabeth Dugan, "Social Isolation, Loneliness and Health Among Older Adults," *Journal of Aging and Health* 24, no. 8 (December 2012): 1346–63, https://doi.org/10.1177/0898264312460275.

31 **One review of seventy studies:** Julianne Holt-Lunstad et al., "Loneliness and Social Isolation as Risk Factors for Mortality: A Meta-Analytic Review," *Perspectives on Psychological Science* 10, no. 2 (March 2015): 227–37, https://doi.org/10.1177/1745691614568352.

33 **Even more troubling:** Timothy D. Wilson et al., "Just Think: The Challenges of the Disengaged Mind," *Science* 345, no. 6192 (July 2014): 75–77, https://doi.org/10.1126/science.1250830.

33 **a full 67 percent of men:** Ibid.

33 **The subjects chose to hurt themselves:** Kirsten Russell, Susan Rasmussen, and Simon C. Hunter, "Does Mental Well-Being Protect Against Self-Harm Thoughts and Behaviors During Adolescence? A Six-Month Prospective Investigation," *International Journal of Environmental Research and Public Health* 17, no. 18 (September 2020): 6771, https://doi.org/10.3390/ijerph17186771; Melinda Reinhardt et al., "A Person-Centered Approach to Adolescent Nonsuicidal Self-Injury: Predictors and Correlates in a Community Sample," *Journal of Youth and Adolescence* 51, no. 9 (September 2022): 1760–73, https://doi.org/10.1007/s10964-022-01628-y.

34 **Rachel Zoffness:** Rachel Zoffness, *The Pain Management Workbook: Powerful CBT and Mindfulness Skills to Take Control of Pain and Reclaim Your Life* (Oakland, CA: New Harbinger Publications, 2020).

34 **John Cacioppo:** John T. Cacioppo and William Patrick, *Loneliness: Human Nature and the Need for Social Connection* (New York: W. W. Norton, 2009); Naomi I. Eisenberger, "Social Pain and the Brain: Controversies, Questions, and Where to Go from Here," *Annual Review of Psychology* 66 (January 2015): 601–29, https://doi.org/10.1146/annurev-psych-010213-115146.

34 **That is why stress hormones:** Robert M. Sapolsky, "Stress in the Wild," *Scientific American* 262, no. 1 (January 1990): 116–23, http://www.jstor.org/stable/24996650; Robert M. Sapolsky, *Why Zebras Don't Get Ulcers: The Acclaimed Guide to Stress, Stress-Related Diseases, and Coping* (New York: Holt, 2004); Daniel M. Campagne, "Stress and Perceived Social Isolation (Loneliness)," *Archives of Gerontology and Geriatrics* 82 (May 2019): 192–99, https://doi.org/10.1016/j.archger.2019.02.007; George M. Slavich et al., "Black Sheep Get the Blues: A Psychobiological Model of Social Rejection and Depression," *Neuroscience and Biobehavioral Reviews* 35, no. 1 (September 2010): 39–45, https://doi.org/10.1016/j.neubiorev.2010.01.003.

35 **Gabor Maté, in his book:** Gabor Maté, *In the Realm of Hungry Ghosts: Close Encounters with Addiction* (Berkeley: North Atlantic Books, 2010), 26, 165.

35 **As smartphones came:** Jean M. Twenge, *iGen: Why Today's Super-Connected*

Kids Are Growing Up Less Rebellious, More Tolerant, Less Happy—and Completely Unprepared for Adulthood—and What That Means for the Rest of Us (New York: Atria Books: 2017).

36 **David Brooks, the writer:** David Brooks, "America Is Having a Moral Convulsion," *The Atlantic,* October 5, 2020, https://www.theatlantic.com/ideas/archive/2020/10/collapsing-levels-trust-are-devastating-america/616581/.

36 **Just before the pandemic:** Jeffrey M. Jones, "U.S. Church Membership Falls Below Majority for First Time," Gallup, March 29, 2021, https://news.gallup.com/poll/341963/church-membership-falls-below-majority-first-time.aspx.

36 **Another recent study argued:** Tyler Giles, Daniel M. Hungerman, and Tamar Oostrom, "Opiates of the Masses? Deaths of Despair and the Decline of American Religion," National Bureau of Economic Research, Working Paper Series 30840, January 2023, http://www.nber.org/papers/w30840.

39 **Restoring their feeling of belonging:** Tyler F. Stillman et al., "Alone and Without Purpose: Life Loses Meaning Following Social Exclusion," *Journal of Experimental Social Psychology* 45, no. 4 (July 2009): 686–94, https://doi.org/10.1016/j.jesp.2009.03.007.

39 **The researchers also found:** Dídac Macià et al., "Meaning in Life: A Major Predictive Factor for Loneliness Comparable to Health Status and Social Connectedness," *Frontiers in Psychology* 12 (February 2021): 627547, https://doi.org/10.3389/fpsyg.2021.627547.

40 **John Henryism, a term coined by:** Gene H. Brody et al., "Is Resilience Only Skin Deep?: Rural African Americans Socioeconomic Status—Related Risk and Competence in Preadolescence and Psychological Adjustment and Allostatic Load at Age 19," *Psychological Science,* 24, no. 7, 1285–93, https://doi.org/10.1177/0956797612471954; Sherman A. James, Sue A. Hartnett, and William D. Kalsbeek, "John Henryism and Blood Pressures Difference Among Black Men," *Journal of Behavioral Medicine* 6 (1983): 259–78, https://doi.org/10.1007/BF01315113; Sherman A. James, "John Henryism and the Health of African-Americans," *Culture, Medicine, and Psychiatry: An International Journal of Cross-Cultural Health Research* 18, no. 2, 16382, https://doi.org/10.1007/BF01379448.

41 **Black Americans report higher levels:** Patricia Louie and Blair Wheaton, "The Black-White Paradox Revisited: Understanding the Role of Counterbalancing Mechanism during Adolescence," *Journal of Health and Social Behavior* 60, no. 2, 169–87, https://journals.sagepub.com/doi/10.1177/0022146519845069; Patricia Louie et al., "Race, Flourishing, and All-Cause Mortality in the United States, 1995–2016," *American Journal of Epidemiology* 190, no. 9 (September 2021): 1735–43, https://doi.org/10.1093/aje/kwab067.

41 **Black parents are more likely than white parents:** Holly M. Hart et al., "Generativity and Social Involvement Among African Americans and White Adults," *Journal of Research in Personality,* 35, no. 2 (June 2001), 208–30, https://www.sciencedirect.com/science/article/pii/S0092656601923189.

42 **Early arrivals to the United States see:** Noreen Goldman, "Will the Latino

Mortality Advantage Endure?" *Research on Aging,* 38, no. 3, 263–82, https://doi.org/10.1177/0164027515620242.

43 **"At one point [in 2021]":** Esther Wang, "Asian America Learns How to Hit Back," *New York Magazine,* September 26, 2022, https://nymag.com/intelligencer/article/stop-asian-hate-crimes-politics.html.

43 **Another finding of the Healthy Minds:** Sarah Ketchen Lipson et al., "Mental Health Disparities Among College Students of Color," *Journal of Adolescent Health* 63, no. 3 (September 2018): 348–56, https://doi.org/10.1016/j.jadohealth.2018.04.014.

43 **Meanwhile, heterosexual students:** Hans Oh, "Flourishing Among Young Adult College Students in the United States: Sexual/Gender and Racial/Ethnic Disparities," *Social Work in Mental Health* 21, no. 4 (December 2022): 347–59, https://doi.org/10.1080/15332985.2022.2155502; Hans Oh et al., "Flourishing and Psychotic Experiences Among College Students in the United States: Findings from the Healthy Minds Study 2020," *The Journal of Positive Psychology* 17, no. 5 (2022): 754–59, https://doi.org/10.1080/17439760.2021.1975162; Nicholas C. Borgogna et al., "Anxiety and Depression Across Gender and Sexual Minorities: Implications for Transgender, Gender Nonconforming, Pansexual, Demisexual, Asexual, Queer, and Questioning Individuals," *Psychology of Sexual Orientation and Gender Diversity* 6, no. 1 (2019): 54–63, https://doi.org/10.1037/sgd0000306; Sarah Ketchen Lipson et al., "Mental Health Disparities Among College Students of Color," *Journal of Adolescent Health* 63, no. 3 (September 2018): 348–56, https://doi.org/10.1016/j.jadohealth.2018.04.014; Sarah Ketchen Lipson et al., "Gender Minority Mental Health in the US: Results of a National Survey on College Campuses," *American Journal of Preventive Medicine* 57, no. 3 (2019): 293–301, https://www.ajpmonline.org/article/S0749-3797(19)30219-3/fulltext.

43 **As Sherry C. Wang:** Alyssa Lukpat, "Hate Crimes and Pandemic Lead More Asian Americans to Seek Therapy," *The New York Times,* October 15, 2021, https://www.nytimes.com/2021/10/15/us/asian-american-therapy-hate-crimes.html.

44 **One 2021 study found:** Patricia Louie et al. "Race, Flourishing, and All-Cause Mortality in the United States, 1995–2016," *American Journal of Epidemiology,* 190, no. 9 (September 2021): 1735–43, https://doi.org/10.1093/aje/kwab067.

45 **can activate our stress system:** Steven W. Cole et al., "Myeloid Differentiation Architecture of Leukocyte Transcriptome Dynamics in Perceived Social Isolation," *Proceedings of the National Academy of Sciences of the United States of America* 112, no. 49 (December 2015): 15142–47, http://www.pnas.org/content/early/2015/11/18/1514249112.full.pdf.

46 **English Longitudinal Study of Ageing:** Daisy Fancourt and Andrew Steptoe, "The Longitudinal Relationship Between Changes in Wellbeing and Inflammatory Markers: Are Associations Independent of Depression?," *Brain, Be-*

havior, and Immunity 83 (January 2020): 146–52, https://doi.org/10.1016/j .bbi.2019.10.004.

46 **The data gathered:** Chloe C. Boyle et al., "Changes in Eudaimonic Well-Being and the Conserved Transcriptional Response to Adversity in Younger Breast Cancer Survivors," *Psychoneuroendocrinology* 103 (May 2019): 173–79, https:// doi.org/10.1016/j.psyneuen.2019.01.024; Steven W. Cole et al., "Loneliness, Eudaimonia, and the Human Conserved Transcriptional Response to Adversity," *Psychoneuroendocrinology* 62 (December 2015): 11–17, https://doi .org/10.1016/j.psyneuen.2015.07.001; Barbara L. Fredrickson et al., "A Functional Genomic Perspective on Human Well-Being," *Proceedings of the National Academy of Sciences of the United States of America* 110, no. 33 (July 2013): 13684–89, https://doi.org/10.1073/pnas.130541911; Barbara L. Fredrickson et al., "Psychological Well-Being and the Human Conserved Transcriptional Response to Adversity," *PLOS One* 10, no. 3 (March 2015): e0121839, https:// doi.org/10.1371/journal.pone.0121839; Shinobu Kitayama et al., "Work, Meaning, and Gene Regulation: Findings from a Japanese Information Technology Firm," *Psychoneuroendocrinology* 72 (October 2016): 175–81, https:// doi.org/10.1016/j.psyneuen.2016.07.004; Sung-Ha Lee et al., "Psychological Well-Being and Gene Expression in Korean Adults: The Role of Age," *Psychoneuroendocrinology* 120 (October 2020): 104785, https://doi.org/10.1016/j .psyneuen.2020.104785; Jennifer S. Mascaro et al., "Flourishing in Healthcare Trainees: Psychological Well-Being and the Conserved Transcriptional Response to Adversity," *International Journal of Environmental Research and Public Health* 19, no. 4 (2022): 2255, https://doi.org/10.3390/ijerph19042255; Teresa Seeman et al., "Intergenerational Mentoring, Eudaimonic Well-Being and Gene Regulation in Older Adults: A Pilot Study," *Psychoneuroendocrinology* 111 (January 2020): 104468, https://doi.org/10.1016/j.psyneuen.2019 .104468; Jeffrey G. Snodgrass et al., "Positive Mental Well-Being and Immune Transcriptional Profiles in Highly Involved Videogame Players," *Brain, Behavior, and Immunity* 82 (November 2019): 84–92, https://doi.org/10.1016/j .bbi.2019.07.035.

Chapter Three:
The Feelings Trap

48 **Epicurus:** Ad Bergsma, Germaine Poot, and Aart C. Liefbroer, "Happiness in the Garden of Epicurus," *Journal of Happiness Studies* 9 (September 2008): 397–423, https://doi.org/10.1007/s10902-006-9036-z; Alain de Botton, "Philosophy: A Guide to Happiness—Epicurus on Happiness," part 2 of *Philosophy: A Guide to Happiness,* Channel 4, February 26, 2014, YouTube, https://www.youtube.com/watch?v=eLPeUWsBRvw.

48 **I name all six:** Paul Ekman, "An Argument for Basic Emotions," *Cognition and Emotion* 6, nos. 3–4 (1992): 169–200, https://www.paulekman.com /wp-content/uploads/2013/07/An-Argument-For-Basic-Emotions.pdf.

50   **Marvin:** Antonio Damasio's patient Marvin is featured in "The Adult Brain,"
     episode 4 of *The Secret Life of the Brain,* PBS, 2002, YouTube, https://www
     .youtube.com/watch?v=G5-HTuRGMmk.

51   **"We've transformed the world . . .":** Anna Lembke, *Dopamine Nation: Find-
     ing Balance in the Age of Indulgence* (New York: Dutton, 2023), 67.

52   **Unlike those in most:** Sieun An et al., "Two Sides of Emotion: Exploring
     Positivity and Negativity in Six Basic Emotions Across Cultures," *Frontiers in
     Psychology* 8 (April 2017): 610, https://doi.org/10.3389/fpsyg.2017.00610;
     Xinmei Deng et al., "Feeling Happy and Sad at the Same Time? Subcultural
     Differences in Experiencing Mixed Emotions Between Han Chinese and
     Mongolian Chinese," *Frontiers in Psychology* 7 (October 2016): 1692, https://
     doi.org/10.3389/fpsyg.2016.01692; Mohsen Joshanloo et al., "Fragility of
     Happiness Beliefs Across 15 National Groups," *Journal of Happiness Studies*
     16, no. 5 (October 2015): 1185–210, https://doi.org/10.1007/s10902-014
     -9553-0; Yuri Miyamoto and Carol D. Ryff, "Cultural Differences in the Dia-
     lectical and Non-dialectical Emotional Styles and Their Implications for
     Health," *Cognition and Emotion* 25, no. 1 (January 2011): 22–39, https://doi
     .org/10.1080/02699931003612114.

52   **Steven Hayes:** Steven C. Hayes et al., "Evolving an Idionomic Approach to
     Processes of Change: Towards a Unified Personalized Science of Human Im-
     provement," *Behaviour Research and Therapy* 156 (September 2022): 104155,
     https://doi.org/10.1016/j.brat.2022.104155.

53   **"The place you suffer . . .":** Susan Cain, *Bittersweet: How Sorrow and Longing
     Make Us Whole* (New York: Crown, 2022).

54   **If we could mitigate:** Roy F. Baumeister et al., "Bad Is Stronger than Good,"
     Review of General Psychology 5, no. 4 (December 2001): 323–70, https://doi
     .org/10.1037/1089-2680.5.4.323; Paul Rozin and Edward B. Royzman,
     "Negativity Bias, Negativity Dominance, and Contagion," *Personality and So-
     cial Psychology Review* 5, no. 4 (November 2001): 296–320, https://doi.org
     /10.1207/S15327957PSPR0504_2.

55   **"Picture a human infant . . .":** Emily A. Austin, *Living for Pleasure: An Epicu-
     rean Guide to Life* (New York: Oxford University Press, 2022), 29.

55   **His contemporary Aristotle:** Julia Annas and Hsin-li Wang, "Aristotle on
     Virtue and Happiness," *Philosophy and Culture* 35, no. 4 (1989): 157–70,
     https://philpapers.org/rec/ANNAOV; Julia Annas, "Happiness as Achieve-
     ment," *Daedalus* 133, no. 2 (Spring 2004): 44–51, https://www.amacad.org
     /publication/happiness-achievement; Corey L. M. Keyes and Julia Annas,
     "Feeling Good and Functioning Well: Distinctive Concepts in Ancient Phi-
     losophy and Contemporary Science," *The Journal of Positive Psychology* 4,
     no. 3 (2009): 197–201, https://doi.org/10.1080/17439760902844228.

60   **This eye-opening chart:** Corey L. M. Keyes et al., "The Relationship of Level
     of Positive Mental Health with Current Mental Disorders in Predicting Sui-
     cidal Behavior and Academic Impairment in College Students," *Journal of
     American College Health* 60, no. 2 (February 2012): 126–33, https://doi.org
     /10.1080/07448481.2011.608393.

Chapter Four:
You Are Not One-Dimensional

65 **overall, the conclusion is:** Ute Habel et al., "Same or Different? Neural Corre-
    lates of Happy and Sad Mood in Healthy Males," *NeuroImage* 26, no. 1 (May
    2005): 206–14, https://doi.org/10.1016/j.neuroimage.2005.01.014; Mark S.
    George et al., "Brain Activity During Transient Sadness and Happiness in
    Healthy Women," *American Journal of Psychiatry* 152, no. 3 (March 1995):
    341–51, https://doi.org/10.1176/ajp.152.3.341; Mario Pelletier et al., "Sepa-
    rate Neural Circuits for Primary Emotions? Brain Activity During Self-
    Induced Sadness and Happiness in Professional Actors," *Neuroreport* 14, no. 8
    (June 2003): 1111–16, https://doi.org/0.1097/00001756-200306110-00003.

66 **There is yet more evidence:** Corey L. M. Keyes, John M. Myers, and Ken-
    neth S. Kendler, "The Structure of the Genetic and Environmental Influences
    on Mental Well-Being," *American Journal of Public Health* 100, no. 12 (De-
    cember 2010): 2379–84, https://doi.org/10.2105/AJPH.2010.193615; Ken-
    neth S. Kendler et al., "The Relationship between the Genetic and
    Environmental Influences on Common Internalizing Psychiatric Disorders
    and Mental Well-Being," *Behavior Genetics* 41, no. 5 (September 2011):
    641–50, https://doi.org/10.1007/s10519-011-9466-1; Kenneth S. Kendler,
    John M. Myers, and Corey L. M. Keyes, "The Relationship between the Ge-
    netic and Environmental Influences on Common Externalizing Psychopa-
    thology and Mental Wellbeing," *Twin Research and Human Genetics* 14, no. 6
    (December 2011): 516–23, https://doi.org/10.1375/twin.14.6.516.

67 **My research on flourishing:** Keyes, Myers, and Kendler, "The Structure of
    the Genetic and Environmental Influences on Mental Well-Being."

67 **strong pathogenic factor:** Jue Lin, Elissa Epel, and Elizabeth Blackburn,
    "Telomeres and Lifestyle Factors: Roles in Cellular Aging," *Mutation Research/
    Fundamental and Molecular Mechanisms of Mutagenesis* 730, nos. 1–2 (Febru-
    ary 2012): 85–89, https://doi.org/10.1016/j.mrfmmm.2011.08.003; Elissa S.
    Epel et al., "Accelerated Telomere Shortening in Response to Life Stress," *Pro-
    ceedings of the National Academy of Sciences of the United States of America* 101,
    no. 49 (December 2004): 17312–15, https://doi.org/10.1073/pnas
    .040716210; Elissa Epel, "How 'Reversible' Is Telomeric Aging?," *Cancer Pre-
    vention Research* 5, no. 10 (October 2012): 1163–68, https://doi.org/10
    .1158/1940-6207.CAPR-12-0370.

68 **David Snowdon's Nun Study:** David Snowdon, *Aging with Grace: What the
    Nun Study Teaches Us About Leading Longer, Healthier, and More Meaningful
    Lives* (New York: Bantam, 2002).

69 **The nuns who had been active:** Anna I. Corwin, *Embracing Age: How Catho-
    lic Nuns Became Models of Aging Well* (New Brunswick, NJ: Rutgers Univer-
    sity Press, 2021).

69 **As new neurons and connections:** Edward Taub, Gitendra Uswatte, and
    Rama Pidikiti, "Constraint-Induced Movement Therapy: A New Family of
    Techniques with Broad Application to Physical Rehabilitation—A Clinical

Review," *Journal of Rehabilitation Research and Development* 36, no. 3 (July 1999): 237–51, https://pubmed.ncbi.nlm.nih.gov/10659807/.

70 **"Neuroscience research reveals . . .":** Rachel Zoffness, "Think Pain Is Purely Medical? Think Again," *Psychology Today,* October 25, 2019, https://www.psychologytoday.com/us/blog/pain-explained/201910/think-pain-is-purely-medical-think-again. See also Rachel Zoffness, *The Pain Management Workbook: Powerful CBT and Mindfulness Skills to Take Control of Pain and Reclaim Your Life* (Oakland, CA: New Harbinger Publications, 2020).

71 **As the twentieth century:** Christopher J. Murray and Alan D. Lopez, "Evidence-Based Health Policy—Lessons from the Global Burden of Disease Study," *Science* 274, no. 5288 (November 1996): 740–43, https://doi.org/10.1126/science.274.5288.740.

72 **A recent CDC study:** Debra J. Brody and Qiuping Gu, "Antidepressant Use Among Adults: United States, 2015–2018," National Center for Health Statistics Data Brief no. 377, September 2020, https://www.cdc.gov/nchs/products/databriefs/db377.htm.

72 **these numbers are consistent:** Laura J. Andrade et al., "Cross-National Comparisons of the Prevalences and Correlates of Mental Disorders," *Bulletin of the World Health Organization* 78, no. 4 (2000): 413–26, https://apps.who.int/iris/handle/10665/268101.

73 **"The good news is . . .":** "The Depression Report: A New Deal for Depression and Anxiety Disorders," Centre for Economic Performance, Mental Health Policy Group, London School of Economics, June 2006, http://eprints.lse.ac.uk/818/1/DEPRESSION_REPORT_LAYARD.pdf.

74 **"While there can be":** T. R. Insel and Edward M. Scolnick, "Cure Therapeutics and Strategic Prevention: Raising the Bar for Mental Health Research," *Molecular Psychiatry* 11, no. 1 (January 2006): 12–13, https://doi.org/10.1038/sj.mp.4001777.

74 **Permanent remission means a cure:** Ibid.

75 **Serotonin deficiency:** Robert Whitaker, *Anatomy of an Epidemic: Magic Bullets, Psychiatric Drugs, and the Astonishing Rise of Mental Illness in America* (New York: Crown, 2011).

76 **At most, the studies suggest:** Irving Kirsch, "Placebo Effect in the Treatment of Depression and Anxiety," *Frontiers in Psychiatry* 10 (June 2019): article 407, https://doi.org/10.3389/fpsyt.2019.00407.

76 **If you have a third episode:** Shysset Nuggerud-Galeas et al., "Analysis of Depressive Episodes, Their Recurrence and Pharmacologic Treatment in Primary Care Patients: A Retrospective Descriptive Study," *PLOS One* 15, no. 5 (May 2020): e0233454, https://doi.org/10.1371/journal.pone.0233454; Stephanie L. Burcusa and William G. Iacono, "Risk for Recurrence in Depression," *Clinical Psychology Review* 27, no. 8 (December 2007): 959–85, https://doi.org/10.1016/j.cpr.2007.02.005; "The Depression Report: A New Deal for Depression and Anxiety Disorders."

79 **"A Tuesday in the Life . . .":** Lahnna I. Catalino and Barbara L. Fredrickson, "A Tuesday in the Life of a Flourisher: The Role of Positive Emotional Reac-

tivity in Optimal Mental Health," *Emotion* 11, no. 4 (2011): 938–50, https://doi.org/10.1037/a0024889.

80 **One study followed:** Alexandra Drake et al., "Daily Stressor–Related Negative Mood and Its Associations with Flourishing and Daily Curiosity," *Journal of Happiness Studies* 23, no. 2 (February 2022): 423–38, https://doi.org/10.1007/s10902-021-00404-2. Stressful work situations didn't correlate with the subjects' languishing. But whether or not they had a supportive work environment did. The study made clear that working in an environment that is both *not* supportive and highly demanding will undermine your well-being and make it more likely that you will languish.

81 **My decades of work:** See also David Brooks, "Should you live for your résumé . . . or your eulogy?," TED, April 14, 2014, YouTube, https://www.youtube.com/watch?v=MlLWTeApqIM.

Chapter Five:
Learn: Creating Stories of Self-Growth

89 **"historians of the self":** Dan P. McAdams, "The Psychology of Life Stories," *Review of General Psychology* 5, no. 2 (2001): 100–22, https://www.sesp.northwestern.edu/docs/publications/430816076490a3ddfc3fe1.pdf.

90 *illusory superiority:* Janey Davies, "What Is Illusory Superiority & 8 Signs You Could Suffer from It," Learning Mind, July 10, 2021, https://www.learning-mind.com/illusory-superiority/.

90 **Indeed, studies have found:** Jeff Haden, "Science Says Stop Infecting Other People with the Better-Than-Average Effect," *Inc.,* October 12, 2020, https://www.inc.com/jeff-haden/science-says-stop-infecting-other-people-with-better-than-average-effect.html.

99 **"step into uncharted . . .":** Pema Chödrön, *When Things Fall Apart: Heart Advice for Difficult Times* (Boulder, CO: Shambhala, 2016), XI.

100 **People with less envy:** Ines Schindler, "Relations of Admiration and Adoration with Other Emotions and Well-Being," *Psychology of Well-Being* 4, no. 14 (August 2014): 1–23, https://doi.org/10.1186/s13612-014-0014-7.

101 **As we turn:** Ibid.

101 **For most people, moving away:** Christine Robitschek and Corey L. M. Keyes, "Keyes's Model of Mental Health with Personal Growth Initiative as a Parsimonious Predictor," *Journal of Counseling Psychology* 56, no. 2 (2009): 321–29, https://doi.org/10.1037/a0013954.

101 **This is why so many people can't escape:** Corey L. M. Keyes and Carol D. Ryff, "Subjective Change and Mental Health: A Self-Concept Theory," *Social Psychology Quarterly* 63, no. 3 (September 2000): 264–79, https://doi.org/10.2307/2695873. Corey L. M. Keyes, "Subjective Change and Its Consequences for Emotional Well-Being," *Motivation and Emotion* 24, no. 2 (June 2000): 67–84, https://doi.org/10.1023/A:1005659114155; Gerben J. Westerhof and Corey L. M. Keyes, "After the Fall of the Berlin Wall: Perceptions and Consequences of Stability and Change Among Middle-Aged and

Older East and West Germans," *The Journals of Gerontology Series B: Psychological Sciences and Social Sciences* 61, no. 5 (September 2006): S240–S247, https://doi.org/10.1093/geronb/61.5.s240.

102 **"Many self-help gurus . . .":** K. C. Davis, *How to Keep House While Drowning: A Gentle Approach to Cleaning and Organizing* (New York: Simon Element, 2022), 15.

104 **We have to *feel*:** Nicholas E. Handoyom et al., "The Importance of Developing Meaningfulness and Manageability for Resilience in Rural Doctors," *Medical Teacher* 45, no. 1 (January 2023): 32–39, https://doi.org/10.1080/0142159X.2022.2128734; James Clear, "The Goldilocks Rule: How to Stay Motivated in Life and Business," Medium, July 12, 2016, https://medium.com/the-mission/the-goldilocks-rule-how-to-stay-motivated-in-life-and-business-399d57d69825; Benedikt Hackert et al., "Towards a Reconceptualization of Flow in Social Contexts," *Journal for the Theory of Social Behaviour* 53, no. 1 (2023): 100–25, https://doi.org/10.1111/jtsb.12362.

106 **But remember:** Giovanni A. Fava, "Allostatic Load in Clinical Practice," *Clinical Psychological Science* 11, no. 2 (2023): 345–56, https://doi.org/10.1177/21677026221121216; Christin Gerhardt et al., "How are Social Stressors at Work Related to Well-Being and Health? A Systematic Review and Meta-Analysis," *BMC Public Health* 21, no. 1 (May 2021): 890, https://doi.org/10.1186/s12889-021-10894-7.

108 **A study of how people:** Abiola Keller et al., "Does the Perception that Stress Affects Health Matter? The Association with Health and Mortality," *Health Psychology* 31, no. 5 (September 2012): 677–84, https://doi.org/10.1037/a0026743.

111 **Researchers at the Stanford University School of Medicine:** Tracie White, "Medical Errors May Stem More from Physician Burnout than Unsafe Health Care Settings," Stanford Medicine, July 8, 2018, https://med.stanford.edu/news/all-news/2018/07/medical-errors-may-stem-more-from-physician-burnout.html.

111 **But research on doctors who:** Margaret Plews-Ogan, Justine E. Owens, and Natalie B. May, "Wisdom Through Adversity: Learning and Growing in the Wake of an Error," *Patient Education and Counseling* 91, no. 2 (May 2013): 236–42, https://doi.org/10.1016/j.pec.2012.12.006.

Chapter Six:
Connect: Building Warm and Trusting Relationships

115 **"In each of my friends . . .":** C. S. Lewis, *The Four Loves* (New York: Harcourt, 1991), 95.

117 **Gangs—of all different kinds:** David C. Pyrooz, " 'From Your First Cigarette to Your Last Dyin' Day': The Patterning of Gang Membership in the Life-Course," *Journal of Quantitative Criminology* 30, no. 2 (2014): 349–72, https://doi.org/10.1007/s10940-013-9206-1; David C. Pyrooz and Gary Sweeten, "Gang Membership Between Ages 5 and 17 Years in the United States," *Journal of Adolescent Health* 56, no. 4 (April 2015): 414–19, https://

doi.org/10.1016/j.jadohealth.2014.11.018; James C. Howell, "Youth Gangs," Office of Juvenile Justice and Delinquency Prevention, December 1997, https://www.ojp.gov/pdffiles/fs-9772.pdf; "Gangs and Children," *Journal of the American Academy of Child & Adolescent Psychiatry* 98 (September 2017), https://www.aacap.org/AACAP/Families_and_Youth/Facts_for_Families /FFF-Guide/Children-and-Gangs-098.aspx; G. David Curry, Scott H. Decker, and David C. Pyrooz, *Confronting Gangs: Crime and Community,* 3rd ed. (New York: Oxford University Press, 2013).

119 **deny and suppress the development:** Daniel H. Pink, *Drive: The Surprising Truth About What Motivates Us* (New York: Riverhead Books, 2009); Edward L. Deci, Anja H. Olafsen, and Richard M. Ryan, "Self-Determination Theory in Work Organizations: The State of a Science," *Annual Review of Organizational Psychology and Organizational Behavior* 4 (2017): 19–43, https://doi .org/10.1146/annurev-orgpsych-032516-113108. For an accessible overview of Self-Determination Theory and the importance of feeling competent, which is the adult version of effectance, see Kendra Cherry, "What Is Self-Determination Theory?," Very Well Mind, November 8, 2022, https://www .verywellmind.com/what-is-self-determination-theory-2795387.

126 **The scale to measure mattering:** Morris Rosenberg and B. Claire McCullough, "Mattering: Inferred Significance and Mental Health Among Adolescents," *Research in Community and Mental Health* 2 (1981): 163–82, https://psycnet.apa.org/record/1983-07744-001.

126 **The midlife adult:** Rosenberg and McCullough, "Mattering: Inferred Significance and Mental Health Among Adolescents."

127 **"internalize thoughts . . .":** Gordon L. Flett et al., "Antecedents, Correlates, and Consequences of Feeling like You Don't Matter: Associations with Maltreatment, Loneliness, Social Anxiety, and the Five-Factor Model," *Personality and Individual Differences* 92 (2016): 52–56, https://doi.org/10.1016/j.paid .2015.12.014. See also Sarah E. McComb et al., "The Double Jeopardy of Feeling Lonely and Unimportant: State and Trait Loneliness and Feelings and Fears of Not Mattering," *Frontiers in Psychology* 11 (December 2020): 563420, https://doi.org/10.3389/fpsyg.2020.563420.

I collected the following results from the first author of these papers and the sample in her 2021 paper "Is Positive Mental Health and the Absence of Mental Illness the Same?" based on personal requests:

Category	Frequencies
Flourishing	45.6% (402)
Languishing moderately	23.5% (207)
Languishing severely	4.1% (36)
Depression (10 or higher on EPDS)	26.9% (237)

Depression is based on a score of 10 or higher (indicating clinically relevant postpartum depressive symptoms) on the Edinburgh Postpartum Depression Scale

Below are the percentages considering the Edinburgh Postnatal Depression Scale (EPDS) cutoff scores from the article using the Beck Depression Inventory to establish cutpoints; see Jennifer E. McCabe-Beane et al., "The Identification of Severity Ranges for the Edinburgh Postnatal Depression Scale," *Journal of Reproductive and Infant Psychology* 34, no. 3 (February 2016): 293–303, https://doi.org/10.1080/02646838.2016.1141346.

Edinburgh Postpartum Depression Scale scores arrayed by depression severity using the Beck Depression Scale cutpoints	Frequencies
None or minimal (0–6)	37.2% (328)
Mild (7–13)	45.4% (400)
Moderate (14–19)	13.8 (122)
Severe (19–30)	3.6% (32)

134 **Having friends from different backgrounds:** "The Power of Diverse Friendships," Centerstone, May 17, 2023, https://centerstone.org/our-resources/health-wellness/the-power-of-diverse-friendships/.

134 **Studies have shown:** "Workplace Diversity Training Works Better with Cross-Race Friendship," I-O AT WORK, November 18, 2020, https://www.ioatwork.com/workplace-diversity-training-with-cross-race-friendship/.

135 **As we age:** Corey L. M. Keyes, "The Exchange of Emotional Support with Age and Its Relationship with Emotional Well-Being by Age," *The Journals of Gerontology Series B: Psychological Sciences and Social Sciences* 57, no. 6 (November 2002): P518–P525, https://doi.org/10.1093/geronb/57.6.p518; Yoh Murayama et al., "The Effects of Reciprocal Support on Mental Health Among Intergenerational Non-relatives—A Comparison by Age Group," *Archives of Gerontology and Geriatrics* 99 (March 2022): 104601, https://doi.org/10.1016/j.archger.2021.104601; Arpana Pandit and Yoshinori Nakagawa, "How Does Reciprocal Exchange of Social Support Alleviate Individuals' Depression in an Earthquake-Damaged Community?," *International Journal of Environmental Research and Public Health* 18, no. 4 (February 2021): 1585, https://doi.org/10.3390/ijerph18041585.

136 **Growing income inequality:** Shigehiro Oishi, Selin Kesebir, and Ed Diener, "Income Inequality and Happiness," *Psychological Science* 22, no. 9 (August 2011): 1095–1100, https://doi.org/10.1177/0956797611417262; Kelly Kirkland et al., "Moral Expansiveness Around the World: The Role of Societal Factors Across 36 Countries," *Social Psychological and Personality Science* 14, no. 3 (2023): 305–18, https://doi.org/10.1177/1948550622110176; Daniel M. Stancato, Dacher Keltner, and Serena Chen, "The Gap Between Us: Income Inequality Reduces Social Affiliation in Dyadic Interactions," *Personality and Social Psychology Bulletin* (April 2023): https://doi.org/10.1177/01461672231164213.

136 **Here, the wealthier you are:** Patrick Sharkey, "To Avoid Integration, Americans Built Barricades in Urban Space," *The Atlantic,* June 20, 2020, https://
www.theatlantic.com/ideas/archive/2020/06/barricades-let-urban-inequality
-fester/613312/.

137 **It is the same sense:** Jun Wu, Xiaochen Hu, and Erin A. Orrick, "The Relationship between Motivations for Joining Gangs and Violent Offending: A
Preliminary Test on Self-Determination Theory," *Victims and Offenders* 17,
no. 3 (2022): 335–49, https://doi.org/10.1080/15564886.2021.1898508;
Caylin Louis Moore and Forrest Stuart, "Gang Research in the Twenty-First
Century," *Annual Review of Criminology* 5 (January 2022): 299–320, https://
doi.org/10.1146/annurev-criminol-030920-094656.

Chapter Seven:
Transcend: Accepting the Inevitable Plot Twists of Life

138 **"A human being is . . .":** Albert Einstein, letter to Dr. Robert Marcus, February 12, 1950, The Library of Consciousness, https://www.organism.earth
/library/document/letter-to-dr-robert-marcus.

142 **". . . a concealed, contagious . . .":** Mary Lamia, "Shame: A Concealed, Contagious, and Dangerous Emotion," *Psychology Today,* April 4, 2011, https://
www.psychologytoday.com/us/blog/intense-emotions-and-strong-feelings
/201104/shame-concealed-contagious-and-dangerous-emotion.

143 **a TEDx Talk:** TEDx Talks, "The Power of Mindfulness: What You Practice
Grows Stronger | Shauna Shapiro | TEDxWashington Square," YouTube,
March 10, 2017, https://www.youtube.com/watch?v=IeblJdB2-Vo.

143 **Shapiro's meditation teacher:** Shauna Shapiro, *Good Morning, I Love You:
Mindfulness and Self-Compassion Practices to Rewire Your Brain for Calm, Clarity, and Joy* (Louisville, CO: Sounds True, 2022), 177–78.

147 **In two experimental trials:** Ernst T. Bohlmeijer et al., "Efficacy of an Early
Intervention Based on Acceptance and Commitment Therapy for Adults with
Depressive Symptomatology: Evaluation in a Randomized Controlled Trial,"
Behaviour Research and Therapy 49, no. 1 (January 2011): 62–67, https://doi
.org/10.1016/j.brat.2010.10.003; Ernst T. Bohlmeijer, Sanne M. A. Lamers,
and Martine Fledderus, "Flourishing in People with Depressive Symptomatology Increases with Acceptance and Commitment Therapy. Post-hoc Analyses of a Randomized Controlled Trial," *Behaviour Research and Therapy* 65
(February 2015): 101–06, https://doi.org/10.1016/j.brat.2014.12.014. See
also Rebecca J. North et al., "From Failure to Flourishing: The Roles of Acceptance and Goal Reengagement," *Journal of Adult Development* 21, no. 4
(September 2014): 239–50, https://doi.org/10.1007/s10804-014-9195-9.

148 **Study after study supports:** Michael M. Prinzing, "Religion Gives Life Meaning. Can Anything Else Take Its Place?," Psyche, April 27, 2022, https://
psyche.co/ideas/religion-gives-life-meaning-can-anything-else-take-its-place.

149 *satisfaction* **with life:** Shigehiro Oishi and Ed Diener, "Residents of Poor Nations Have a Greater Sense of Meaning in Life than Residents of Wealthy Na-

tions," *Psychological Science* 25, no. 2 (February 2014): 422–30, https://doi
.org/10.1177/0956797613507286.

149 **"Religiousness may foster . . .":** Michael Prinzing, Patty Van Cappellen, and
Barbara L. Fredrickson, "More Than a Momentary Blip in the Universe? Investigating the Link Between Religiousness and Perceived Meaning in Life,"
Personality and Social Psychology Bulletin 49, no. 2 (December 2021): 180–96,
https://doi.org/10.1177/01461672211060136.

150 **The results showed:** Laura Upenieks, Scott Schieman, and Christopher G.
Ellison, "Does Religiosity Buffer the Adverse Mental Health Effects of Work-
Family Strain? Examining the Role of an Overlooked Resource," *Review of
Religious Research* 65, no. 1 (March 2023): 7–36, https://doi.org/10.1177
/0034673X231171788.

151 **The Indigenous Language Institute:** Steph Koyfman, "What Was, and
What Is: Native American Languages in the United States," *Babbel Magazine*,
June 8, 2023, https://www.babbel.com/en/magazine/native-american
-languages-in-the-us.

151 **In their research, they discovered:** Michael J. Chandler and Christopher E.
Lalonde, "Cultural Continuity as a Hedge Against Suicide in Canada's First
Nations," *Transcultural Psychiatry* 35, no. 2 (June 1998): 191–219, https://
doi.org/10.1177/13634615980350020; Michael J. Chandler and Christopher E. Lalonde, "Cultural Continuity as a Protective Factor Against Suicide
in First Nations Youth," *Horizons* 10, no. 1 (January 2008): 68–72, https://
www.researchgate.net/publication/239921354_Cultural_Continuity_as_a
_Protective_Factor_Against_Suicide_in_First_Nations_Youth; Brittany
Barker, Ashley Goodman, and Kora DeBeck, "Reclaiming Indigenous Identities: Culture as Strength Against Suicide Among Indigenous Youth in Canada," *Canadian Journal of Public Health* 108, no. 2 (June 2017): e208–e210,
https://doi.org/10.17269/cjph.108.5754.

151 **They also found:** Darcy Hallett, Michael J. Chandler, and Christopher E.
Lalonde, "Aboriginal Language Knowledge and Youth Suicide," *Cognitive Development* 22, no. 3 (July 2007): 392–99, https://doi.org/10.1016/j.cogdev
.2007.02.001; Jeffrey Ansloos, "Rethinking Indigenous Suicide," *International Journal of Indigenous Health* 13, no. 2 (December 2018): 8–28, https://
doi.org/10.32799/ijih.v13i2.32061.

151 **Through their native language:** Jessica Saniguq Ullrich, "For the Love of Our
Children: An Indigenous Connectedness Framework," *AlterNative: An International Journal of Indigenous Peoples* 15, no. 2 (February 2019): 121–30,
https://doi.org/10.1177/1177180119828114.

154 **researchers looked at two groups:** Sharon Begley, *Train Your Mind, Change
Your Brain: How a New Science Reveals Our Extraordinary Potential to Trans-
form Ourselves* (New York: Ballantine Books, 2007).

156 **Some sutras promise:** Bellur Krishnamachar Sundaraja Iyengar, *Light on the
Yoga Sutras of Patanjali* (San Francisco: Aquarian/Thorsons, 1993), 82.

158 **A full yoga practice:** Alyson Ross et al., "Frequency of Yoga Practice Predicts
Health: Results of a National Survey of Yoga Practitioners," *Evidence-Based*

Complementary and Alternative Medicine 2012 (August 2012): 1–10, https://doi.org/10.1155/2012/983258.

160 **that "religious attendance is associated . . .":** Sunshine Rote, Terrence D. Hill, and Christopher G. Ellison, "Religious Attendance and Loneliness in Later Life," *The Gerontologist* 53, no. 1 (February 2013): 39–50, https://doi.org/10.1093/geront/gns063.

162 **thousands of studies show:** Bassam Khoury et al., "Mindfulness-Based Stress Reduction for Healthy Individuals: A Meta-Analysis," *Journal of Psychosomatic Research* 78, no. 6 (June 2015): 519–28, https://doi.org/10.1016/j.jpsychores.2015.03.009; Juan Li et al., "Effectiveness of Mindfulness-Based Interventions on Anxiety, Depression, and Fatigue in People with Lung Cancer: A Systematic Review and Meta-Analysis," *International Journal of Nursing Studies* 140 (April 2023): https://doi.org/10.1016/j.ijnurstu.2023.104447.

Chapter Eight:
Help: Finding Your Purpose (Even in the Mundane)

165 **"the place where . . .":** Frederick Buechner, *Wishful Thinking: A Seeker's ABC* (New York: Harper and Row, 1973), 19.

165 **The journalist Po Bronson:** Po Bronson, *What Should I Do with My Life? The True Story of People Who Answered the Ultimate Question* (New York: Random House, 2002).

165 **But purpose is not:** Larissa Rainey, "The Search for Purpose in Life: An Exploration of Purpose, the Search Process, and Purpose Anxiety," Masters of Applied Positive Psychology Capstone Projects, University of Pennsylvania, August 2014, https://core.ac.uk/reader/76383860; David B. Newman, John B. Nezlek, and Todd M. Thrash, "The Dynamics of Searching for Meaning and Presence of Meaning in Daily Life," *Journal of Personality* 86, no. 3 (June 2018): 368–79, https://doi.org/10.1111/jopy.12321; Michael F. Steger et al., "Understanding the Search for Meaning in Life: Personality, Cognitive Style, and the Dynamic Between Seeking and Experiencing Meaning," *Journal of Personality* 76, no. 2 (April 2008): 199–228, https://doi.org/10.1111/j.1467-6494.2007.00484.x.

169 **Research shows that:** Patrick L. Hill et al., "Sense of Purpose Moderates the Associations Between Daily Stressors and Daily Well-Being," *Annals of Behavioral Medicine: A Publication of the Society of Behavioral Medicine* 52, no. 8 (August 2018): 724–29, https://doi.org/10.1093/abm/kax039.

170 **resilience in military veterans:** Kayla Isaacs et al., "Psychological Resilience in U.S. Military Veterans: A 2-Year, Nationally Representative Prospective Cohort Study," *Journal of Psychiatric Research* 84 (2017): 301–09, https://doi.org/10.1016/j.jpsychires.2016.10.017.

171 **Conceptions of good health portray:** Carol D. Ryff, "Happiness Is Everything, or Is It? Explorations on the Meaning of Psychological Well-Being," *Journal of Personality and Social Psychology* 57, no. 6 (1989): 1069–81, https://doi.org/10.1037/0022-3514.57.6.1069; Carol D. Ryff and Corey

Lee M. Keyes, "The Structure of Psychological Well-Being Revisited," *Journal of Personality and Social Psychology* 69, no. 4 (October 1995): 719–27, https://doi.org/10.1037//0022-3514.69.4.719.

171 **The psychiatrist Viktor Frankl:** Viktor E. Frankl, *Man's Search for Meaning* (New York: Simon and Schuster, 1959).

171 **Social contribution is:** Corey L. M. Keyes, "Authentic Purpose: The Spiritual Infrastructure of Life," *Journal of Management, Spirituality and Religion* 8, no. 4 (November 2011): 281–97, https://doi.org/10.1080/14766086.2011.630133.

174 **Matilda Riley:** Matilda White Riley et al., *Age and Structural Lag: Society's Failure to Provide Meaningful Opportunities in Work, Family, and Leisure* (New York: John Wiley & Sons, 1994).

176 **A study of youths:** Heather Malin, Parissa J. Ballard, and William Damon, "Civic Purpose: An Integrated Construct for Understanding Civic Development in Adolescence," *Human Development* 58, no. 2 (June 2015): 103–30, https://doi.org/10.1159/000381655. See also William Damon and Heather Malin, "The Development of Purpose," in *The Oxford Handbook of Moral Development: An Interdisciplinary Perspective,* ed. Lene Arnett Jensen (New York: Oxford University Press, 2020), 110; Seana Moran, "Purpose: Giftedness in Intrapersonal Intelligence," *High Ability Studies* 20, no. 2 (December 2009): 143–59, https://doi.org/10.1080/13598130903358501; Seana Moran et al., "How Supportive of Their *Specific* Purposes Do Youth Believe Their Family and Friends Are?," *Journal of Adolescent Research* 28, no. 3 (2013): 348–77, https://doi.org/10.1177/0743558412457816; Kirsi Tirri and Brandy Quinn, "Exploring the Role of Religion and Spirituality in the Development of Purpose: Case Studies of Purposeful Youth," *British Journal of Religious Education* 32, no. 3 (July 2010): 201–14, https://doi.org/10.1080/01416200.2010.498607.

177 **Studies suggest:** See, for example, Moran et al., "How Supportive of Their Specific Purposes Do Youth Believe Their Family and Friends Are?"; Damon and Malin, "The Development of Purpose."

178 **Asian American families have:** Gloria Guzman, "Household Income: 2021. American Community Survey Briefs," U.S. Census Bureau, October 4, 2022, https://www.census.gov/library/publications/2022/acs/acsbr-011.html.

178 **But this just isn't true:** The findings reported are from the combined 2007 and 2009 data from the Healthy Minds Study of college undergraduates, and the analyses presented here combined two years from this study when the study used the MHC-SF, which resulted in data from 9,296 undergraduate college students (6,955 white students, 563 African American students, 760 Hispanic students, and 1,018 Asian American students). The findings reported here, although they may seemed old or outdated, have been replicated in the Healthy Minds data that are much more recent and use an eight-item scale called the Flourishing Scale.

178 **The stereotype is:** Han Na Suh et al., "The Role of Model Minority Stereotype on General Self-Efficacy and Depressive Symptoms," *The Counseling Psycholo-*

gist 51, no. 1 (2023): 62–83, https://doi.org/10.1177/00110000221130016; Tiffany Yip et al., "Development Against the Backdrop of the Model Minority Myth: Strengths and Vulnerabilities Among Asian American Adolescents and Young Adults," in *APA Handbook of Adolescent and Young Adult Development*, ed. L. J. Crockett, G. Carlo, and J. E. Schulenberg (Washington, DC: American Psychological Association, 2022), 359–74, https://doi.org/10.1037 /0000298-022; Lazar Stankov, "Unforgiving Confucian Culture: A Breeding Ground for High Academic Achievement, Test Anxiety and Self-Doubt?," *Learning and Individual Differences* 20, no. 6 (December 2010): 555–63, https://doi.org/10.1016/j.lindif.2010.05.003.

178 **Compared to other racial:** Chuansheng Chen and Harold W. Stevenson, "Motivation and Mathematics Achievement: A Comparative Study of Asian-American, Caucasian-American, and East Asian High School Students," *Child Development* 66, no. 4 (1995): 1215–34, https://doi.org/10 .2307/1131808; Jamie Lew, *Asian Americans in Class: Charting the Achievement Gap Among Korean American Youth* (New York: Teachers College Press, 2006); So Yoon Yoon and Marcia Gentry, "Racial and Ethnic Representation in Gifted Programs: Current Status of and Implications for Gifted Asian American Students," *Gifted Child Quarterly* 53, no. 2 (April 2009): 121–36, https://doi.org/10.1177/00169862083305; Scott J. Peters et al., "Effect of Local Norms on Racial and Ethnic Representation in Gifted Education," *AERA Open* 5, no. 2 (May 2019): 1–18, https://doi.org/10.1177 /2332858419848446.

179 **Asian American youths reportedly:** Shelley Sang-Hee Lee, *A New History of Asian America* (New York: Routledge, 2013); Rachel U. Mun and Nancy B. Hertzog, "The Influence of Parental and Self-Expectations on Asian American Women Who Entered College Early," *Gifted Child Quarterly* 63, no. 2 (January 2019): 120–40, https://doi.org/10.1177/00169862188235.

179 **Their abilities and academic interests:** Mun and Hertzog, "The Influence of Parental and Self-Expectations on Asian American Women Who Entered College Early."

179 **Since 1990, there has been:** Thomas Curran and Andrew P. Hill, "Perfectionism Is Increasing over Time: A Meta-Analysis of Birth Cohort Differences from 1989 to 2016," *Psychological Bulletin* 145, no. 4 (2019): 410–29, http:// dx.doi.org/10.1037/bul0000138.

179 **This shift has occurred:** Matthias Doepke, Giuseppe Sorrenti, and Fabrizio Zilibotti, "The Economics of Parenting," *Annual Review of Economics* 11, no. 1 (February 2019): 55–84, https://www.nber.org/papers/w25533; Matthias Doepke and Fabrizio Zilibotti, *Love, Money, and Parenting: How Economics Explains the Way We Raise Our Kids* (Princeton, NJ: Princeton University Press, 2019).

180 **parents' rising expectations:** Carol D. Ryff, Pamela S. Schmutte, and Young Hyun Lee, "How Children Turn Out: Implications for Parental Self-Evaluation," in *The Parental Experience in Midlife,* ed. C. D. Ryff and M. M. Seltzer (Chicago: University of Chicago Press, 1996), 383–422.

This chapter reviews evidence that the top two goals parents have when
they reach midlife and see their kids go off to college is for them (1) to get
a good education at college and (2) to be happy. That was true of both
mothers and fathers.

180 **People who are more self-compassionate:** Juliana G. Breines and Serena
Chen, "Self-Compassion Increases Self-Improvement Motivation," *Personality
and Social Psychology Bulletin* 38, no. 9 (September 2012): 1133–43, https://
doi.org/10.1177/0146167212445599; Jia Wei Zhang and Serena Chen,
"Self-Compassion Promotes Personal Improvement from Regret Experiences
via Acceptance," *Personality and Social Psychology Bulletin* 42, no. 2 (February
2016): 244–58, https://doi.org/10.1177/0146167215623271; Jia Wei
Zhang, Serena Chen, and Teodora K. Tomova Shakur, "From Me to You:
Self-Compassion Predicts Acceptance of Own and Others' Imperfections,"
Personality and Social Psychology Bulletin 46, no. 2 (February 2020): 228–42,
https://doi.org/10.1177/0146167219853846; Jofel D. Umandap and Lota A.
Teh, "Self-Compassion as a Mediator Between Perfectionism and Personal
Growth Initiative," *Psychological Studies* 65 (August 2020): 227–38, https://
doi.org/10.1007/s12646-020-00566-8.

180 **discourage maladaptive perfectionism:** Hyun-joo Park and Dae Yong Jeong,
"Moderation Effects of Perfectionism and Meaning in Life on Depression,"
Personality and Individual Differences 98 (August 2016): 25–29, https://doi
.org/10.1016/j.paid.2016.03.073.

180 **Viktor Frankl argued:** Michael F. Steger, Shigehiro Oishi, and Selin Kesebir,
"Is a Life Without Meaning Satisfying? The Moderating Role of the Search
for Meaning in Satisfaction with Life Judgments," *The Journal of Positive Psychology* 6, no. 3 (September 2011): 173–80, https://doi.org/10.1080/174397
60.2011.569171; Nansook Park, Myungsook Park, and Christopher Peter-
son, "When Is the Search for Meaning Related to Life Satisfaction?," *Applied
Psychology: Health and Well-Being* 2, no. 1 (February 2010): 1–13, https://doi
.org/10.1111/j.1758-0854.2009.01024.x.

183 **Most adults (56 percent):** James C. Davidson and David P. Caddell, "Religion and the Meaning of Work," *Journal for the Scientific Study of Religion* 33,
no. 2 (June 1994): 135–47, https://doi.org/10.2307/1386600; Amy Wrzes-
niewski et al., "Jobs, Careers, and Callings: People's Relations to Their Work,"
Journal of Research in Personality 31, no. 1 (March 1997): 21–33, https://doi
.org/10.1006/jrpe.1997.2162; Sarah J. Ward and Laura A. King, "Work and
the Good Life: How Work Contributes to Meaning in Life," *Research in Organizational Behavior* 37, no. 3 (January 2017): 59–82, https://doi.org/10
.1016/j.riob.2017.10.001.

184 **Without attributing causality:** Davidson and Caddell, "Religion and the
Meaning of Work."

184 **C. B. Macpherson:** C. B. Macpherson, *The Political Theory of Possessive Individualism: Hobbes to Locke* (Oxford, UK: Clarendon Press), 1962.

188 **In a recent study on kindness:** S. Katherine Nelson et al., "Do unto Others
or Treat Yourself? The Effects of Prosocial and Self-Focused Behavior on Psy-

chological Flourishing," *Emotion* 16, no. 6 (September 2016): 850–61, http://dx.doi.org/10.1037/emo0000178.

191 **adults who identified themselves:** Corey L. M. Keyes, "Social Functioning and Social Well-Being: Studies of the Social Nature of Personal Wellness," PhD diss., University of Wisconsin–Madison, 1995. See also Elisabetta Magnani and Rong Zhu, "Does Kindness Lead to Happiness? Voluntary Activities and Subjective Well-Being," *Journal of Behavioral and Experimental Economics* 77 (December 2018): 20–28, https://doi.org/10.1016/j.socec.2018.09.009; Ricky N. Lawton et al., "Does Volunteering Make Us Happier, or Are Happier People More Likely to Volunteer? Addressing the Problem of Reverse Causality When Estimating the Wellbeing Impacts of Volunteering," *Journal of Happiness Studies* 22, no. 2 (February 2021): 599–624, https://doi.org/10.1007/s10902-020-00242-8.

Chapter Nine:
Play: Stepping Out of Time

195 **a touching *New York Times* article:** Kerry Egan, "No Love Is Ever Wasted," *The New York Times,* March 10, 2023, https://www.nytimes.com/2023/03/10/style/modern-love-no-love-is-ever-wasted.html.

196 **Stuart Brown, a psychiatrist:** Stuart L. Brown, *Play: How it Shapes the Brain, Opens the Imagination and Invigorates the Soul* (New York: Avery, 2009).

200 **HighScope Perry Preschool Study:** Lawrence J. Schweinhart et al., "The HighScope Perry Preschool Study Through Age 40: Summary, Conclusions, and Frequently Asked Questions," HighScope Educational Research Foundation, 2005, https://nieer.org/wp-content/uploads/2014/09/specialsummary_rev2011_02_2.pdf; James J. Heckman et al., "The Rate of Return to the HighScope Perry Preschool Program," *Journal of Public Economics* 94, no. 1–2 (February 2010): 114–28, https://doi.org/10.1016/j.jpubeco.2009.11.001; Greg Parks, "The HighScope Perry Preschool Project," Office of Juvenile Justice and Delinquency Prevention, October 2000, https://www.ojp.gov/pdffiles1/ojjdp/181725.pdf.

202 **Joe Frost, one of the leading:** Joe L. Frost and Paul J. Jacobs, "Play Deprivation: A Factor in Juvenile Violence," *Dimensions of Early Childhood* 23, no. 3 (Spring 1995): 14–20, 39, https://eric.ed.gov/?id=EJ501994; Joe L. Frost and John A. Sutterby, "Outdoor Play Is Essential to Whole Child Development," *Young Children* 72, no. 3 (July 2017): 82–85, https://openlab.bmcc.cuny.edu/ece-110-lecture/wp-content/uploads/sites/98/2019/11/Frost-Supperby-2017.pdf.

203 **"arbitrariness, skill-lessness . . .":** C. Thi Nguyen, "The Right Way to Play a Game," *Game Studies* 19, no. 1 (May 2019): 1, https://gamestudies.org/1901/articles/nguyen.

206 **I might argue:** This is the point that Mihalyi Csikszentmihalyi made in his seminal work on flow. When adults are engaged and engrossed in leisure or work activities, not only do they experience the mental state of flow, but the

state of being in flow is conducive to creativity and enjoyment, fun, and well-being. See Mihaly Csikszentmihalyi, "Flow and Creativity," *NAMTA Journal* 22, no. 2 (Spring 1997): 60–97, https://eric.ed.gov/?id=ej547968; Mihaly Csikszentmihalyi, Sami Abuhamdeh, and Jeanne Nakamura, "Flow," in Mihaly Csikszentmihalyi, *Flow and the Foundations of Positive Psychology: The Collected Works of Mihaly Csikszentmihalyi* (New York, Springer, 2014): 227–38; Nicola S. Schutte and John M. Malouff, "Connections between Curiosity, Flow and Creativity," *Personality and Individual Differences* 152, no. 1 (January 2020): 1–3, https://doi.org/10.1016/j.paid.2019.109555.

206 **Josef Pieper:** Josef Pieper, *Leisure: The Basis of Culture* (San Francisco: Ignatius Press, 2009).

207 **This, like play:** Robert Snape, "Leisure in Middletown: Cultural Change and Social Capital in an Inter-war American Community," *World Leisure Journal* 64, no. 3 (March 2022): 290–303, https://doi.org/10.1080/16078055.2022 .2043425.

207 **people find contentment:** Pink, *Drive*.

210 **Real leisure was sitting:** Snape, "Leisure in Middletown."

211 **Yet more people:** James Sherk, "Upwards Leisure Mobility: Americans Work Less and Have More Leisure Time than Ever Before," The Heritage Foundation, August 31, 2007, https://www.heritage.org/jobs-and-labor/report /upwards-leisure-mobility-americans-work-less-and-have-more-leisuretime -ever#:~:text=Americans%20work%20fewer%20hours%20and,focus%20 on%20their%20own%20pursuits; Marian L. Tupy, "We Work Less, Have More Leisure Time and Earn More," HumanProgress, November 15, 2016, https://www.humanprogress.org/we-work-less-have-more-leisure-time-and -earn-more-money/; Rich Miller, "Americans Are Working Less than Before the Pandemic as They Embrace Work-Life Balance," *Financial Post,* April 5, 2023, https://financialpost.com/fp-work/americans-working-less-embrace -work-life-balance.

211 **People in the latter sector:** Sherk, "Upwards Leisure Mobility"; Derek Thompson, "The Free-Time Paradox in America," *The Atlantic,* September 13, 2016, https://www.theatlantic.com/business/archive/2016/09 /the-free-time-paradox-in-america/499826/.

211 **Studies have shown:** See Paul Smeets, Ashley Whillans, Rene Bekkers, Michael I. Norton, "Time Use and Happiness of Millionaires: Evidence from the Netherlands," *Social Psychological and Personality Science,* 11, no. 3 (2020), 295–307, https://doi.org/10.1177/1948550619854751.

212 **People who spend their money:** Cassie Mogilner and Michael I. Norton, "Time, Money, and Happiness," *Current Opinion in Psychology* 10 (August 2016): 12–16, https://doi.org/10.1016/j.copsyc.2015.10.018.

212 **Experiences, in reality:** Wan Yang, Ye Zhang, and Yao-Chin Wang, "Would Travel Experiences or Possessions Make People Happier?," *Journal of Travel Research* 62, no. 2 (2023): 412–31, https://doi.org/10.1177 /00472875211064631.

217 **In Gay's book:** Ross Gay, *The Book of Delights: Essays* (New York: Algonquin Books, 2019).

Conclusion

222 **"Everything passes away . . .":** Mikhail Bulgakov, *The White Guard* (New York: Rosetta Books, 2016), 245.

Index

ABOUT THE AUTHOR

COREY KEYES is a sociologist and professor emeritus at Emory University whose research on mental health has had wide-reaching policy implications. Over the course of his career, he's advised the CDC as well as governmental agencies in Canada, Northern Ireland, and Australia.

ABOUT THE TYPE

This book was set in Garamond, a typeface originally designed by the Parisian type cutter Claude Garamond (c. 1500–61). This version of Garamond was modeled on a 1592 specimen sheet from the Egenolff-Berner foundry, which was produced from types assumed to have been brought to Frankfurt by the punch cutter Jacques Sabon (c. 1520–80).

Claude Garamond's distinguished romans and italics first appeared in *Opera Ciceronis* in 1543–44. The Garamond types are clear, open, and elegant.